GOING TO EXTREMES

First published in 2001 by Channel 4 Books, an imprint of
Pan Macmillan Ltd, Pan Macmillan, 20 New Wharf Road,
London N1 9RR, Basingstoke and Oxford.

Associated companies throughout the world

www.panmacmillan.com

ISBN 0 7522 2016 0

3 5 7 9 8 6 4

A CIP catalogue record for this book is
available from the British Library.

Designed and typeset by seagulls
Colour reproduction by Aylesbury Studios
Printed and bound in Great Britain by Mackays of Chatham plc

This book accompanies the television series *Extremes*
made by Keo Films for Channel 4.
Executive producers: Zam Baring and Andy Thomson
Series Producer: Andrew Palmer

GOING TO
EXTREMES

Mud, Sweat and Frozen Tears

Nick Middleton

Contents

Acknowledgements

A lot of people put a lot of energy into this book and the accompanying television series. Most of them live in the world's extreme places and appear in these pages. I am grateful to them all for so generously contributing their time and assistance. I would also particularly like to thank those whose names follow, though in no particular order.

At Keo Films: Will Anderson, Alethea Palmer, Annette Gordon, Havana Marking, Katherine Perry and Claire Hamilton.

In Siberia: Andrey Koriakine, Olga Vasilievna Ulturgasheva, Dima Govorukhin, Usik Igor, Guy Pugh, Godfrey Kirby and Tom Holland.

In Chile: Christian Gonzales, Pablo Osses, Ana Monzon-Monzon, Dennis Beauchamp, Michael Tien and Gethin Aldous.

In Ethiopia: Valerie Browning, Ishmael Ali Garde, Mr Bisrat, Tony Hickey, Mohamed Fayez Marei, Paul Paragon and Dudu Douglas-Hamilton.

In India and Bangladesh: Runa Marre, Khandaker Badrul Alam ('Babu'), Dulci Wallang, Maan Barua, Rajan Chakravarty, James Perry, Claudia Morris, Ali Kazimi and Lainie Knox.

In Britain: Toby Sculthorp, Mark Carwardine, Thierry du Bois, Anabel Leventon, Katherine Vincent, Robert Twigger, Tahir Shah, Andrew Goudie, Alan Downes, Kevin Duncan, Margot Eardley, Shayne Jackson, Debbie Willett, Emma Tait and Julian Flanders.

Special thanks go to David Tibballs – director of the films in Chile and India – for his good humour and amazing stamina, and Zam Baring, film editor extraordinaire. Extra special thanks go to Andrew Palmer – director of the films in Siberia and Ethiopia – who had faith in the project from the word go and the extraordinary energy to see it through; Doreen Montgomery for her encouragement, enthusiasm and eagle eye; and Lorraine Desai for her support throughout a long year.

Introduction

The man in the city-slicker shirt carried his bottle over to my table as I was finishing my dinner and asked if he could join me. He sat down and introduced himself as Charles. Charles was interested to know about England, he said, starting with where it was. He furrowed his brow as if he were trying to remember, 'It's near the USA, isn't it?'

'Not really,' I said, 'closer to France and Portugal.'

'Ah, yes,' he nodded knowingly, and took a swig from his beer bottle. 'Is it cold there?' he asked.

'Yes,' I told him, 'especially in these months.'

'Is there hail and snow?'

I nodded.

'Gosh!' he exclaimed, 'there's no hail, snow or even ice here – it's a normal climate. In England I would die in one day.'

Ideas are curious things, and you don't always recognize them when they creep up on you. I didn't realize it at the time, but that brief exchange in a restaurant in central Mozambique had sown the seed for a book that wasn't to germinate for almost ten years.

I was sitting at my desk at home, gazing out into my back garden as the sun beat down, when that snippet of conversation with Charles came back to me. After writing travelogues on Outer Mongolia and Mozambique, my last two volumes had taken me to places closer to home. Europe and the US southern states had been interesting but to my mind they hardly counted as real adventures. And a real adventure was what I was searching for as I sat comfortably in middle England, at the heart of the mid-latitudes, reaching middle age.

The memory of that exchange with Charles all those years before had been prompted by a report on the television news of another drought in Britain. British people are obsessed with the weather. It's a constant topic of conversation, and TV weather presenters can become national heroes. The Scandinavians have a similar interest, but their passion doesn't quite match up to that of the Brits. Whether it's too hot or too cold, we moan about it. A flood usually causes a national outcry, but only until the next drought comes along, and then we wonder what happened to all the floodwaters.

But, if the truth be told, the weather we get in Britain is never really extreme. It's actually very moderate and middle-of-the-road. Like the British themselves, their weather is all very temperate and restrained. What then, I thought to myself, was it like in places where they *really* have something to complain about? After several days of wading through reference books, I had an idea of where I could go to find out. The world's hottest, coldest, wettest and driest inhabited towns were spread across three continents and their climatic records left me speechless. The annual temperature in Dallol, Ethiopia averaged a searing 34.5°C (94°F), whereas Oymyakon in Siberia had recorded a staggering low of -71.2°C (-96°F). Every year, Mawsynram in India received an extraordinary 11,872 mm (nearly 39 feet) of rainfall, while Arica in Chile got virtually none at all.

I wanted to investigate the day-to-day challenges of life at the planet's maxima and minima, to compare and contrast the climatically excessive and the meteorologically destitute. Thirty years after putting the first man on the moon, how good was human society at coping with our own planet's extremes? And why did people live in such places? Were they pioneers battling against the elements in search of untold riches? Were they society's outcasts, relegated to inhospitable climes? Or were they so assimilated to their local climatic peculiarities that they hardly noticed?

I felt I needed a dose of something extreme to get the juices flowing, so I set out to see some properly severe and excessive weather.

COLDEST

Oymyakon

Siberia

ONE

A week before leaving I checked the daily weather report for Siberia and saw a deep purple patch on the temperature map of Russia depicting less than -40°C (-40°F) for virtually the whole of the area I would be travelling through. Oymyakon, the coldest town on Earth, was enjoying a balmy -53°C (-63°F). I was rather pleased with myself. I couldn't have timed it better.

I became rather less content when the British media started running stories about Siberia's cruellest winter in living memory. I watched sorry pictures of a hospital in Irkutsk as the voice-over said that its staff had been overwhelmed by 200 frostbite victims in a fortnight. The BBC's woman on the spot matter-of-factly stated that the surgeons had run out of anaesthetic after performing 60 amputations that week. Faint screaming could be heard coming from the operating theatre behind the reporter. This was followed by pictures of Nikolai Dobtsov, a driver whose truck had broken down a long way from anywhere. After six hours in the biting cold, he had managed to fix his vehicle and drive to hospital. When he got there, they had to cut off his hands and feet. I was beginning to think that perhaps this wasn't such a great idea after all.

Sitting in my nice warm home in Oxford planning the trip, I'd read numerous articles about survival in extreme cold. I had learned how to prevent, recognize and treat frostbite, hypothermia and a range of other cold-weather injuries. I knew about the dangers of snow blindness, and the importance of maintaining my body's core temperature. But reading all this advice was one thing, seeing Nikolai Dobtsov with all four limbs reduced to bandaged stumps was quite another. And this guy *lived* in Siberia. He must have been well aware of the dangers, even adapted to them up to a point. What chance would I have, a mid-latitude man who had read a few books about winter-related illnesses? To say that my blood ran cold would be understating the matter.

But it was too late. I'd paid for my flight and worked out my itinerary. Vehicles had been booked and people were expecting me. There was nothing for it but to buy yet another pair of thermals and make a start. I'd wanted an adventure, now I was going to get one.

It hit me as soon as I stepped out of the railway station at Irkutsk. I felt a tingly feeling in my nostrils that was caused by the hairs in my nose instantaneously freezing. I took a deep breath and immediately regretted it because the shock of the cold air in my lungs set me off on an extended bout of coughing that felt like I'd been smoking forty a day since before puberty. Half a minute later, as the coughing subsided, the skin all over my face began to feel as if it were burning. I had already lost contact with my toes and my fingers were heading the same way. It was -41°C (-42°F) and I'd arrived in Siberia. During the five minutes I waited for the arrival of my driver, I was seriously concerned that my nose might fall off.

My face, fingers and toes became more painful as they warmed up on the short journey to the Hotel Angara. As you would expect in January, the streets of Irkutsk were lined with chest-high piles of shovelled snow beside the pavements, but the roads were well gritted and clear except for a light sprinkling of fresh snow on the compacted ice. At home, anyone fool enough to be out for a drive in such conditions would be doing so with extreme caution, but here the familiarity of a seven-month winter had bred total contempt. Everyone was driving like maniacs.

We swept past old wooden houses and lines of Soviet-style tenement blocks, on one occasion getting stuck behind a lumbering bus as it accelerated away from its stop. It billowed white exhaust fumes like an ancient steam engine, temporarily reducing our visibility to near zero.

I had found my driver through a local non-governmental organization called Baikal Environmental Wave, dedicated to conserving the world's deepest freshwater lake, which is situated a few kilometres down the road from Irkutsk. Dima was an environmental inspector with the organization, but like so many Russians today he was not averse to doing a bit of freelance work on the side.

Founded about 350 years ago, Irkutsk started out like many Siberian settlements, as a wooden fort surrounded by a stockade built by Cossacks who came to the great Siberian wilderness in search of furs. The fur trade still plays a significant part in the city's commerce, and Dima drove me past its fur market, 'the largest one in Siberia' he said. It only works three days a week and today was not one of those days, so all I saw was lines of deserted wooden stalls in the open air. I did a double take. 'The market is outside?' I asked incredulously. 'Of course,' replied Dima. 'Isn't it rather cold?' I enquired. 'We don't think so,' he said breezily.

I was still reeling from this revelation when we pulled up outside the hotel, which dominated one side of a vast park full of ice sculptures shimmering in the midday sun. Irkutsk has attracted numerous admiring sobriquets during its history. In many ways the city lies at the heart of Siberia, with its proximity to Lake Baikal, its status as a major hub on the trans-Siberian railway and a fine legacy of classical wooden mansions and grandiose public buildings dating from a gold-rush period in the late nineteenth century. I had passed through it once on the trans-Siberian and had always yearned for a closer look at the 'Paris of Siberia'. My first glimpse of the Hotel Angara gave me the distinct impression that the former Soviet authorities had baulked at the comparison with such a potent symbol of western decadence. So they put up a horrible pile of 1960s' plate glass and characterless concrete instead.

Its appearance wasn't the only vestige of the old USSR that was alive and well in the Hotel Angara. I spent an extended period in nearby Mongolia in the late 1980s, where I had my first taste of a Westerner's life under the old Soviet regime, and the Hotel Angara provided more than a few doses of déjà vu. The first came in the form of the carpet that led me to my room down a corridor of interminable proportions. It was mostly red, with a green and yellow border. It was exactly the same design that had adorned the floors of the Hotel Ulan Bator in Mongolia nearly 15 years previously. I had seen it elsewhere too, in Mongolian government buildings and in hotels in Moscow. Goodness only knows how many thousands of miles of this carpet had been produced, probably in a single carpet factory somewhere in the old Soviet Union.

Inside my room, attached to one wall, was another throwback to those heady days. It was an oblong, blue and white plastic radio with just one knob, the volume control. In the Hotel Ulan Bator in 1987 this infernal machine had very nearly driven me insane. It was permanently tuned to the state radio station that broadcast a staple diet of military marching music and stirring pronouncements on the latest production targets achieved by the country's heroic herdsmen. The worst thing about the radio was that it was impossible to turn off. You could turn down the volume, but never to an inaudible level. As a result I had spent many an unpleasant night in the Hotel Ulan Bator with my pillow over my head trying in vain to block out the triumphalist Soviet tunes.

On entering my room in the Hotel Angara I immediately confronted the plastic radio, which, as expected, was playing a little light marching music. The memories of sleepless nights were so immediately vivid for me that I was fully prepared to commit an instant act of wanton destruction. I reached for the volume control and turned it. To my surprise, the music faded to absolute silence. At least some progress had been made in post-Soviet Russia.

Down in the restaurant that first night, the trip down Soviet memory lane continued with a fat and surly waitress who stood glaring over me as I went through the menu. She could have saved us both a lot of time if she'd come straight out and told me that all the items on the extensive menu were off except what they had. This was *pilmeni* (mutton parcels in a light broth) and chicken Kiev, the latter straight out of a packet. As it was, it took almost 15 minutes of enquiries after the availability of various unobtainable delicacies before she told me what I was going to eat for dinner.

Loud, tinny, melancholic Russian rock music, played on an electric organ, seeped out of a large loudspeaker mounted somewhere out of sight as I surveyed the scene. The only other occupied table in the substantial eatery was populated by a group of drunken Russian men who were nearing old age but well past the inebriation stage. It was Saturday night and their intentions were clear.

The surly waitress banged a bottle of Baltika beer down on the table in front of me. The beer was warm, as it turned out to be everywhere else in Siberia when it was available. Unsurprising, I suppose, given the sub-zero temperatures outside. But the heating was off, so it cooled down pretty fast.

The restaurant walls were all in shiny polished wood panelling, adorned with cock-eyed paintings of terrible landscapes, leavened here and there with reproductions of old prints of Irkutsk. Plastic ivy dangled from a central column. The floor was pink and white mock crazy paving. Six of the eleven ceiling lights were working. As I ploughed my way through the cardboard chicken Kiev, I noticed a small token of twenty-first century Russia in the retro restaurant scene. The paper serviettes, softer than the toilet paper, but only just, were decorated with Christmas holly motifs. All religious festivals had been frowned upon by the former communist regime.

But some things are timeless. As I finished my beer, the old guys were just getting into their stride. I knew it was going to turn into a serious session when one of them turned up the music and grabbed the crabby waitress by her substantial midriff, whirling her into a lurching waltz. To my surprise she offered little resistance. In fact, she almost smiled. I left as two of the other old guys started fighting.

For my baptism in Siberia I had made contact with a group of people in the city of Angarsk, a short drive from Irkutsk up the Angara River, the only river flowing out of Lake Baikal. Baptism it was literally going to be, because these hardy Angarsk residents were members of what is known as a walrus club. Russians have long been partial to winter bathing and those brave enough to swim in ice holes are known as walruses.

I'd read a bit about the Russians' soft spot for this type of behaviour and learned that in pre-revolutionary times it was traditional to take a dip through an ice hole during Epiphany, usually dressed in a long shirt. Decades of communist-inspired atheism had discouraged this tradition, but in recent years the walrus clubs have been making a comeback. I'd just missed Epiphany, but it didn't matter. Every Sunday during winter, the Angarsk walrus club drove in convoy to a spot on the frozen Kitoy River, a tributary of the Angara, and took the plunge through a hole in the ice.

I had to admit to having mixed feelings about the whole concept. I had contacted the Angarsk walrus club in a fit of child-like enthusiasm about things Siberian while the idea was still a romantic dream. But as we drove north-west out of Irkutsk through the snowscape I was beginning to have my doubts. The temperature that morning was -38°C (-36°F). Despite the fact that stripping off and going for a swim in seriously sub-zero temperatures was supposed to be good for your health, I was not convinced. Lots of unpleasant things are promoted as 'good for you' and one of the advantages of being an adult is supposed to be that you can decide for yourself on such issues. On further consideration, having now arrived in the midst of Siberia's cruellest winter in living memory, I decided that joining a walrus club for the afternoon would not be good for me. On the contrary, I had an inkling that it might be positively dangerous to my health. Indeed, the possibility of having a heart attack came to mind.

As we drove up the main street of Angarsk, the lamp-posts adorned alternately with metal silhouettes of a red star and a hammer and sickle, my mind started racing. I thought perhaps I could feign heart palpitations. Or maybe I could contrive some other excuse, like it was too soon after lunch, or too long after Epiphany. Perhaps I could just say I'd forgotten my swimming trunks. It was -38°C, for God's sake! Perhaps that would be enough.

Dima parked our vehicle outside a large public building opposite a standard tenement block, one entire wall of which featured a giant coloured mural of Lenin with his fist raised, possibly in protest against the existence of religiously motivated walrus clubs. It was odd to think he might actually have been on my side.

Almost immediately a small group of people dressed in colossal topcoats and huge fur hats appeared through a heavily padded door in a building on my side of the road and walked towards us. Greetings were exchanged and a young woman whose name was Natasha looked at me sorrowfully. 'We regret to say that today it is too cold for us to go swimming,' she said in heavily accented English. I could have hugged her. Instead I opened my mouth to voice my disappointment, but before I could utter a word she continued. 'However, my father has found some volunteers who are prepared to swim.' My heart did a pretty good impression of a palpitation. Natasha was still talking. 'Some members of our club have dug the hole in the river yesterday, the ice is 1 metre thick.'

Groaning inwardly, I said 'Oh good,' with as much enthusiasm as I could muster, and thanked her and her father for going to so much trouble. In the circumstances it would be churlish for me to back out now. Their kindness had sealed my fate. I was going to be a walrus for the day. We all piled into an array of motley vehicles lined up at the roadside and drove off to find the hole in the ice in the frozen Kitoy River.

As we neared the fateful spot, a perfect Christmassy scene with spruce trees on the riverbank wreathed in thick snow, I turned to Dima and asked if he would be going in for a dip. Dima looked at me with a perplexed smile on his face that said he wasn't mad. I took that as a 'no'.

The Kitoy River was about 50 metres wide at this point and its frozen surface was covered in a fine layer of snow. The walrus club stalwarts, led by Natasha's father and two walrus lookalikes – identical middle-aged brothers with large moustaches who between them carried a shovel with holes in its business-end like a sieve and long poles with serious spikes on – showed me where to descend the steep bank. The hole, shaped like a mini swimming pool about 4 metres long and 2 metres wide, was right in the middle and surrounded by piles of ice that had been excavated the day before. Two neat steps had been carved in one end of the pool. I peered down into it and saw not flowing water but more ice. The moustachioed brothers immediately set to with their spiked poles, smashing at the newly formed layer with glee. 'Yes, it was cold last night,' Natasha said from over my shoulder. 'This new ice is very thick.'

It took the moustache brothers a good three-quarters of an hour of determined hacking to break the new ice layer into giant pieces that were scooped out with the sieved shovel. By this time their moustaches had completely frozen, leaving them looking exactly like a couple of walruses in their woolly hats and army camouflage combat jackets. The fact that these two completed the entire procedure without gloves just added to my feeling of trepidation. These people were made of different stuff. Through the sparkling water now revealed, I could see down to the pebbles on the riverbed but it was impossible to say how deep it was. One of the walrus twins looked at me with a broad grin beneath his frozen moustache. He pointed a gnarled finger down into the shimmering depths and then put the finger on me. 'Kamikaze!' he yelled, bursting into a fit of laughter and slapping me on the back with such force that I nearly went in with all my clothes on. The walrus twins at least were going to enjoy this.

The small assembled crowd retired back up the bank to a position among the spruce trees where they set about building a bonfire to warm the swimmers after the event. I retired to my vehicle in a vain attempt to warm myself before the event. To add to my worries, one of the small toggles that hold my spectacles to my nose had broken. It was made of plastic and had simply snapped in the cold. It was definitely a bad sign. I sat hunched over the heater trying to bind my glasses with sticking plaster and rationalize my present predicament. Just standing out there watching the walrus twins hack away at the ice had left me feeling numb, not just mentally, but physically too in my hands and chin and cheeks. In what seemed like no time at all I had encountered difficulty in talking to Natasha because my jaw was freezing up. It felt as if I'd had a marathon session at the dentist.

I had asked her why the walrus club had been formed. It was to strengthen the immune system, she explained. 'Walrus club members hardly ever suffer from colds,' she said. 'They are always feeling strong and healthy thanks to their swimming. It is also good for the soul.' 'And how do you think I will fare?' I asked her. Natasha looked at me seriously from beneath her fur hat. 'It is important to have the right mental attitude to enjoy this healthy experience,' she said.

So I sat there wrapping sticky tape round my spectacles, with hands that were not properly responding to central command because they were too cold, trying desperately to achieve the right mental attitude. Then a tap came at the window and there was Natasha pointing towards a short procession of men and women who were making their way down the slope of the riverbank carrying towels. The time had come.

A number of women went first. One by one, each undressed a few metres from the hole while standing on a small plastic mat that had been brought for the purpose. Before walking the short distance in their swimwear to the mini pool, each made a worshipful gesture to the sun that sat in a cobalt sky providing brilliant light but apparently no warmth. The motion involved waving the arms above the head in a manner similar to that of gymnasts at the end of a performance. The swimmer was helped down into the pool by the walrus twins who stood on either side of the ice steps and held the swimmer's hands as she descended into the icy depths. Some simply dunked themselves up to their necks in the water and immediately climbed out while others swam the short length of the pool and back before scrambling out to towel down and dress quickly.

I studied the women taking their dips to see if there were any special techniques that I should mimic. The only tip I picked up was that none of them put their head under the water, presumably because their hair would freeze immediately on exit. Otherwise the only solace I took from the ritual was the fact that nobody screamed with pain. Neither did anyone spend longer than about 15 seconds actually in the water.

My time had come. I sat down on the small plastic mat and struggled to remove my boots. Next came two pairs of thermal trousers as a few in the assembled crowd cracked what were pretty clearly jokes about the number of clothes the Englishman was wearing. Putting my disabled glasses to one side, I pulled off my four top layers and stood up. A ripple of amusement went through the crowd when they saw my boxer shorts sporting coloured maps of Europe. I pointed out the small sliver of Russia that was shown and received a minor roar of appreciation.

Facing the sun, I closed my eyes and raised my arms in salute before turning to walk the short distance to the pool. The walrus twins grabbed my outstretched hands as I put my foot on the top step, which was incredibly slippery. They let me go as I sank into the icy water.

It wasn't actually cold, I don't think. In my near panic at the thought of taking part in this foolhardy exercise I had completely forgotten the obvious fact that the water itself would not be particularly cold. If it was water it had to be above freezing, and relative to an air temperature of -38°C (-36°F) it could have almost been described as warm. I struck out with a couple of breaststrokes and touched the opposite end of the pool, turned and swam back. It felt good. After all the anxiety over the build-up, it felt very good indeed. 'I'm a walrus,' I cried. 'I'm a walrus.'

Now I had to get out. I hadn't fully realized that this would be the dangerous bit. Feeling both elated and relieved I padded across the snow to the mat to dry myself. I lost the plot very quickly along with all feeling in my toes. Sitting on the mat I became obsessed with rubbing my left forearm to get it dry. I couldn't feel the arm. It was as if it belonged to someone else. I just knew that it should be perfectly dry before putting on any clothes because any residual moisture would instantly turn to ice.

People were all around me shouting. Someone pulled my two woolly hats on over my head. One of the walrus twins had grabbed me under the armpits and was trying to make me stand. I didn't particularly want to stand, but the shouts were becoming more insistent. Natasha was nowhere near to translate so I had no idea what it was they were urging me to do. Besides, I wasn't entirely sure that the shouts were aimed at me. They sounded as if they were far off. Perhaps there was some other event going on that I was unaware of. I was far too busy getting this forearm dry to be too concerned.

Then I was on my feet and one of the walrus twins was gesturing that I remove my boxer shorts. Briefly, my brain kicked back in. My God, of course, I had to take off my boxer shorts because they were wet. I couldn't get dressed with them on. They disappeared to be replaced with my thermal leggings and I could sit down again to concentrate on that forearm. Someone was rubbing my back with another towel. It was my back, but at the same time it wasn't. The vigorous rubbing made it difficult for me to sit upright, but I couldn't actually feel the towel on my back.

A red plastic cup was thrust under my nose and I took a gulp of what looked like water, although having a drink was really the last thing on my list of priorities. I filled my mouth with the liquid before realizing that it was vodka. Swallowing hard, the fiery liquid disappeared, much to the delight of the walrus twins, and a brief flash of warmth rippled down inside me.

Someone was drying my feet and offered me a sock. I bent to pull it on, but for some strange reason I couldn't get my foot beyond the sock's heel. I pulled and pulled. My foot was stuck. I couldn't understand why. Perhaps I had been passed the wrong sock? Or maybe someone had put glue in it or something? My mind just couldn't work it out. My arms were pulled back and up as another layer of clothing went over my head. I had forgotten about that forearm. The sock challenge was much more interesting. My foot was permanently stuck in the heel. It was baffling. To me it was clear I needed assistance but no one was bothering about getting that sock on properly. It was all very disturbing.

The other sock went on, followed by another layer on my top half. Like a rag doll I was lifted to my feet again. One of the walrus twins grabbed my wrist and proffered me a stiff, frost covered version of my geographical boxer shorts. They had frozen rigid almost instantly. Natasha appeared, 'Go to the car now,' she said, 'and get warm.' Her words were just what I needed, clear instructions in the English language. I took off at a run, the sock still only half on my foot.

It was only later that evening that I realized I must still be in shock. Two other things also dawned on me. One was that if the walrus twins hadn't been there to dry and dress me I would probably still be sitting there now, frozen to death. The other was that my foot had still been wet when I'd tried to pull on that sock. The water had turned to ice and had stuck the sock to my heel. It felt good to have resolved that conundrum.

TWO

Irkutsk has taken on several roles during its long history, including expedition base for explorations of Siberia and gold-rush town. In the early nineteenth century it also became a dumping ground for political exiles. Perhaps the most important group in this vein was the Decembrists, whose failed *coup d'état* in 1825 earned the lucky ones a one-way trip to oblivion (the others were sentenced to death). The Decembrists were followed by numerous other groups of unfortunates deemed undesirable in Moscow, and by the late nineteenth century it was said that up to a third of the city's population was comprised of deportees. In the early twentieth century, Irkutsk's exile population was further swelled at various times by some of the most notable protagonists of Marxism. These included Joseph Stalin himself, Felix Dzerzhinsky (first head of the Soviet secret police, later to become known as the KGB), Vyacheslav Molotov (a future secretary of the Central Committee of the Communist Party and the inspiration behind the world's first undrinkable cocktail) and Sergei Kirov (later to be assassinated, probably on Stalin's orders, while boss of the Leningrad Communist Party).

Walking the streets of Irkutsk I got a taste of the shock that those exiles who had arrived in winter must have felt. I didn't actually see a great deal of the city on foot because I could only stay outside for maybe 20 minutes before everything started to hurt. My toes would go numb, as would my nose, followed closely by my chin. My hands were OK just so long as I kept them firmly in the pockets of my over-coat, but every time I pulled out my camera to take a photograph my fingers began to throb with the cold. I had taken the precaution of wrapping zinc oxide tape around that part of the camera that might come in contact with my face as I composed a shot, for fear that my skin would stick to the metal body, but this did little to protect my hands. I had brought two pairs of gloves, a silk inner pair and some heavier outer ones, but I had to remove the heavier pair to operate the camera and consequently I only managed a couple of photos at a time before I was forced to shove the camera back inside my coat in order to pull on my gloves again. This was probably just as well for the camera too, since batteries have a notoriously short lifespan when the temperature drops below about -20°C (-4°F).

All in all, it was a pretty miserable introduction to Siberia. The only solace I found was in seeing numerous residents of Irkutsk scur-rying along the snowbound streets holding their noses. Perhaps not everyone was completely immune to the weather after all.

Two days after my initiation with the Angarsk walrus club, Dima arrived at the hotel having made arrangements for a trip to Lake Baikal. The lake usually freezes over in January and the ice does not break until May, so I was keen to see it in its frozen state. I had also asked Dima to see if he could arrange a meeting with anyone who worked in the nearby Pribaikalsky National Park because I wanted to talk to someone who spent long periods working outside in the winter. I thought I might be able to pick up some tips in advance of my journey to Oymyakon.

Early the following morning we left Irkutsk shrouded in thick, grey, freezing fog. Siberian cities are renowned for their heavy winter smogs, created by a blend of vehicle exhaust and industrial emissions, which tend to sit over urban areas unmoved by the light or nonexistent winds. The theory was confirmed once we had reached the outskirts of the city, because the fog had virtually disappeared and a pallid sun was doing its best to shine in a watery kind of way. As on the Kitoy River a few days previously, the best the sun could manage was to give some light to the proceedings. Providing warmth seemed to be beyond its capabilities in the depths of a Siberian winter.

What had been a sealed road soon gave way to a rough icy track as we drove south-east through the spruce trees towards Baikal. Small villages with steep, snow-capped roofs nestled in wide valleys, wisps of smoke from their chimneys one of the few signs of human habitation. Another was the relentless march of telegraph poles that followed the track. As in Britain, each pole was a spruce tree trunk, but here the pole itself was not driven into the ground. Each one was strapped to a half-buried concrete post because concrete is better able to withstand the seasonal freeze and thaw that characterizes the soil in these latitudes.

As the trail began to climb, it cut through thick coniferous woodland, a tiny part of a broad swathe of forest known as *taiga* that stretches the entire width of Russia from the Siberian Far East through northern Finland to the Atlantic coast of Norway. The trees of the *taiga* are supposed to be evergreen, with needles that lose less water and shed snow more easily than broad leaves. But I wouldn't have known this by looking at the spruce that whipped past our windscreen. Here the trees were heavily laden with snow and the only colours to break up the ethereal landscape were browns and greys. Green didn't enter into it.

At the top of a pass, Dima pulled over to the side of the track. 'Time for a toast,' he said, putting his fur hat on his head and grabbing a bottle of pepper vodka from the glove compartment in the dashboard before jumping out. This threw me somewhat. It was still only 9.30 in the morning and I hadn't put Dima down as a drinker. He was a fresh-faced guy with rosy cheeks and an air of innocence about him that reminded me of Tintin. As he was rummaging in the back of the van I opened my door to see lots of empty vodka bottles by the roadside. Dima emerged from his excavation clutching a couple of tin mugs, a loaf of bread and a thick liver sausage. He produced a lengthy knife from his boot and sliced the sausage along with thick hunks of bread.

'Now we toast the spirit of the mountain,' he declared as he poured generous measures of pepper vodka into the mugs. 'No, Nick,' he cried as I raised the mug ready for a toast. 'First we do like this.' Dima dipped the third finger of his left hand into the alcohol, touched the finger to the vehicle and then flicked it twice into the air. 'For a good journey,' he said, downing the vodka in one and immediately tucking into a liver sausage open sandwich.

I was surprised, not by the toasting procedure but because I had come across it before. The three finger flicks are common practice as a tribute to the spirits in Mongolia, and although an area round Lake Baikal is home to Buryat Mongolians, I had not expected to be reintroduced to the custom by a Russian.

An hour later we stopped at the top of another pass and toasted the spirits again, only this pass was the highest of our journey so we had to do it three times. As before, the drinking was punctuated with bread and liver sausage that tasted very good, but within half a minute the bread had frozen so it was quite challenging to eat. Another drawback to the triple session was that I had to remove my left-hand glove for the duration in order to do the flicking and by the end my fingers had turned a waxy white colour. Even in my inebriated state I remembered that this was the first sign of frostbite, so I was more than grateful when Dima announced that we should get going again.

The sun was colourless and watery above the hillside and it started to snow very light, tiny flakes as I climbed back into the cab to warm my hand. It was 10.30 in the morning and I was totally smashed. I just hoped that Dima was more accustomed than me to drinking so early in the day.

By the time we reached the shore of Lake Baikal, a beach of rounded granite pebbles dusted with snow, I had more or less sobered up. I needn't have bothered because before Dima would venture out on to Baikal's icy surface we had to pay our respects to the spirit of the lake. A fresh half-litre of pepper vodka appeared along with the remains of the bread and a hunk of ham. Just when I thought we were ready, Dima drew his knife and dashed off away from the shore to attack a birch tree. He walked back clutching some desiccated pieces of bark that he placed carefully on the ground and then set alight with a match. After toasting the god of Baikal, we fed the small fire with slivers of ham.

Lake Baikal's vital statistics are on a scale appropriate for the vast wilderness of Siberia. It nestles in a continental rift, a yawning slit in the Earth's crust more than 8 kilometres deep. Much of this is buried in sediment, but the lake itself is still the world's deepest, its crystal clear waters bottoming out at more than 1,620 metres. It's the largest freshwater lake on Earth and at perhaps more than 25 million years old, the oldest as well. Its 23,000 cubic kilometres of water, which cover an area the size of Belgium, constitute one fifth of the world's reserves of surface fresh water. It is said that it would take all the rivers of the world nearly a year to fill it. Of course, it's also one of the world's most diverse lakes with 1,085 species of plant and 1,550 species of animal. Eighty per cent of the animals are found nowhere else on Earth. They include the Baikal seal, one of the world's only two freshwater species.

In winter, up to a metre of its surface waters freeze, enabling vehicles to drive over the ice. During the Russo–Japanese war, when the trans-Siberian railway used ships to traverse Lake Baikal, the crossing became impossible in the particularly severe winter of 1904 because the ferries were ice-bound. Desperate to get reinforcements to the Far Eastern front, the authorities organized huge teams of men and horses to drag more than 2,000 munitions carriages and 65 locomotives across ice that was more than 150 centimetres thick.

Before dragging this lot they had tried laying track across the icy surface, using especially long sleepers to spread the load. But the first engine to test the rails came to a weak spot and plunged into the icy depths to leave a gaping hole more than 22 kilometres long. I felt suitably sobered by the memory of reading about this incident as Dima revved the engine and drove down the pebble bank and on to the ice.

The experience was surreal. The view from the cab was not that of a frozen lake, it looked more like a photograph of the liquid version. For the first 100 metres the waters were flat, while beyond this a slight ruffling of the surface resembled the small ripples that might be produced by a light wind on water. As we crossed the glassy plain, the ripples materialized as a stretch of jagged ice that Dima turned to avoid.

The lake's petrified shell stretched out before us like an enormous ice rink. Where patches of snow covered the surface the tyres were able to grip, but a glassy section offered little traction and sent us into a spin, which was met with chuckles of delight from Dima. Away from the pebble beach the bank closed in as steep cliffs, their lower sections swathed in dramatic ice formations that looked like a Siberian Goliath had been dripping wax from a dinner-party candle over the rocks.

We stayed close to the shore as we drove north-east, heading towards a hunting lodge in the Pribaikalsky National Park which hems the south-western rim of the lake. Our route was a tortuous one that Dima had taken before. Every so often our way was barred by a lengthy stretch of jagged ice, like gigantic glass shards thrust up to half a metre into the air and several metres in width. If the water had been liquid, these sections would have been waves. As it was they looked like ice sculptures, or Nature's attempt at frozen barbed wire.

Every so often Dima would stop and get out to investigate something. He carried a long spiked pole, like the ones the walrus twins had used to excavate the swimming pool. It was the ideal instrument to test the thickness of the ice, which in its weakest spots was less than 20 centimetres and definitely unsuitable to drive across.

Daily temperature fluctuations and warm subsurface currents give rise to these intricate assemblies of cracks and minor crevasses that resemble collision zones between rival ice plates. Walking and sliding across the smooth parts of the lake surface produced squeaky noises from my rubber-soled shoes, which offset the ominous creaks and occasional deep booming sounds that signified great ice movements. Beneath my feet, a dark-green abyss of water reminded me of the absurdity of my actions. I was out for a stroll on the world's deepest lake. I had complete confidence in Dima's ability to get us through this eerie ice field, despite the fact that he must have been half-cut like me. The alternative didn't bear thinking about.

Nikolai was everything I could have hoped for from a Siberian forest ranger. His face wasn't skin-covered but shaped from a tough hide, with eyebrows that met on the bridge of his nose and eyes that betrayed the faint almond shape of Siberian stock. His hands were the hardest hands I'd ever seen and one of his thumbs bore a deep, roughly healed gash, the result of a slip with his knife that had left him with no feeling in his eastern extremity. He was a man of few words, as silent as the wilderness he inhabited.

His self-built wooden hunting lodge stood surrounded by a series of outhouses right on the shore of the petrified lake. He also had a house in a village ten hours' walk away where his children were at school. But this was where he preferred to live with his wife, most of their food the result of hunting trips into the forest interior, their water hacked from the lake as blocks of ice.

Dima and I had arrived in time for dinner. Other than at the entrance, there were no doors inside the lodge, where all rooms led off the warm kitchen with its stove built into the central support wall. Vodka was served before we tucked into a feast of pickled salads and a thick venison stew. This was followed by a couple of typical Siberian dishes, both of them raw and frozen solid. On one plate was a large frozen deer's liver, on another a couple of frozen raw fish, not unlike medium-sized trout to look at. I like liver when it's fried, but the raw frozen version is never likely to become a favourite. I found the fish, which Nikolai shaved into thin strips with his hunting knife, more palatable. The shavings were dipped in salt before eating and tasted very good when washed down with vodka.

We each drank a generous shot of the oily alcohol between every course and when Dima placed a second bottle on the table in front of us he did so with the announcement that, 'to have a good conversation you have to drink vodka – it is food for the soul.'

Dima had a point, because with each drink Nikolai had become a little more talkative. I had already learned from my driver that Nikolai was employed by the National Park authorities to safeguard the area from poachers. Pribaikalsky was rich in wildlife, including brown bear, deer, fox, wild boar, sable and lynx. As a ranger, Nikolai had a licence to hunt. 'Do you hunt to sell the hides or for food?' I asked him. 'I hunt to live,' he replied, with Dima translating. We had been eating the fruits of his labours, but he also provided skins on contract to a hunting organization. Sables were among the more profitable species, he told me, since their skins made the best fur hats. But they were not easy to hunt. I asked him if he set traps. '*Niet*,' he replied, and I thought that was all I was going to get until he added, 'I track a sable with my dogs. It takes one or two days.'

Once the dogs had a sable's scent the hunt was on, the aim being to chase the small animal until it took refuge in a tree. Then Nikolai would build a fire beneath the tree and wait. 'When the sable jumps from the burning tree to the next, that's when I shoot it.' 'It has to be in the head,' Dima added, translating as Nikolai spoke, 'or the fur is spoiled.'

Silently, Nikolai had left the table and reappeared holding two small gleaming brown pelts. I examined them and found the bullet entry holes in the heads. To shoot such a diminutive creature while flying through the air with this accuracy was a sign of an extraordinary marksman. I said as much and Nikolai gave me a barely perceptible shrug before looking away. 'I hunt wild animals,' he said finally, 'but I couldn't kill a chicken.'

'I have hunted since I was a child,' he added by way of further explanation. 'I used to run away from kindergarten to go hunting.' He told me he remembered catching his first perch when he was four years old in northern Siberia. 'It pulled so hard I fell off the jetty trying to haul it in,' he added with the slightest of twitches at the ends of his mouth that I took to be a rare smile. It was the most expressive gesture he'd made all evening.

'And what about bears?' I asked him. 'Do you hunt bears?' He nodded. 'There are too many bears in these parts,' he said. But bears were unpredictable, he added, and therefore difficult to hunt. The meat was plentiful but a bearskin was too heavy to make into a coat. He used it to make pads for hunting seals on the ice. 'A dead bear is also heavy,' he continued. 'Once my boat nearly sank when I brought back a bear in it.'

'Wolves are a big problem also,' he went on. When Nikolai killed a deer that was too large for him to drag back home, he would skin it and cut the carcass into quarters. One quarter he would carry back, the others he would wrap in the hide and bury for another time. But if wolves found his kill, there wasn't another time.

The evening continued with understated stories of encounters with wolves and bears and when the vodka appeared to run dry I produced a half-litre of Scotch whisky as my contribution. Dima lifted the bottle to inspect it and made a comment to which Nikolai nodded his agreement. 'Whisky tastes like moonshine,' Dima announced as he unscrewed the cap, 'but we will try it.'

They did, looked at each other again and nodded some more. 'Yes, moonshine,' declared Dima and he left to find another bottle of vodka.

That night I slept beneath a bearskin. It was very heavy.

The following morning, Nikolai joined us in the van to drive further up the coastline. We were heading for a lair that he had built in the forest the last time he had spent the night out on a hunting trip. When we had parked the vehicle, Dima and I had our work cut out to keep up with Nikolai as we trudged through the thick snow deep into the forest. Our boots were no match for his short skis with pelts on their bottoms.

The lair was constructed of coniferous logs and branches and was open along one side to face a log fire. The inside of the lair was lined with plastic sheeting to reflect the fire's heat. It was the longest period I had yet spent outside and I was truly grateful when Nikolai set about lighting the fire and settled down with his knife to shave strips off a frozen fish that he had produced from his pocket. From another pocket he pulled a small jam jar of salt and we sat down to enjoy the fish. Dima delved into the small distillery he kept inside his coat and produced the usual bottle of pepper vodka along with three tin mugs.

Sitting inside the makeshift shelter I was surprised at how warm it felt once the fire had got going, although I still wouldn't actually have wanted to spend a night here. Nikolai told me that if I was going to places colder than this, which I was, I should buy a proper coat made of fur and a hat to go with it. 'Fur is the only thing to keep you warm,' he told me as he looked with his usual deadpan expression at my greatcoat and two woolly hats.

During the previous night's dinner I had warmed to this undemonstrative Siberian hunter-cum-forest ranger and this morning he was decidedly more talkative, suggesting perhaps that he had warmed to me too. He looked away from my coat as he lifted his mug to his lips and drank another shot of vodka; then put his eyes directly on mine. His face was a piece of Baikal driftwood carved to look like a man but his eyes appeared to be sizing me up like a quarry. Here was a man who could remain stock-still but totally alert for hours, while waiting for the right moment to shoot.

'A piece of advice,' he said finally. 'Always stay warm in Siberia. If ever you have the opportunity to go inside a car or a house, take it.'

THREE

The road ran through this part of north-eastern Siberia like an artery, kilometre after kilometre of frozen gravel stretching from the ice-bound port of Magadan at one end towards the ice-bound city of Yakutsk at the other. The heavy trucks that plied the Kolyma Route supplied the chain of towns and villages that unfolded across the land-scape like a string of fairy lights in a forgotten void. We drove across frozen rivers trapped in a winter time warp that lasted so long no one bothered to build any bridges; huge barges ferry the traffic across during the brief summer months. The trail snaked its way through a terrain of breathtaking beauty, the endless *taiga* forest sitting silently beneath a shield of snow. Each tree looked snug in its winter coat and it was difficult to imagine that the winter would ever pass.

Every day the panorama was bathed in a crisp clean sunlight, making it Christmas-card pretty. But the vista was deceptive, a honey trap that lured you into a world barely fit for human habitation, to a place of such searing cold that it bites through layers of clothing as if they weren't there.

Yet I was feeling more confident about the weather after kitting myself out with fur clothing, as Nikolai had advised, in Yakutsk. In the central market I had bought a raccoon fur hat and a pair of boots made of fur taken from the legs of a reindeer. They were both light and remarkably warm. But the centrepiece was my sheepskin coat that was so heavy it felt as if I was carrying an entire flock around on my back. I'd been sad to leave Dima in Irkutsk but the flight to Yakutsk had put me on this road that would lead me to my destination, the coldest town on Earth. The sense of penetrating deeper into the heart of Siberia was palpable. I was nine hours ahead of London, on the same longitude as Australia and I felt as if I had entered another dimension. Flying into Yakutsk had been like landing on a different planet. The frozen River Lena, among the longest in the world but one I had barely registered previously, was shrouded in heavy mist and the sun that sat on the horizon was ghostly, like the yellow planet Venus or a moon of Pluto, wreathed in a vaporous miasma.

The city itself was otherworldly too, a settlement constructed entirely on permafrost, ground that remains frozen to great depths throughout the year. Building on this icy substrate requires special measures because a heated house placed directly on permafrost can partially melt the surface layers, which heave and subside in their struggle to throw off the unnatural intrusion. The results were plain to see in the succession of old wooden dwellings that lined the road into town from the airport. Some were partially sunken, their windows now resting at road level; others had been reduced to drunken edifices with neither a horizontal nor vertical line to their names.

Modern engineers and architects have met the challenges of building in the permafrost zone by preserving the Earth's thermal equilibrium. Every contemporary structure in Yakutsk stands above the ground on concrete stilts. It's as if the buildings know they really shouldn't be there, so they stand on tiptoe as a mark of respect to Nature. Pipes too are difficult to bury, so the urban landscape is a maze of heavily lagged pipelines winding their way all over town like bloated spaghetti to feed the apartments and office blocks with hot water and to remove their waste.

My awe at this floating cityscape was strengthened by a respect for the people who lived there. The market where I bought my winter clothing was in the open-air, the stallholders just standing around in -41°C (-42°F). I couldn't quite believe it. Who were these people? I decided that there must be something physiologically different about them, which both eased my feeling of envy at their resilience but at the same time deepened my sense of insecurity. This meant an additional challenge for me as a mid-latitude man. I could come here and feel the cold, only more so because I was not on an even playing field.

The fact that Yakutsk was in a different cold league from Irkutsk was clear. Several people I spoke to just laughed when I asked about Siberia's cruellest winter in living memory. 'That is in the south,' they told me, 'they don't get proper winters there.' Other little things confirmed this viewpoint. In Irkutsk every public building came with double doors against the cold, but in Yakutsk the entrance doors came in threes. Many of the vehicles I saw on the streets, including the one I was now travelling in, had been equipped with home-made double-glazing. Roughly cut pieces of glass had been attached to the outside of all the windows using double-sided sticky tape like the draught-excluding strips I have round the windows of my house in England. I could see how effective they were because beyond each double-glazed panel in my vehicle the metal window frames were permanently covered in frost on the inside.

Yet at the same time I was definitely becoming accustomed to the cold. The temperature in the morning in Yakutsk was significantly less of a shock to my system than the temperature in the morning in Irkutsk. This realization, along with the furry additions to my wardrobe, gave me hope as we drove further north and east towards Oymyakon.

I had been joined for this leg of my journey by Andrei, my new interpreter. He was a gentle man who worked as a researcher in a Yakutsk economics institute after doing a series of jobs that included hotel manager and street trader. Like Anatolie, my fixer, who was usually a university lecturer in anthropology, Andrei could take leave from his job to do better-paid work on an ad hoc basis. Both men were Asiatic in appearance, members of local nationalities that are still dominated numerically by ethnic Russians, although it should be said that much of the power in this region is now in the hands of the Yakuts.

The area in question is Yakutia, or the 'Republic of Sakha (Yakutia)' as it is now officially known. It is Russia's largest region, occupying one fifth of the country's territory, stretching 2,000 kilometres from north to south and 2,500 kilometres from east to west. It has three time zones. Yakutia's incorporation into the Russian state dates from 1632 when Russian Cossacks, sent by the Czar in search of furs, built a fort on the bank of the Lena River, from which the city of Yakutsk developed. The Yakuts have a legend that deals with these events. It says that two blue-eyed, blond people arrived one day and were enslaved for a couple of years before they escaped and disappeared on a boat up the Lena. Three years passed before a large number of people looking like the escaped ones arrived on big rafts and asked the Yakut ruler to grant them a piece of land the size of an ox-hide. On receiving approval, the Cossacks cut the hide into thin strips and encircled a huge area on which they built their wooden fortress. Realizing their mistake, the Yakuts tried in vain to destroy the fort, and soon after they submitted to the Russian Czar. Using Yakutsk as their base, the Russians went on to conquer the rest of Siberia all the way to the Pacific Ocean.

Long an autonomous republic within the Soviet Union, Yakutia signed a Declaration of State Sovereignty in 1990 and created its own government and parliament. It has a Yakut president who presides over a series of ministries, but I was hard-pressed to discover exactly what these government bodies did. One local cynic described them to me as 'toy ministries', because the fact remains that Moscow still calls the shots. And it is unlikely ever to let go because Yakutia is the archetypal Siberian treasure house of mineral wealth awaiting exploitation. Oil, gas, coal, antimony and iron ore are here in abundance, but diamonds and gold top the region's impressive list of natural resources. Yakutia turns out about a quarter of the world's diamond production, and more gold nuggets are found here than anywhere else on Earth.

It was the discovery of gold in the Kolyma region of Yakutia that inspired the building of the road we now travelled on. Known in polite circles as the Kolyma Route, Russians have also dubbed it 'the road built on bones' because it was constructed by inmates of Stalin's gulags who froze to death and could not be buried in the permafrost, so their skeletons were used as ballast for the road. The few survivors called Kolyma the 'White Hell'.

Construction of the Kolyma Route started in the 1920s at Magadan and continued inland. The road stretches for more than 1,200 kilometres and they say that every metre cost a human life. I had heard a lot of talk about the soul in Siberia and until today my soul had been having a pretty good time. The walrus dip was supposed to be good for the soul, the frequent shots of vodka were good for the soul, but the day we started driving along this 'Road of Bones', my soul's condition took a definite turn for the worse.

I kept thinking that it was obscene just to be here and that I shouldn't be doing it. But then I thought that it would be just as obscene not to drive along this road since it was here and all those people had perished in its making. Then the driver would stop and we'd all pile out for a pee and I'd be standing there with the matter in hand and suddenly I'd start to feel guilty because I was probably pissing on some poor bastard's grave. Then a wind would get up and the cold would begin to bite, making all exposed areas of skin start to burn and the full horror of the convicts' plight would begin to sink in. The Kolyma region was a white cold furnace that Stalin had stoked with human bodies in order to fuel a great socialist search for gold that would pay for his experiments.

Let's face it; Stalin was the best mass murderer the twentieth century ever saw. The boy from Georgia done good. His exploits make Cambodia's Pol Pot look like a cuddly toy, makes Adolf Hitler's extermination of the Jews seem like a training exercise. Twenty million ... thirty million people, no one will ever know. The system he devised for mass killing was the best. Send them out to Siberia, don't clothe them properly, don't give them enough to eat and just work them to death. And when they are about to die you just leave them outside in the 'White Hell'. You don't even have to waste a bullet or develop some special gas canister to do away with them. And finally, the ultimate irony, get them to die on the road and hey presto there's the next metre of aggregate for you in the morning. It was all so fiendishly simple.

And who was it that wanted this road anyway? Not the people who lived in this region. They were just a bunch of nomadic reindeer herders. What would they have wanted with a road? No, the reason was more convoluted in its logic, in a way that typified the Soviet Union. Old Joe Stalin, sitting with his cronies in the nice warm Kremlin, set up Kolyma's gulags to build a road to go to other gulags that manned the mines to produce the gold to pay for the system that ran the gulags. That was it.

It's a strange place, Siberia. I really hadn't expected to come all this way to get so irate about a piece of transport infrastructure.

Stalin was by no means the first to see Siberia as a dumping ground for Russian subjects he didn't like. The practice may have begun as early as 1591, when 500 insurrectionists were said to have been exiled by Boris Godunoff, later a very unpopular Czar. The historical accuracy of this tale is questionable, but not that of several thousand undesirables who were dispatched in chains to various parts of Siberia after an uprising in Ukraine towards the end of the seventeenth century. The idea of banishment to Siberia as both a punishment but also as a means of settling the vast tracts of bountiful wilderness had become firmly established by the mid-nineteenth century. Hence the range of crimes that earned their perpetrators a one-way ticket east was widened to include a number of more petty offences. Murderers and political offenders were joined by those convicted of eluding military service, vagrancy, horse stealing, debt and insubordination to lawful authority. Even in the latter half of the nineteenth century, these miserable exiles were still forced to walk to Siberia in chains. The journey from Moscow to Yakutsk was more than 8,000 kilometres. It took them two and a half years. At least Stalin offered transport.

After the gulag system was officially disbanded in the late 1950s, the stick was superseded by the carrot as forced occupation of Siberia was replaced by the 'long rouble'. Workers were lured to the region by the offer of salaries as much as eight times higher than corresponding Moscow wages, along with low prices and abundant supplies. Thousands of remote communities sprung up to serve the Soviet mining, oil and nuclear power industries, attracting pampered pioneers who dreamt of making a quick killing in the permafrost and retiring to the warmer latitudes of the 'mainland' – non-Arctic European Russia.

Nezhdaninskoye was more of a village than a town, stuck out in the middle of nowhere with the sole purpose of excavating gold from the Verkhoyansk mountains that hemmed it in on all sides. In its heyday in the 1980s, it drew so many volunteers that they had to live in railroad cars while waiting for enough housing to be built. The thriving community supported a kindergarten, a school, a gym, a library and a small hospital. They even had a music institute with its own brass band. They were still building the post office when the state-owned mining company pulled the plug. Today it is like a post-Soviet version of the *Mary Celeste*, just a dot on the map that Moscow has tried to rub out.

I wandered into a two-storey wooden apartment block where doors had been pulled off at the hinges and burnt by people left behind after the village was liquidated in 1998 and the coal supplies had run out. A kitchen was littered with broken bits of equipment, a lonely pepper shaker and some dried mushrooms scattered across the room. There were frozen piles of human excrement surrounded by soiled pages pulled from books. Old shoes lay forlornly on the floor.

In another dilapidated apartment was a child's exercise book, its first few pages full of spelling tests that had lost their significance. Floorboards had been ripped up and broken glass lay everywhere, partially concealing a torn picture of the Madonna and child. It was a sad epitaph for Moscow's attempts to colonize Siberia. I guess in this case Siberia won.

Few of the village's inhabitants had been local people. According to an old legend, a rare and beautiful firebird once flew over Yakutia and dropped her gold feathers that turned into the belts of alluvial and ore deposits of precious metal common to the area today. The Yakuts believe that finding this gold brings misfortune. Andrei told me that when the pioneers were evacuated from Nezhdaninskoye they were taken on ships up the river to Yakutsk and from there further west. But although many had relatives in western parts of Siberia and European Russia, Nezhdaninskoye had been their home. 'It was very traumatic for them to leave,' Andrei said simply.

The evacuation had been slow, leaving a few to fend for themselves. As winter set in, not only were they burning anything that they could lay their hands on, but the village dogs started mysteriously disappearing until someone admitted that the local canine community was helping to keep the remaining human population alive. A village of golden dreams had turned into a prison camp without the barbed wire.

I was beginning to get used to Siberia's little surprises, but Andrei still shocked me when he declared that we would spend the night in this ghost town. 'Where exactly?' I asked tentatively. 'You will see,' he said.

On the outside the tenement block that was to be our 'hotel' for the night had been finished with such appalling attention to detail that it gave the concrete a stucco effect. The same plasterer had been assigned to the interior décor on the bunker-like walls that appeared through the usual heavily padded double doors. I realized that this place must still be inhabited when I saw a single bare, but lit, light bulb. It revealed a tangle of electric cables running along the walls and a rickety wooden staircase that looked as if it had never been new. Beneath the staircase on the cracked concrete floor stood an ancient iron bedstead, a couple of metal buckets and a dirty cardboard box. I put my hand on an antique radiator. It was warm, but still unable to disperse a growth of ice that clung to the concrete above the doorway like a giant white fungus.

The surprises had only just begun. A figure appeared from the stairway and moved towards me. The young man's Yakut face peered out from beneath a bouffant of shoulder-length black hair that he flicked from his eyes to give me a glimpse of the gold stud adorning his earlobe. 'Welcome,' he said in a broad North American accent, 'welcome to our happy home.' The leather of his trousers, black to match his flowing locks, gave off the faintest creak as he proffered an outstretched hand. 'My name's Sasha by the way. Did you have a good journey?'

The fact that Nezhdaninskoye is still considered to be a world-class gold deposit is testament to the efficacy of Soviet economics. Three years after the village's liquidation, a small part of the settlement was up and running again courtesy of a Dublin-based natural resources company that had bought a 50 per cent stake in the mine. Sasha was an interpreter, one of the small Celtic Resources team that at the time of my visit only included one expatriate, an electrical engineer named Chris. The company was still waiting for all the paperwork concerning their operation in Yakutia to be processed. This meant there wasn't a great deal of interpreting for Sasha to do. He told me that his main duties were to translate Chris's daily report and the menu in the canteen. 'What do you do the rest of the time?' I asked him. 'We have some videos in the canteen. I listen to music,' he replied in the Midwestern accent he had picked up from an American English teacher in Yakutsk. 'But most of the time I just hang out, y'know.'

Chris was originally from Wales. I talked to him briefly when I arrived that evening, although not exactly in person. We spoke through the door of his bedroom. Although it was only 8 o'clock he had already turned in and he wasn't going to get up for an idle chat with an itinerant Englishman. There was something about this behaviour that struck me as slightly odd.

Although born in Wales, Chris had lived in Australia for the last 20 years. There were plenty of mines in Australia, he told me the following morning when we met face-to-face, and he had worked in most of them. He was a red-haired giant of a man who had also done stints in several other far-flung places. How did this compare, I wondered. He looked at me from behind the cover of one of the small desks in his office. The desks were really tables, covered in plastic tablecloths that came with a flowery design. 'It's the most bizarre,' he said simply. 'I've been in mines in a lot of remote spots all over the world, but this is the most remote.'

Chris's office was on the ground floor opposite the canteen. It had no doubt originally been part of an apartment. A computer sat on one flowery desk next to a pile of glossy brochures for belt conveyors and power tools and a guide to satellite communications pulled from a magazine. A short row of airport paperbacks rested against one wall. Pinned to another was a Russian technical drawing of some kind of industrial processing plant. Lined up on the chunky windowsill was a display of old metal serial number plates from Soviet mining equipment made in Novosibirsk by a company named Trud, which means 'labour'. There was a major accumulation of ice on the inside of the double glazed windows.

'But I have e-mail,' Chris continued, 'I'm not completely cut off here, and Sasha and the other guys are good company. It could be worse.' I did a good job of not saying that I found it difficult to imagine how.

Chris was well into a three-month stint at Nezhdaninskoye that had included Christmas and New Year. He wasn't very forthcoming when I asked him how he'd spent the festive period, but he did tell me he had gone for a walk each day. 'I walked up the track, up this side of the valley,' he said. During the shortest days the ghost town had never emerged from the shadows of the surrounding mountains. Chris's daily stroll up the hillside was so that he could see the sun. 'I felt that was important,' he told me.

Meanwhile, he had set about organizing his personal life as best he could. 'There's a woman who gets me beer,' he said. 'She commissions truck drivers to bring it to town. I wander down to her shop most days to see if there's been a delivery. It's a bit of exercise too, although it's a bloody cold walk.' 'There's a shop here?' I asked incredulously. 'But this is a ghost town.' 'It's only a little shop,' he said almost apologetically. 'There are a few people still living here, but I don't think she can make much of a living out of it. I buy what I can, but there's not much of a selection.' Chris's major complaint was the lack of decent chocolate. 'She only ever has Mars bars, and I hate Mars bars. It's the caramel that doesn't agree with me.'

I joined Chris for his daily constitutional down towards Nezhdaninskoye's shop. A bright sun was hovering above a sharply drawn horizon, bathing the surrounding wooded peaks in a primrose glow. 'They've all got names ...' Chris said, squinting at the mountaintops, 'the highest one's called Fairytale. There's another mountain they say looks like the Sleeping Beauty in profile, her face, nipples, everything. But you have to switch on your fantasy button to see it.'

We passed the shattered remains of several wooden houses and the music institute before coming to the snow-covered airfield that Chris told me had last been used a couple of months previously. The small wooden terminal building, topped by a sagging windsock, looked as if it might indeed still be operational. A snow shovel was propped beside its brown door, which was locked with a padlock. Nailed on the wall beside the doorway was a large painted sign in English that read 'Nezhdaninskoye International Airport'. I couldn't decide whether this was in hope or in jest.

The shop had a brightly painted sign too. It said Magazin in red on a white background bordered by blue and white stylized flowers.

The red lettering seemed incongruous in the snowscape. The sign sat above a long window with six panes of glass, none of which I could see through because they were thick with frost. The lady who ran the shop smiled broadly to reveal a gold front tooth when Chris appeared through the doorway. She welcomed me too, but conversation was limited because neither Chris nor I could speak more than a handful of words in Russian. It felt all wrong to be among the few inhabitants of a ghost town and not be able to talk to each other.

The shop was actually a corner of the woman's front room equipped with rough wooden shelves bearing neat piles of stock. There were tins of Nesquick and coffee, little gherkins in jars, cans of peas and sweetcorn, as well as several types of fish. Four bottles of beer, two each of two different brands, sat on the top shelf alongside four bottles of what looked like Russian champagne. At one end of this shelf were three huge white tubs of Golden Mayonnaise with yellow tops. At the other, a large black cat that had its eyes fixed on the lady's fur hat as she stood, arms folded, waiting for our order. Down below were packets of biscuits and tea and a row of snow-white eggs. Several brands of cigarettes were also available. Chris's hated Mars bars were in a box next to a pile of garlic bulbs. Oddly enough, there was a postcard of a girl with big bosoms stuck on the wall beside them.

Beneath the window, where a blanket had been laid to keep out the weather and had become set fast inside a great wad of ice, there were cartons of milk, tubes of shampoo and a cardboard box full of frozen fish. Beside this were more giant tubs of Golden Mayonnaise.

Chris bought a plastic litre-bottle of very red fizzy pop and asked the woman whether there were any pistachio nuts. She smiled and shook her head. 'They do have pistachios sometimes,' he mused, 'but not today, right out of supplies.'

I felt for Chris, stuck out in the middle of nowhere with so little to do that a trip to the shop had become the highlight of his day. So much so that I gave him one of my prized chocolate bars before I left.

His eyes lit up. 'Oh boy! Thanks mate.' I imagined him secretly scoffing it in his bed at 8 o'clock that evening.

Ever since I'd arrived, I had been having trouble pronouncing the ghost town's name. As we drove off the following morning, I asked Andrei if he could translate 'Nezhdaninskoye'. Andrei paused for a short while and said, 'Approximately, this word means "unexpected".'

FOUR

We continued along the Road of Bones through kilometre after kilometre of virgin territory. The occasional fenced corral for horses or cattle that had marked our first day out of Yakutsk had long gone with the flat plain of the Lena River. The road twisted and turned as it took us further into the untouched hills and mountains where the slopes became steeper and the valleys deeper. For an entire morning, the heavy frost and snow that covered every bush and tree looked as though the make-up department had tried to simulate a nativity scene but had overdone it. Then the trees became skeletal, with no needles that I could see, just black and dark brown silhouettes against the snow, some of them leaning over drunkenly. They had climbed up the mountainsides as far as they could go and had grown weary with the effort. As they thinned out into the distance the mountains looked as if they were sporting stubble.

The landscapes came in all shades of white, from pure blinding light, through hazy blues to misty greys. Only at sunrise and sunset did the rest of the spectrum make an appearance when the peaks were splashed with amber and golden yellows and, for the briefest of moments, a spectacular array of fiery reds.

After the usual early morning ritual of warming the axles and wheel hubs with flaming torches, coaxing our frozen vehicles back to life after a night in the deep freeze, we wound our way up mountainsides to gaze over rivers that slept in their gorges and down again to creep across narrow wooden bridges so as not to disturb them. Whenever we stopped to stretch legs and relieve bladders I would walk far enough away from the vehicle's engine to stand and marvel at the serenity of it all; not a breath of wind, not a twitter of a bird, just a majestic silence.

There's a map of the world pinned to the wall of my study at home and I often sit there looking at it thinking what a pimply little afterthought Europe is on the western end of Asia. Asia is a really serious, man-sized continent and Siberia occupies almost a third of it. Though you can get a certain handle on the scale of things by looking at a map, it was only now that I'd been here for a couple of weeks that I was beginning to get a feel for Siberia's size.

Even after the break-up of the Soviet Union, Russia emerged as by far the largest country in the world and three quarters of it is Siberia. Siberia is unimaginably vast. It could swallow up the largest countries in South America, Africa *and* Europe and still have more than a million square kilometres of elbow room. This 'sleeping land', as its name translates literally, possesses a million lakes, 53,000 rivers and a staggering wealth of natural resources. It spans eight time zones for God's sake.

Down in a wide valley we stopped to pay our alcoholic respects to the spirit of a hot spring beside the road. It was immediately obvious in the snowscape thanks to its shroud of mist. Seeing hot running water seep from a land that was otherwise set in suspended animation, it was easy to understand the pagan origins of the ritual. All the trees around the spring were festooned with bits of rag tied by Nature's parishioners. Other people had left messages, cigarettes and an empty vodka bottle.

Hot tea, sausage and bread were waiting for us in the back of the van after our toast and we ate greedily with the engine running to maintain the heater. Although thirsty after the alcohol, I stopped myself from drinking the tea straight away because I remembered something in one of the medical articles I'd read about how drinking hot liquids straight after coming in from very low temperatures raises the likelihood of shattering your teeth. So I let it go cool.

The sun had already vanished behind the mountains by 3 o'clock in the afternoon. We passed other patches of thick fog signifying open water and more hot springs as the last rays of sunshine splashed yellow beams on to the snow-clad peaks. At about 6 o'clock, a good hour after the sun had set, the moon came up at the end of the valley. But this was no ordinary moon. If I hadn't just seen the sun disappear I'd have said that this was it, because the thing perched on the horizon was a huge, really bright, orange vitamin-C lozenge. It seemed to just sit there radiating an incredible light vertically upwards. Like a gigantic bonfire, orange flecks were being fired towards the heavens. The phenomenon lasted for perhaps ten minutes before we were left with just the tunnel of light from our headlights as we pushed on through the snowy scene.

I heard three theories on why Oymyakon, the coldest town on Earth, is situated where it is. One said that it was in a meadow on the Indigirka River because historically this was where nomadic reindeer herders would spend the summer in a sort of semi-permanent settlement. The second said that this was the spot where Stalin, when he introduced collectivization in the 1930s, told the nomads to settle down. The third was that the town was a regional administrative centre. The three ideas were not necessarily mutually incompatible.

I felt a rising sense of excitement on our final day of driving along the Road of Bones. The valley had widened and the mountains had given way to hills set back from the road, which looked more like piles of white sand or flour. From this distance, the spruce trees clustered around the base of the piles took on the appearance of black currants. We were scuttling through a Siberian giant's kitchen as he prepared to knead a currant loaf.

Wildlife had begun to appear. A snow-white ptarmigan shot out almost from underneath our wheels, invisible but for the two black triangles on its tail feathers. It moved gently through the air like a kite until it hurtled across the grey ice of the road and became briefly visible as a bird flapping its wings before disappearing again over the snow.

Still 150 kilometres from Oymyakon we pulled off the road up a steep incline to a wooden house that commanded the best view of the valley. It was a lonely meteorological station, manned by a young man who lived in the middle of nowhere with his wife and two dogs. I wondered how he felt, being posted to this isolated spot in the heart of Siberia, so close to the world's coldest town and yet not quite there. He took me to inspect his compound of instruments, a difficult operation when I ventured from his well-trodden path because the snow was thigh-deep in places. He put his foot on the step up to his Stevenson screen, opened the louvered door designed to protect a thermometer from direct solar radiation that would warm it up beyond the temperature of the air, and examined the instrument. 'It's 32,' the young man told me. I peered over his shoulder. The liquid inside the instrument's thin tube was at -32°C (-26°F). 'You don't say "minus" here?' I asked. 'No,' he replied, 'it's obvious.' There was no answer to that.

But it felt colder. A light wind was blowing, burning my face and slicing through my gloves to freeze my fingers. I was relieved when he invited us in to drink a cup of tea. The meteorological observer wore thick, bottle-bottom glasses, and like me he suffered from the tedious problem of their frosting up as soon as we entered his house in billows of what seemed like steam as the cold air mixed with the warm inside. It was a handicap that I'd learned to live with since my arrival in Siberia. The frosted lenses had to be warmed before I could see again and it was unwise to venture out a second time before they had, because the condensation would freeze, potentially ruining the spectacles. But this man introduced me to a clever solution. He removed his glasses and held them over the hot stove, evaporating the condensation in no time at all.

Several factors contribute to Oymyakon's record low temperature. Siberia is cold in winter and eastern Siberia particularly so, because it has the highest degree of continentality on Earth, being far from the effect of the sea in dampening down extremes of temperature. This severe continental climate is dominated by cold air from the Arctic in winter when the region is under the influence of an area of high pressure. Winter means short days and little energy from the sun, but the cold is intensified by the dominant high pressure that produces clear skies. Clear weather promotes strong radiation from the snow surface during the long winter nights, hence what little heat is available during the day is lost rapidly after the sun sets. Winter in this part of the eastern Siberian *taiga* is typically severe and dry, with relatively little snow, few clouds and only light winds.

Eastern Siberia's generally low winter temperatures are lower still at Oymyakon thanks to the local topography. Although the town lies at an altitude of 740 metres above sea level, it is situated in a valley 10 to 20 kilometres wide and below the general level of the Oymyakon Plateau, which in turn is enclosed on all sides by mountains at a height of 1,500 to 2,000 metres.

Just as hot air rises, cold air tends to sink, so cold air accumulates in the valley. In winter at Oymyakon there is hardly any wind to disturb this cold air and the air is effectively trapped in the valley by a more-or-less permanent 'inversion': typically, there is an increase in temperature with height in the air through the first 500 to 1,000 metres above the surface of Oymyakon's valley floor (in most parts of the world, air temperature decreases with height). I tested the inversion theory for myself one day, managing to scale one of the hills at the side of the valley carrying the portable meteorological station I'd brought for the purpose. To my delight, the temperature at the top of the hill was a whole 4°C (7°F) warmer than at the bottom. This inversion also means there is little wind to disturb the cold air sitting in the valley bottom and the coldest temperatures coincide with the calmest periods. The average January temperature at Oymyakon is -50.1°C (-58.2°F) and the lowest temperature recorded was -71.2°C (-96.2°F) during a Russian expedition to the then unknown mountains of Yakutia in the 1920s.

When finally we arrived in the world's coldest town I asked that we drive directly to the monument erected to commemorate that occasion. The memorial to 'Oymyakon – Pole of Cold' was in the middle of town, a stone's throw from a small area of forest. Set in a stone base, surrounded by a low wire fence, it consisted of a mock thermometer recording the record low set next to a plaque honouring Sergei Vladimirovich Obruchev (1891–1965), journalist, geographer, traveller and writer, who holds the honour of having recorded the lowest temperature of -71.2°C during the expedition of 1926–29. Andrei translated the inscription for me, 'For his glory already nothing is needed. He is needed for our glory.'

Above the plaque, set on stakes, was a metal snowflake and wind vane, and above them the hammer and sickle. As a geographer, I suspected that Obruchev would have been disappointed with the circular metal globe that accompanied these symbols because North America was woefully thinner than it should have been, no doubt to give added prominence to the USSR, picked out in red.

After leaving the ghost town of Nezhdaninskoye we had passed several other sad and depleted settlements along the Road of Bones. Their outskirts were marked by derelict houses abandoned as the towns had contracted following the closure of a state-run enterprise or industry, leaving a core of survivors in the centre of a withered community. But Oymyakon was not like that. Spread out across the plain of the Indigirka River, it had many hallmarks of a thriving hamlet. Each neat wooden house was hemmed in by paddocks enclosing haystacks and grazing horses or cows, the school was well attended, the shop well stocked and a new sports hall had only recently been built. During my stay there I learned that the town was not without its problems but people were coping well enough because virtually every family was basically self-sufficient thanks to their animals.

The head of the family I boarded with (there was no hotel) worked at the town's electricity generating plant that ran on diesel. He worked 12 hours on, 24 hours off, and was glad of the extra income I brought because he hadn't received his salary from the power plant for more than a year. 'I do get advances on my wages,' he told me, 'but it is not unusual to go for three months with nothing.'

This was a story I was to hear repeated numerous times during my stay in the world's coldest inhabited place. The electricity generating plant was important, but its sister plant, the town's boiler house, was simply essential to life. Much of Oymyakon's housing consisted of farmhouses spread out across the plain, loosely linked by a network of rough tracks, but the central part of town was more tightly organized in a few conventional streets of housing, the kindergarten, the school, shop and bakery. While the farmhouses had their own wood-burning stoves, the centre of town relied on the boiler house for heat. The hot water was pumped across the permafrost through pipes enclosed in a wooden casing that looked like very short fences running along the sides of the roads.

The boiler house ran on coal, but the state did not have enough trucks to distribute it from the Yakutsk coalfields in the south. Of the 1,300 tonnes they needed in a year usually only about 900 arrived. Nikolai, the manager, shrugged when he told me this while we stood outside his small plant with its two pencil-like chimneys billowing smoke into the crisp air. Behind us, two grimy figures were shovelling black nuggets from an undersized pile into an iron wheelbarrow that looked as if it remembered the great October Revolution and had come out of it badly.

'So we burn whatever else we can,' Nikolai said. 'I have a team who chop wood in the forest and we dismantle abandoned houses to feed the boilers.' And if the boiler house stopped working, I asked him, what then? 'It would be a crisis,' he said simply, almost as if the thought had never occurred to him. 'There would be no bread, the schools would have to shut and a lot of houses would have no heat.'

The situation had happened in other Siberian towns that winter. Some had had to be evacuated when the fuel ran out, the heating ground to a halt and houses rapidly sank below freezing point. A roof over your head is a bare essential in the icy wastes of winter, but a house without heat is like no house at all.

'That would be the first problem, but worst of all the hot water pipes would freeze and fracture. They would have to be replaced. It would take many months to get new ones.'

Nikolai didn't tell me he hadn't been paid for ten months. Andrei informed me as we were leaving the plant after looking inside. Three huge brick furnaces gobbled coal and splintered doorframes to heat the boilers. Tangles of antiquated pipes and valves were encrusted in black coal dust. It was Dante's *Inferno* incarnate. I offered to contribute some shovelfuls of coal to the furnaces' fiery bellies and within minutes was almost overcome by the dust that penetrated to the depths of my lungs.

'Nothing at all?' I asked Andrei. 'No, he gets no advance on his wages, but the bakery allows him to buy bread on credit. He lives with his mother and he says her state pension is paid regularly. He has his own animals too.'

I thought of my own life at home in England. What chance would there be of me continuing to write or teach if no one paid me for ten months? But Nikolai still turned up for work each day to organize his small workforce, to keep the heart of Oymyakon pumping because he knew that if he didn't there would be little of his community left.

'He is a true hero,' Andrei said as we made our way up the main street past the school where children played in their break time in the snow, 'a hero without reward.'

About the only compensation of a job in Oymyakon's Dickensian boiler house was the fact that the workplace was warm. The following day Andrei suggested I might like to see what life was like working at the other end of the spectrum, so we drove to the outskirts of town to join up with a man named Alexei as he rounded up his horses.

Yakut horses are hardy beasts, left to forage for themselves through the harshest months. They have short legs and heavy compact bodies that mean the ratio of their surface area to their volume is low, helping them to preserve heat. Their stature mirrored that of all the people I had come across in Yakutia: small and compact. So much so that I kept banging my head on low doorways, even though at five foot nine I am hardly a giant myself. There was no doubt in my mind that the distinct lack of tall thin people among these northern inhabitants was evidence of a physical adaptation to the cold.

I had already seen some of the horses from the Road of Bones, standing in small groups scraping at the snow with their front hooves to uncover tussocks of dry grass below. But although well adapted for life in the freezer the horses still rely in part on human help. Every couple of months in the winter, Alexei rode out to round up his herd, to brush them down with heavy metal combs and scrapers. Snow collected on their backs, he told me, and turned to ice, both a heavy burden for the animals and an icy threat to their health.

Alexei would typically spend eight or nine hours a day outside while finding his horses and rounding them up. He was well dressed for the operation, wreathed in a thick sheepskin coat and huge fur hat like my own. The only difficulty he encountered was plain to see on his face. His prominent cheeks were red and raw where frostbite had taken a grip. But it wasn't painful, he said, and would heal come springtime. Nevertheless, for me the prospect of spending all day outside was still a disturbing one. It was clear that Oymyakon's residents were made of sterner stuff. Indeed, they were well prepared for this kind of life from an early age. In the school, naughty children are not made to stay behind after class for detention but simply locked out in the cold after lessons have begun. This punishment is not practised in all weathers, however. Classes are suspended and the youngest children sent home when the thermometer sinks to -52°C (-62°F).

The middle classes hold out to -54°C (-65°F) and for the oldest children classes continue until the temperature reaches -56°C (-69°F).

Other than a few cattle, horses made up the core of most people's livestock holdings. They are an excellent source of meat and the mares produce milk throughout the spring and summer period. Although the family I stayed with occasionally served reindeer, horsemeat was the mainstay of their diet, as it was for most of Oymyakon's inhabitants. It was usually boiled and dished up in large hunks for each person to attack with a knife on their own personal chopping board. By the end of a week, I longed for someone to roast the meat, but the oven in the family cooker had clearly never been used for anything other than storing bread.

Vegetables were conspicuous by their absence – unsurprisingly given the impossibility of growing anything in the permafrost – with the exception of raw onion and garlic bulbs. The latter were particularly loved by Andrei who popped one or two at breakfast each morning telling me how good raw garlic was for preventing colds. Otherwise, the lack of fresh produce from the ground took some getting used to; especially since I had to sit down to eat each day beneath a huge poster of fresh fruit on the wall in the kitchen. But everyone I consulted on the matter in Oymyakon informed me that fruit and vegetables were a waste of time. They provided little energy, I was told, since they burned up too quickly. Vegetable matter was what their livestock ate. A high-protein, meat diet was what people needed in winter.

It gave me reason to think about the phrase 'to eat like a horse'. I don't know where it came from since all horses eat is grass. A better phrase would be 'to eat like a Siberian'. These guys ate vast quantities of meat and anything else they could lay their hands on (mostly bread and milk products like ice cream). They really threw it down their throats. And I did too because I was always hungry in Siberia. I ate what seemed to me vast quantities but never felt full. My body was like the boiler-house furnaces that needed constant stoking.

If I had consumed as much at home I would have had permanent indigestion, but not in Siberia. Nevertheless, devouring horsemeat morning, noon and night was something my intestines took a bit of time to get used to. Three or four days into my stay at Oymyakon my stomach began to make constant groaning noises, as if there was a whole horse inside there trying to get out. I knew what the problem was but just the thought of resolving it made me weary. I had left the land of flushing toilets far behind. I remembered the last one, in a truckers' stop on the Road of Bones. The converted apartment only had hot water, no cold, including in the loo. It had been a very peculiar, rather pleasant feeling to sit on the bowl and have my bottom warmed from beneath.

But there were no such luxuries in Oymyakon. The apparatus in question was located outside in a little wooden hut raised up above the ground at some distance from the house. Number ones were no problem, a fast and efficient operation, swiftly completed. But the prospect of squatting down over a hole in the floorboards, straining to evacuate the unprocessed remnants of an entire stallion at -45°C (-49°F) was daunting. I left it for another day, hoping against hope that we were due for a warm spell. Doing it at -30°C (-22°F) would make a great deal of difference, I felt. The next day I could wait no longer, because I was becoming seriously disturbed by the thought of my belly splitting. I checked my portable meteorological station but its electronics had frozen solid. My backup conventional thermometer said it was -52°C (-62°F). It served me right. The only consolation lay in the lavish supply of toilet paper. It was a book to tear up; a 1983 Soviet volume entitled *New World*.

My encounter with Siberian toilets was just one in a series of everyday activities that took on quite different dimensions in the cold. The unfortunate incident involving my glasses just prior to the walrus dip had been followed by a series of similar breakages of the plastic straps on my boots, brought from England, which had been advertised by a well-known Danish footwear specialist as suitable for temperatures down to -50°C (-58°F). It was -38°C (-36°F) when the plastic snapped. I had expected the ink to freeze in my pens (which it did) so I'd brought a Dictaphone to make notes on, being very strict about keeping it deep inside a pocket next to my body so that the batteries wouldn't conk out. The machine worked after a fashion but when I listened back to my tapes in the evenings they came with ghostly silent patches that were inexplicable other than as some sort of reaction to the cold.

For my personal safety, investigation of the medical literature had been supplemented by advice from several people at home on the sorts of dangers I could expect in Siberia in winter. Some also suggested how I might avoid them. Worried (unnecessarily as it turned out) about vicious Siberian dogs, I went to see a nurse who gave me a rabies jab. She went all goggle eyed when I told her the temperature might sink as low as -50°C. 'Your eyeballs will freeze,' she said with complete authority. What was the best precaution I could take to prevent this type of injury, I enquired. 'Don't go,' she replied.

My sister Margot came up with a more useful source of advice, a friend of hers who had trained Special Forces in Arctic survival. He warned of the dangers of frostbite and recommended I buy some silk underwear to keep me warm. Cotton is no good in the cold apparently because it absorbs your sweat and rapidly loses heat when wet. He also told me I should get kitted out in whatever local people wore, which would probably be animal skins.

His opinion had been echoed by the words of Nikolai, the hunter-cum-forest ranger from Lake Baikal, and the dead animals that I'd chosen had served their purpose very effectively. Apart from significant discomfort and the temporary loss of feeling in the extremities, including a couple of occasions when Andrei had startled me by reaching out to hold my nose ('It is white,' he would say with customary understatement, 'this is not a good sign.'), I had survived my trip to date medically undamaged. The only drawback of my animal furs was the weight of my sheepskin coat, a significant cause, I suspected, of my voracious appetite. I had to eat a pound of meat a day just to keep up the strength to walk while wearing it.

But the danger that had loomed largest in my mind ever since I had set out on my journey to Oymyakon had come from my reading of the medical literature. Simply breathing at extremely low temperatures can kill you. Very cold air brought too rapidly into the lungs can damage bronchial tissue and cause potentially fatal internal haemorrhaging. When I read this it sounded to me like a good reason for smoking in Siberia: warm the air before it goes into your lungs to avert the mortal dangers of breathing.

Hence there was additional cause for concern the night I ventured forth to the small wooden cabin in -52°C (-62°F) to 'see a man about a horse' as they say so aptly in Mongolia. The temperature was a new personal best, but I was too busy concentrating on staying alive to celebrate. When I finally left the cabin, joyous after my success both at avoiding internal haemorrhaging and in finally embracing the opportunity to dispatch a few more pages of *New World* to the frozen stalagmite of history, I was met by another curious quirk of life in the deep freeze. As I walked down the snow path back towards the house with my torch I became aware of a slight rustling sound. It was barely audible, but was in the region of the very faintest rustle of leaves in a breeze, or of sand sliding down a dune face.

I stopped, held my breath and pricked up my ears to listen. Nothing. Not even the rumour of a noise. Then I let out my breath and heard it again, a magical sound like grain being poured in some distant elevator, the smallest amount of noise as if in respect for Siberia's primeval silence. It was the noise produced by the freezing of water vapour in my breath. I looked up at the perfectly clear night sky and was met by a spectacular array of stars. As I stood spellbound by the marvellous heavenscape, I realized that I could now hear the rustling continuing between my breaths. It was a phenomenon only perceptible on especially clear and cold nights, a weak, continuous strange rustling which the Yakuts call the 'whisper of the stars'. It is the sound caused by the settling of tiny ice particles produced by sublimation – when water vapour, a gas, freezes directly to become solid ice – at these very low temperatures. Even the soft voices of the stars seemed happy at my success.

FIVE

I had come to Oymyakon with preconceptions, half expecting to find a miserable place full of hopeless people trapped in a post-Soviet nightmare of slough and despondency. I had arrived in Siberia with visions of the world's coldest town as a gulag leftover, or a dilapidated mining settlement, populated by forgotten souls, desperate to get away but with nowhere else to go. I couldn't have been more wrong. Whenever I asked anyone how they coped in such a God-forbidding climate they would look at me as if this was a curious question, one that had not crossed their minds before. 'This is our home. This is where we live,' they would say, and that would be the end of the matter. The outsized poster of ripe watermelons and juicy peaches adorning the wall in the kitchen of my hosts was not a cry for a transfer to another world, just a nice colourful picture of fruit that might become available when winter passed.

No one was champing at the bit to get out of Oymyakon. They all seemed rather happy with their lot, in spite of the delayed salaries and the wintry weather. Not once did I hear a bad word about Moscow or the Soviet Union, despite the rigours of the past. Just the opposite in fact. Wages were paid on time during the Soviet period. If anything,

The drunken edifice of wooden housing built on permafrost in Yakutsk. A heated building partially melts the surface layers of the frozen ground causing heaving and subsidence.

Chopping a hole in the ice in preparation for a spot of river fishing.

The 'Road of Bones', Stalin's main contribution to development in the 'White Hell' of the Kolyma region.

One of the moustache brothers, a walrus club stalwart.

Andrei the interpreter examining the author's nose for signs of frostbite.

Olga and two of the herders offering advice on how to ride a reindeer.
Staying in the saddle was largely driven by the fear of losing an eye on its antlers.

Sunrise over a Siberian truckers' stop.

The author testing the medical effects of extreme sub-zero
temperatures at the monument to 'Oymyakon – Pole of Cold'.

times had been better then. But no matter what the complexion of the government more than 9,000 kilometres away, people here just got on with things. In many cases this seemed to mean reverting to subsistence level, but there was nothing wrong in that.

Self-sufficient the people of Oymyakon were, in terms of food, but water was provided by a municipal truck that drew it from a warm spring in the nearby river and delivered it to your door. Every time I walked or drove through the town, admittedly much more often the latter than the former, I saw a parade of red flags hung on poles outside houses signifying that the residents were in need of water from the truck. After a few days, however, it became clear that the flags were never taken down. Each day they became a little more encrusted with frost until in some cases it was difficult to tell what colour they were.

I asked Andrei what was going on. 'The truck is not delivering,' he told me. 'Why not?' I wondered. 'It has broken down.' I paused, disappointed because I had rather hoped to be able to join the water delivery man on his rounds. 'Also, the driver is drunk,' Andrei added, rather disapprovingly.

When the full story was revealed it transpired that the driver, a man with the improbable name of Guy, had gone on a binge after failing to fix his truck. I imagined Guy lying face down on his back somewhere in a pile of straw, having drowned his sorrows. 'Perhaps he'll sober up tomorrow,' I ventured. 'I don't think so,' Andrei replied, 'he started drinking two weeks ago.'

So while they dutifully kept their red flags flying, awaiting the return of Guy from his trip to oblivion, the residents of Oymyakon were obliged to be self-sufficient in collecting water too. This meant harnessing a bullock or a couple of horses to a sledge and driving it down to the river. No one had the wherewithal to pipe water from the spring, and besides there was a danger that the sledge would get stuck, so they visited frozen parts of the watercourse and hacked great chunks of river ice to take back home. Consequently, every house had a pile of ice lumps outside next to the neat pile of chopped firewood.

Another aspect of life in the permafrost zone that fascinated me was the challenge presented to gravediggers by deeply frozen ground. The issue had caught my interest many years ago, as a student, when I read a book about economic development in Siberia. Death caused its own unique problems in the coldest place in the world. Simply digging a hole in the iron-hard ground of winter is difficult enough, but the most macabre aspect of the business comes much later. Although permanently frozen to a depth of 100 metres or more, the surface layers of permafrost often thaw during the summer and freeze again seasonally. This cyclical nature of freeze-thaw has the effect of forcing large buried objects to rise towards the surface. In old cemeteries, the book stated, bodies buried in coffins are pushed to the surface where they thaw.

I sought advice from Andrei on the accuracy of the story. He confirmed that it was correct, adding that putting the dead in the ground was a settlers' custom brought from European Russia. 'Traditionally, the local tribes in these parts, the Evens and Evenks, bury their dead in trees.' The thankless task of re-interring the returning dead was a grisly symbol of the fact that the north does not easily tolerate the lifestyle of newcomers.

Andrei was not keen to discuss the matter further. He told me it was not a polite topic of conversation, so I didn't pursue it. I had wandered through Oymyakon's graveyard where the snow was deeper than elsewhere, reaching my thighs in places. I saw no exposed coffins, just a surprising number of deceased drivers, their headstones marked by a steering wheel, often with their photograph set in the middle. The potential foolishness of my enquiries into the ways of the dead was brought home to me towards the end of my stay in the world's coldest town. The week before I'd arrived a little girl had contracted pneumonia and had been flown to Moscow for treatment. She died during my stay and her body was flown back to Oymyakon for burial.

The little girl's father and brothers had to thaw the permafrost with a bonfire, enabling them to dig down about a foot before building another bonfire in the shallow hole, to warm up the frozen ground again and dig further. It took them two days to dig a hole deep enough to bury her coffin.

Much of my last day before leaving was spent in the town of Tomtor, Oymyakon's nearest neighbour. Oymyakon was set back some 30 kilometres from the Road of Bones, but Tomtor was situated right on the region's major highway. It was for this reason that the mayor of Tomtor had erected a second monument to the Pole of Cold, a towering column topped by a globe that could be seen a kilometre or two before reaching the town. It was dramatically larger than the memorial in Oymyakon, and it soon became clear to me that there was a certain rivalry between the two settlements for the title of coldest town on Earth. Standing in the snow outside Tomtor's museum were another two monuments to the record minimum temperature.

A small, wooden memorial that resembled a truncated telegraph pole had apparently been brought to Tomtor from its original position somewhere in the forest between Tomtor and Oymyakon. Behind the wooden monument was another in stone engraved with the magic -71.2°C (-96.2°F) and a further figure of 109.2°C (228.6°F) which is the difference between Tomtor's lowest and highest recorded temperatures, also claimed as a world record. In summer, temperatures here could reach as high as 30°C (86°F).

At least part of the confusion over the exact location of the Pole of Cold lay in the fact that Oymyakon no longer had a meteorologist to record its daily temperature. When I found my way to the Tomtor meteorological station I was told that records had not been kept at Oymyakon since 1996 when a man named Ipatiy Atlasov, who had taken the temperature readings for the previous 17 years, had become so dissatisfied at not receiving his salary for a whole year that he simply stopped. Apparently, he gave the thermometer to the local school and burned all his notes.

In consequence, Tomtor was the nearest operational meteorological station to the world's coldest inhabited place, and thus its authorities felt a certain justification in claiming the record for themselves. But there was no doubt in the mind of Tomtor's chief meteorologist that Oymyakon was the real Pole of Cold.

The meteorologist's assistant, a young woman called Natasha, took me to see their compound of instruments. Natasha was straight out of university in Moscow and looked far too glamorous to be a meteorological observer. She was blonde and beautiful, dressed in an ankle-length fur coat, and totally disinterested in my questions about life stuck out in Tomtor. Talking to her was like taking a time warp back to the Soviet days when the only comments a Westerner could extract from a Russian were either '*niet*' or '*da*', and at least two '*niets*' to every '*da*'.

'Do you like living in Tomtor?' I asked her, in an effort to break the ice. '*Da*' she replied. Pause.

'Don't you find it rather cold here compared to Moscow?' '*Niet*', she explained.

I decided to change tack and ask her more specific questions about her work. Stations in these cold climates use ethyl alcohol thermometers rather than standard mercury ones because mercury freezes at -38.8°C (-37.8°F) whereas ethyl alcohol freezes at -115°C (-175°F). But the man with the bottle-bottom glasses at the station on the ridge where we'd stopped on our journey to Oymyakon had told me he had to use both, since his dogs broke the spirit-filled instruments to drink the alcohol inside.

'Another meteorological observer told me that he has trouble with his dogs breaking the ground thermometers,' I said to Natasha. 'Do you have similar problems here?' Natasha looked at me with piercing eyes that could have melted my soul. She began to giggle. I knew what was coming. '*Niet*' she said.

I had avoided kind invitations to spend long periods outside during my stay in Oymyakon partly through cowardice and partly because I had managed to arrange to spend my last week in Siberia with some reindeer herders who were still more-or-less nomadic. I had seen the world's coldest town. Now I wanted to get away from the 'comforts of civilization' (the toilets notwithstanding) to taste a life that was as close as you can get to this inhospitable climate.

When the time came I drove with my new translator, Olga, past Tomtor and back along the Road of Bones for 100 kilometres or so before turning off just after a large wooden bridge. On the journey to Oymyakon I had secretly cursed the Road of Bones for its lumps and bumps that had us lurching and reeling all over the vehicle as we drove. I had thought that although the Soviet Union had produced some notable achievements, that road was not one of them, quite apart from the million-odd people who had died in its construction. Now that we were proceeding in a south-westerly direction towards the valley where the reindeer herders had arranged to meet us, I thought differently. The Road of Bones was like a snooker table compared to the track we followed.

We drove straight towards the sun, which was more brilliantly blinding than at any time during my stay in Siberia, through another stretch of winter wonderland populated by trees wearing their snowy winter coats, before following the welcome flat of a frozen river. After too brief a time on its sweeping meanders we ploughed off again over-land at no more than 10 kilometres an hour, penetrating deeper into a landscape of quite incredible beauty, the virgin snow only touched by the tracks of deer or rabbit, the trees now looking as if they had been decorated with big blobs of cotton wool.

Tucked away on one side of the valley, hard up against a steep wooded slope, was the reindeer herders' camp, a simple affair consist-ing of two canvas tents and a couple of wooden huts. Surrounded by piles of firewood, chunks of drinking water ice and wooden sledges, it was fronted by three large wooden posts, which bore a slight resemblance to totem poles, used for tying up reindeer. We were met by the head of the family, Petya, a wiry old man with a shock of grey hair, a leather face and a droopy moustache, and his wife, Shura, a woman whose main distinguishing feature was her bulbous red cheeks. The vehicle left me after I had made an arrangement with the driver to return after my week in the wilderness.

Petya and Shura were Evens, an ethnic group indigenous to the Siberian north-east, most of whom have long reared reindeer and hunted for their living. Spread wide across Yakutia and neighbouring areas, they probably number fewer than 20,000, including a semi-settled group on the Okhotsk Sea coast who fish and hunt sea mammals, using dogs rather than reindeer as draught animals. But Petya and his family were reindeer people, with a herd of nearly a thousand, which his four sons were out with when I arrived.

Their life was unaffected by electricity and unlike in Oymyakon I had to supply my own knife at mealtimes. The biggest blade on my Swiss Army knife looked decidedly puny beside their large hunting knives. Like everywhere else I had stayed in Siberia, I was accepted into the camp with genuine warmth, especially by Petya and Shura's seven-year-old daughter Nadia after she had spent the first day checking me out. Soon Shura replaced my daily diet of horse with a daily diet of reindeer, relieved by the delightful appearance at breakfast of a sort of rice pudding and on one occasion by a delectable stew of wild mountain goat.

I had already begun to wonder whether it was the cold that made people so hospitable, providing a common bond against the elements, a sense of community based on fellow feeling. In part this was true. In Irkutsk, Dima had told me that during this severe winter he had noticed a distinct thawing in the usual reserve people maintained on the city's buses and in the shops. The cold had made them more talkative, wanting to share their stories of wintry adversity. And all along the Road of Bones the driver would slow down or stop whenever he saw another vehicle potentially in trouble beside the track. However, what clinched the cold weather theory of community for me were the dogs. When I first arrived in Siberia I had been wary of them, a distrust based on my experiences in Mongolia where they were beasts to be feared. But after some tentative first encounters with canines in Yakutia, I found even the most ferocious looking husky to be friendly. A bark there may be, but on approach every hound simply sought a pat on the head or a scratch behind the ear, a bit of human warmth in the icy wastes. The same was true among the reindeer herders, despite their warnings that their dogs, which they kept tied up outside, were dangerous. When one joined us to help herd the reindeer, it was friendlier than I could ever have expected, especially since it looked more like a wolf.

In Oymyakon, the sense of community had been palpable, enhanced when I discovered that everyone seemed to be related to each other, a fact borne out by the very small number of family names in the town. I was rather pleased with how my theory was progressing until Andrei pointed out that none of the limited number of surnames were of local origin. When the nomads were settled there in the 1930s the use of their indigenous languages was 'discouraged', as Andrei put it, by the authorities. Everyone was required to take Russian names and only a limited number were made available. My faith in kinship ties was restored among the reindeer herders, however, when Olga, who had been brought up in a village more than 200 kilometres away, announced that she'd discovered that she and Shura were cousins.

I was surprised by the fact that Petya's family had avoided the permanent settlement that had followed the collectivization of many reindeer herds in the 1930s, and surprised again when I learned that their animals were still owned by the state. Although seemingly so free of outside interference here in their idyllic valley, Petya, Shura and their sons were all state employees. At first glance, little appeared to have changed since Soviet times, with the exception that the salaries they earned were now usually late and when they did arrive their buying power was significantly smaller than ten years previously. The size of their herd was still checked twice a year by government inspectors and any animals that had accidentally died in the interim had to be accounted for on the appropriate forms. Hearing the situation from Shura, via Olga, I saw the stark contrast with a herding life that in its day-to-day practice had changed little for centuries.

When the day came to join Petya and his sons in rounding up the herd and moving it, the boys brought a dozen reindeer into the camp, which they tied to the totem poles before harnessing them to sleds. The animals waited patiently, sniffing the crisp air and the ground around them. The lucky ones found yellow urine patches in the snow, a good source of salts.

Olga took me on one side and politely explained that Shura thought I needed a change of outfit. My sheepskin coat was too unwieldy for riding reindeer and the boots that I'd bought in Yakutsk were fine for city wear but no good for the country. I was mildly disappointed to have to shed my coat, which I'd become rather attached to despite its weight, but the boots I was happy to part with because the felt heels had warped and I found them increasingly difficult to walk in. In their place, Shura provided me with a reindeer hide coat that was so thin and light compared to my sheepskin that I initially doubted its ability to keep me warm. The replacement reindeer boots were made of the softest chamois-leather with the fur on the inside. On the soles of my feet they felt like moccasins.

As Olga and I sped away in the convoy of sleds, the temperature sank rapidly with the wind generated by our movement. In protest, my nose and chin broke off diplomatic relations almost immediately, but the rest of my body was quite happy beneath its layers of reindeer skin. Fur keeps animals warm because it traps air within the hairs to provide insulation. Air is a poor conductor of heat so it retains warmth. It's the principle employed by the string vest, invented for an expedition to the Antarctic in 1920: the holes between the strings trap the air. Reindeer fur is particularly warm because each individual hair is hollow. I have sympathy with animal-rights activists and vegetarians at home in the West when they argue against the maltreatment of God's other creatures. But I suspect that not many of them have been to Siberia where there is no substitute for meat as human fuel, and animal skins are still the best means of staying warm. Although some of the clothing I'd seen during my journey had been stylish, these people weren't making fashion statements. They were simply conserving body heat by using the best materials available. Mind you, I still felt a tinge of guilt being pulled along by a couple of reindeer while wearing their cousins on my back.

We found the herd only a few kilometres away but kept going towards a ridge to where we would be driving the animals. 'How does Petya know where to take them?' I shouted to Olga who sat in front of me on the sled. 'The reindeer know where is the best grazing,' she called back. 'They just follow them.'

When we got to the ridge we set up camp – a large canvas tent. Petya's sons set about chopping firewood and stripping spruce trees of their branches, which were laid on the ground inside the tent to provide a layer of insulation beneath a floor of hides. A battered metal stove was positioned inside the door, its chimney poking out through a hole in the flap, and rapidly filled with logs. Petya cut shavings with his knife to make kindling and we were soon drinking hot tea and chewing meat before settling down for the night, fanned out with our heads all pointing towards the dying embers of the stove.

It was one of the most uncomfortable nights that I can remember. My sleeping bag, a construction of animal skins, was excellent, keeping my entire body snug. When I covered my head with my hat and coat, that was fine too, except for one serious drawback – I couldn't breathe. Twice in what seemed like quick succession I was woken by nightmares. In the first I was doing a sponsored fast (something I've never done) in a cellar that someone had freshly painted. The fumes woke me up gasping for breath. Later I was awoken again when I dreamt I'd been buried alive.

The solution to this problem presented me with a new dilemma. I left an air hole in my folded coat but although the air it admitted was breathable, it was also perilously cold. I spent most of the rest of the night shifting from one position to another, first freezing my ear, then my cheek, followed by my nose, the other cheek, the other ear and so on. Somehow I did manage to get off to sleep again, but I only knew this when I was woken a third time by another bad dream. I was playing in my parents' garden on a bright summer's day with my childhood friend David Williams. We were using magnifying glasses to burn holes in dead leaves. Bored with this, I suggested to David that he turn his glass on my forehead to see what it would be like. I woke up when the tiny centre of light started to burn my flesh and was surprised to find myself not only considerably older but also wrapped in animal skins in a tent in Siberia in winter. David Williams was nowhere to be seen.

Kiasha, one of Petya's sons who had the telltale signs of severe frostbite on his cheeks, had briefed me on the basics of riding a reindeer the day before. I quickly realized that the most difficult bit would be simply getting on the beast since there were no stirrups hanging from the shapeless lump of felt that served as a saddle. The trick was to launch the left foot straight on to the felt and then push yourself up with a long stick, later to be used to drive the animal and maintain balance. If I'd been a practicing ballet dancer this would probably have been an undemanding task, but seeing as how I had spent much of the last month sitting on my arse in a vehicle trying to keep warm, the procedure presented problems. When Kiasha leapt into the saddle it looked so easy. The first time I tried it, I inevitably fell flat on my back. When the snow broke my fall it was the first time I truly appreciated the stuff.

Docile and uncomplaining, the reindeer just stood there awaiting my next attempt. With a great shove from Kiasha, I made it onto its back. 'Sit forward,' Olga said as I settled into the saddle. I edged a little further towards the towering antlers. 'Further,' she urged. My nose came within a matter of millimetres of the furry horns. 'Yes,' she called. I was sitting on the animal's neck. 'You lean forward to balance,' Olga added, a piece of advice that seemed like madness because if I leant any further forward I'd be impaled on the antlers. 'OK?' Kiasha asked me with his thumb up in anticipation. 'OK,' I replied, lying fluently.

He showed me how to drive: a pull on the rein to turn right, a tap on the muzzle with the stick for left. Kiasha warned me not to poke the stick in the reindeer's eye. Moving was a simple matter of kicking with my heels, like on a horse. If that sounds like I have ridden horses before, it's misleading. I have, but only twice in my entire life and one of those occasions had been in Mongolia where 'ridden' is not the appropriate word. If I remember correctly, the longest I stayed in the saddle was about four seconds.

So it was with no small degree of trepidation that I set off. It felt like riding a cow, an unhurried and stately pace that was only interrupted when Rudolph decided his head needed a shake, which he did while bending his neck down towards the ground. I don't know how I stayed in the saddle but I think it was something to do with the fear of putting my eyes out on his antlers.

The remainder of the day passed in a blur and not just because I had removed my glasses before mounting the reindeer on the advice of Kiasha. In fact, my eyesight seemed to me significantly improved in the cold air if that is medically possible.

The reindeer moved in their hundreds yet as one flowing whole save for the occasional splinter group that was soon absorbed back into the herd. I impressed myself by maintaining my perch and actually managed to provide some minor assistance in driving the herd, although Kiasha did most of the work, backed up by the dog and Petya who brought up the rear on his sled. The dog was easily the fastest to move across the snowscape, and continually dashed back and forth in response to Kiasha's whistles, to cut off stragglers and keep the herd moving.

We drove them across a frozen lake where the sound of their hooves on the ice was that of a gale through trees, and up a snowy bank where the air reverberated with the clacking of horn against horn. When we finally reached the tent I flaked out, exhausted and aching all over but especially in the legs, renewing my acquaintance with muscles I'd forgotten I owned. That night, I had no trouble at all in sleeping.

I like to think of myself as adaptable and I was pleased with my performance on the reindeer drive. I had managed to stay outside for most of the day without freezing to death and for me that was a significant achievement. The concentration needed to stay on board my reindeer was part of the explanation, as were the rare moments when I could sit and gaze across the valley in wonderment at Nature's splendour. But I also felt that I'd adapted to the cold in some rudimentary fashion.

Rudimentary it was, however, because at the same time the weather was getting to me after a month in Siberia. Everything was so relentless: the cold, the constant eating, and the daily ritual of pulling on so many clothes. Prior to the reindeer drive I had started to wake up in the mornings longing for the day when I could walk out of the hut wearing just shirtsleeves. The conditions were grinding me down. Everything was such an effort. I felt as if I'd been to the edge and looked over, but I wasn't going to cross. The prospect of spending an entire winter in Siberia was unimaginable. If I had to do it, I probably could, but in my heart of hearts I knew that I could only do so by mimicking the behaviour of Chris, the Australian at Nezhdaninskoye. I'd be in bed by 8 o'clock every evening and would refuse all visitors until I felt ready. This might not be until springtime.

One day during our drive along the Road of Bones to Oymyakon, I had asked Andrei what Siberia was like during the summer. 'It is very hot and much of the *taiga* is marshy,' he told me, 'then the mosquitoes come out. They are very good at biting. This part of Yakutia also receives swarms of giant insects in some years.' 'What sort of insects?' I asked him. He paused. 'They are like grasshoppers ...' he said finally, '...only flying.' 'Locusts?' 'Yes, locusts.'

I told Andrei that in my opinion Siberia ranked as the most hostile environment on Earth. 'The whole place is frozen solid for eight months of the year thanks to the lowest temperatures in the world, then it gets too hot and turns into a swamp with swarms of mosquitoes and plagues of locusts!' Andrei just smiled, obviously unconvinced at my assessment. Later he told me that of all the extreme places I was visiting he thought that Siberia must be the one that was easiest to live in. We agreed to disagree on this point.

Yet, despite its drawbacks, Siberia was still a magical wilderness and I couldn't help feeling how unfair it was that it was so inextricably linked in the European mind with exile and hardship, a land of woe symbolized by unutterable suffering. Misery and torment there had been, of course, on an unrivalled scale, and my soul had felt it on the Road of Bones. But the landscapes along that sorry trail had also been awe-inspiring, and somehow the reindeer herders' valley had taken me beyond awe. The stars at Oymyakon had been brilliant, but here they were better. I had marvelled at the otherworldly silence heard elsewhere in the *taiga*, but here it was more so. I tried to think of words to express it, but failed. I just drank it in instead. Siberia had surpassed herself. I felt that I had truly penetrated her heart and found a wonderful place.

But it was still cold, and I was glad to be going home.

DRIEST

Arica

Chile

ONE

Don Cecilio lost his hand when he was hit by lightning as a child. The shock of the strike put him into a coma for three days. In a sense, he was lucky. He might never have regained consciousness. Had this happened in Europe, Don Cecilio would have been forever relegated to a position of pity. He'd just be another cripple who couldn't hold his knife and fork properly. But it's not like that in South America.

For three days and three nights, his mother sat by his bedside and watched anxiously as her son wrestled with the visions that were floating through his mind. When eventually he came to, he was a different boy from the one who was caught out in the Puna by a rare thunderstorm. He awoke with the power of foresight, and so began his career as a soothsayer and shaman for the village of San Pedro de Atacama.

I had arrived in San Pedro in a small aeroplane that flew low over the high-altitude desert. This was the elevated section of the Atacama, the world's driest desert, here known as the Puna de Atacama after the local name for altitude sickness. Approaching the Andes in the early morning, the mountains had seemed at first like clouds on the horizon, but soon materialized as a series of brown peaks with snowy summits, that looked as if someone had painted them white so that passers-by wouldn't trip over them in the dark. Down below, the arid landscape was the closest in reality I'd seen to pictures of Mars. The desert was coloured with a palette of terracottas, browns and burnt siennas. It was red and dead, with not a tree, or bush, or blade of grass in sight. The airstrip we landed on was just that, a ribbon of tarmac on a gravel plain with a limp windsock and nothing else, at all.

San Pedro exists in this desolate terrain because it is on a river, the Lican, which rises in the foothills of the Andes and peters out in one of the many salt lakes that puncture the landscape of northern Chile. But green though the village was, it couldn't totally escape its barren surrounds, its baked mud streets and adobe houses respiring dust in the desert sun. My consultation with Don Cecilio took place one evening as a dry wind was getting up to blow in from the Puna, adding a slightly spooky edge to my sense of expectation. I had decided to confer with Don Cecilio about my passage down from the highlands, across the Atacama to Arica, the driest city on Earth. I was keen to learn what I should expect from my journey, but my enthusiasm was tempered by consternation at the possibility that the soothsayer might prophesy bad luck. As I made my way to Don Cecilio's house beyond the village street lights, clutching my offerings in kind – a bottle of pisco, the local firewater, and a packet of cigarettes – I was wrestling with the pros and cons of the man's part-time profession.

The very fact that I was prepared to consult him reflected my readiness to accept his prognosis, but another part of my brain wanted me to hedge my bets. If Don Cecilio's forecast was bad, I thought to myself, I could always dismiss it as an interesting, yet doubtful, piece of local anthropology. But this rational argument from my cynical European mind had fast lost ground during the day that I'd spent asking around to find Don Cecilio's abode. Everyone I spoke to talked about him in hushed and revered tones. There was no doubting his elevated position in the community. He was clearly the top banana on all matters futuristic and spiritual. The only glimmer of hope for my sceptical side was Don Cecilio's daytime job as a maintenance man for the local water company. It was not the sort of occupation I would have expected of a man who could look into the future.

He greeted me at his gate and led me into a shadowy garden where we sat on opposite sides of an ancient low table, he on a rickety chair and me on a pair of breeze blocks. A single electric light bulb dangled from an overhanging tree. Don Cecilio had the appearance of a kindly old hawk, with a creased leather face and piercing eyes that he used to look at me only sparingly, as if just a glance was enough to see deep into my soul.

From inside his windbreaker, he pulled a cloth that he laid carefully over the table top. He produced an old plastic bag from his trouser pocket and emptied its contents onto the cloth. 'Coca,' he said simply, as he piled the dry leaves into the centre of the cloth with his right hand. 'They are not fresh, they are from Bolivia.' He selected a couple and popped them into his mouth to chew, then another, which he offered to me. The leaf had little taste; it was like munching on dry privet. I saw him tuck his wad into the corner of his cheek, so I did the same, resisting the temptation to spit it out. Don Cecilio then carefully folded the sides of the cloth over the dry coca leaves and pulled a very old pair of spectacles from his windbreaker. Holding the glasses in his left claw, he opened them and placed them crookedly on his nose. He checked the cloth, tugging at one corner and flattening the bundle with his good hand, then removed his spectacles to place them on top of the cloth between us.

He accepted my offerings, lit himself a cigarette and bent down into the shadows beneath the small table to produce two small glasses that he filled with pisco. Before drinking, he poured some onto the ground beside the table. 'For the god of the earth,' he said quietly. Then he lifted his head and drained the glass.

It took another cigarette and a couple more slugs of pisco before Don Cecilio announced that I should ask him a question. I explained the nature of my journey and made my request. 'How will my trip go?' I enquired.

Don Cecilio nodded and proceeded to unwrap the cloth bundle to reveal the desiccated leaves. He spread them out with his good hand and studied them intently. The look of concentration was evident in his eyes, but the larger part of my brain remained sceptical as Don Cecilio selected seemingly random leaves, picked them up, turned them over, and examined them. Some he dropped back into the pile, others he popped into his mouth to add to his wad. It looked as if he selected only the smallest leaves, but that might just have been my need to observe method in an apparently haphazard process. I had expected to be a bit more involved, to have to ruffle the coca leaves, or shake them in the folded cloth, at least to touch the leaves before he read them.

The procedure took place in silence, with just the desert wind rustling the tree above us. A moth, attracted to the scene by the electric light bulb, fluttered in and out of my vision. Don Cecilio sighed and I held my breath, but he discarded the leaf in his fingers. Then finally he spoke. 'Your journey will be a happy one,' he said without looking at me. He picked another leaf from the pile in front of him for examination. 'The roads will be clean.' He dropped the leaf and selected another, rubbing it gently between his leathery fingers. 'Yes, all the roads will be clean.' He lifted his head and gave me a kindly look. I gave him a smile of nervous relief in return. Don Cecilio went back to the coca leaves, gently spread them out further with his fingertips, and picked another from the pile. He lifted it close to his nose for examination, dropped it, and quickly selected another. This one he held by its tiny stem and turned over and over. He held it further from his nose, so better to catch the light from the bulb above us. 'There will be one problem,' he announced, twisting the leaf under the light. My heart sank. 'But just a small problem,' he added, discarding the leaf. There was a very long pause. The moth landed on the table beside the coca leaves. Don Cecilio ran his fingers casually through the pile again and the moth flew off to circle the light once more. Don Cecilio ruffled the leaves a final time. 'But otherwise,' he said slowly, 'your journey will be a good one.'

Despite being more than 2,400 metres above sea level, I had not felt any effects of the altitude at San Pedro. Headaches, nausea, and difficulties with sleeping are all problems that can potentially hinder the unwitting traveller further while he or she is struggling to catch their breath at high altitude. More serious problems can occur above 3,000 metres, and that was where I was heading. Acute mountain sickness has been likened to a bad hangover, but without the pleasures of getting drunk first. It can entail vomiting, migraines and severe problems with sleeplessness. The human body can also succumb to ataxia, a constitutional unsteadiness in the use of your arms and legs. It becomes difficult to think clearly and to concentrate, and people can fly into violent rages for little apparent reason. It all sounded like it might be quite fun.

With its backdrop of snow-capped volcanoes, I headed out of San Pedro northwards. I had joined up with a local guide who had agreed to drive me along my route to Arica. Zahel was a quiet man with long black hair and a penchant for reflective sunglasses. At our initial meeting, he seemed rather remote, corroborating my first impressions of him as a cross between an ageing hippy and a Latin American revolutionary. His radical credentials were confirmed when we drove past the local militia station fronted by a green sign that read '*Carabineros de Chile – un amigo siempre*' (always a friend). The slogan was a post-Pinochet attempt to polish their tarnished image in the eyes of the populace. 'Are they?' I asked Zahel. 'Never,' he replied. 'How can anyone who carries a gun ever be your friend?'

Ruta Nacional 23 sliced its way north-west across a landscape of unrelenting aridity towards Calama, 'a land of sun and copper', as the town's welcoming signpost announced. Calama is the nearest town to Chuquicamata, the largest of Chile's numerous copper mines, and acts like a safety valve for many of its miners to let off steam.

'Calama is the richest town in Chile,' Zahel announced as we drove round its ring road, 'but intellectually the poorest. It is full of prostitutes, homosexuals and transvestites; an awful place.'

Off in the distance, through the desert haze, I caught a glimpse of the mineworking itself, a giant hole in the hillside sitting beneath its own little milky cloud of contamination generated by the copper-processing plant. Zahel told me that pollution from the plant was blown across the Andes to Bolivia and Paraguay and that Chile had started paying them in compensation. 'Locals know Chuquicamata as *Chuqui que mata* (the mine that kills).'

We climbed slowly away from Calama back towards the Andes, briefly following the Loa River, the only waterway to make it across the Atacama Desert from the mountains all the way to the Pacific coast. As we gained altitude, the landscape began to sport some meagre vegetation, but it was just clumps of tough-looking grass and the occasional wiry bush. A brown eagle sat momentarily in the middle of the road, before flying off at a leisurely place. After the tarmac ended, a dirt track followed a chain of gigantic *salars*, salt lakes that spend most of their time without water, their arid surfaces cracked into polygonal patterns by the sun. Mini sand dunes, no more than half a metre high, began to appear along their shores as the perfect cones of volcanic peaks crept closer and closer.

Signs of human habitation became fewer and further between, just the occasional small village where men laboured in the rarefied atmosphere, filling sacks with salt from the *salars*. Otherwise, there was just the dirty track we drove along, its very presence casting doubt on the Don's soothsaying skills, and a small-gauge railway line that didn't look like it got much traffic. It amused me that every time the track crossed the railway, Zahel religiously applied the brakes to halt at the stop sign, despite the fact that the clear lack of trains was apparent from a vast distance away. From a stationary position, he would look both ways, before engaging the gears once more and setting off.

Up on the Altiplano, a grand plateau shadowed by snow-capped summits, the browns and reds of the desert had given way to gleaming black boulder fields spat forth from ancient volcanic furies, and dark lava flows fossilized in position down mountain flanks. The track followed a pipeline that Zahel told me carried water from the mountains down to the desert town of Calama and to the city of Antofagasta on the coast, the latter more than 200 kilometres distant. We stopped to stretch our legs on a plain of small pumice stones, the size you use in your bathroom, which made a glassy clinking sound when I kicked them. I put my ear to the pipe and heard the strange sound of water flowing through the parched landscape. The pipe provided a lifeline for Calama and Antofagasta, Zahel told me, but left small Andean villages with water problems.

We stopped at a Carabineros checkpoint on a mountain pass in the middle of nowhere, which a sign beside a tiny old steam train declared was at 3,966 metres above sea level. Just over the pass, the brilliant white salt of the *Salar de Ascotán* gleamed like a sheet of pearls in the late afternoon sun and we stopped beside it at the foot of a volcano to set up camp for the night.

We couldn't have picked a worse spot. As the sun set behind the mountains, a hurricane-force gale picked up to make pitching the tents a virtual impossibility. This was not helped by the fact that the tent pegs just sunk straight into the volcanic gravel and gave no hold whatsoever. After manfully struggling for an hour, Zahel and I managed to secure a single tent and gave up on the other one when I decided to sleep in the car. Zahel produced some dried coca leaves, which he used to make an infusion of coca tea, supposedly a good antidote to altitude sickness, but it was one of the most uncomfortable and cold nights I've ever spent camping. As I struggled to get some sleep, my mind took me back to Don Cecilio's pronouncement that I should expect a small problem en route to Arica. I supposed that this was it. I didn't think I would like to see his idea of a large problem.

I had the vague suspicion of a headache that night, but other than that and some difficulty in getting off to sleep, I was blissfully unaffected by the altitude. Except, that is, for wind. I don't think I burped more than usual, but my rear end was producing at a phenomenal rate. It wasn't a symptom mentioned in any of the medical literature I'd read on the subject.

Zahel's tent was drenched in dew the following morning and I noticed that the white patches on the gravel, that I had mistaken for snow the previous night, were in fact salt. At five past seven, the sun made an appearance just above the volcano and transformed the nightmarish scene back into a terrain of beauty. Wisps of high cirrus clouds appeared on the horizon in the biggest, brightest, deepest blue sky I have ever seen.

Down on the *salar*, which had open water at its northern end, six flamingos stood motionless a few hundred metres from the shore. I walked down to the bright green tussocks of grass at the water's edge and sat on a heap of salt that had the appearance of brain coral. The lake was a perfect pane of glass, mirroring the volcanic peaks and the six pink birds. The glare from the sun on the water and the white salt was quite blinding. Total silence reigned, other than when one of the flamingos called 'caw'.

The town of Ollagüe looked just like a movie set thrown up for a spaghetti western. Sheltering beneath the active Ollagüe volcano, which sent forth ominous wisps of smoke into the mountain air, it sat just a couple of kilometres from the frontier on the edge of a *salar* that wound its way past the volcano and on into Bolivia. It was a border town and not much else, just two dusty streets, one each side of the railway line which boasted one train a week to Calama.

We hadn't been intending to spend any time at Ollagüe, but as luck would have it, Zahel got talking to a man from whom he asked directions, and 20 minutes later we were heading off past the outskirts of town towards a tiny hamlet where the man we'd met was supervising a llama sacrifice.

Llamas are members of the camel family, but look more like mutant sheep that have spent time being tortured on a rack. Their legs have been stretched and their necks rightly belong on a herd of giraffes. They are kept for their wool, meat and milk and as high-altitude beasts of burden. Finding pasture for llamas is a constant worry on the dry Altiplano, so every now and again one of their number is offered up to the gods to secure the future for the rest of the herd. It had rained in this area a couple of weeks before, so now was an appropriate time, Donato, the local master of ceremonies, explained. He was a middle-aged man of Quechua Indian origin, with jet-black hair and a very low forehead. His face looked the part, but his indigenous features sat somewhat at odds with his pullover, which bore a picture of a football and goal nets with the words '*Francia '98*' emblazoned across them. 'It is an ancient tradition in the Andes,' he explained, 'to thank *Pacha Mama*, (Mother Earth), for good pastures.'

Donato was quite happy for me to witness the ceremony, which would last for an hour or two, he said. 'You could also help,' he added with a kindly smile as we bumped along a dirt track out of town, 'a llama is too strong for a single man to hold down.' I thanked him but I wasn't entirely sure whether an active part in the ceremony was what I wanted. Despite Donato's modern attire, I had visions of an Inca-style procedure involving a beating heart being ripped from a still-warm chest.

'How do you kill the llama?' I asked him tentatively. 'We cut out its heart,' he replied.

About 30 llamas were wandering about on a hillside where a small spring of sparkling water nurtured a bright green gash of grass and some stunted bushes. On a slight rise, a house and paddock were fashioned from drystone walls. Most of the llamas looked up from their munching as we pulled to a halt and got out of the car. Several came over with inquisitive looks on their faces and proceeded to check me out at close quarters. To my surprise, several llamas sported tufts of pink and orange wool on their ears and some also had coloured tufts on their backs. 'They have been dressed for the sacrifice,' Donato told me.

While llamas look docile and cuddly, they also look very stupid, but this didn't make me feel any better about the idea of whacking one. Stupid or not, these were still nice furry creatures and the suggestion that I should help to cut one open and rip out its heart was bothering me.

But I didn't have time to dwell on the matter because Donato was already introducing me to the llamas' owner, a very old Quechua woman named Felicia who seemed delighted that I had come to her ceremony. 'Welcome *Caballero!*' she cried with a wrinkly smile.

Herding the llamas was not a challenging task. For most of the way to the stone-walled paddock, the roles were reversed. All we had to do was walk there and the llamas trotted along behind us, blissfully unaware of the fate that awaited one of their number. But as we neared the walls, Donato signalled Zahel and me to circle round behind the herd and issue them up and into the corral.

Inside, at one end of the dusty compound, sat a table bedecked with stems of foliage, a bottle of pisco, a carton of red wine, a motley collection of glasses and some plastic bags filled with what I correctly suspected were coca leaves. Donato took charge and explained that the ceremony had to begin with a request to *Pacha Mama* to ensure that this was an auspicious occasion. He emptied one of the bags of coca on to the table and stuffed most of the dry leaves into a coloured pouch that he hung round his neck. The rest he popped into his mouth to chew.

Donato then told me to hold out my hands and he proceeded to fill them with coca leaves from his pouch. He did the same for Zahel and Felicia and a couple of other guys who had appeared to help with the llama kill. We were instructed to sprinkle the leaves over the table in front of us, while making a chant that translated as, 'Make this a good time.'

A similar procedure followed in which we each took a glass of wine, poured some of it on to the earth around the table for *Pacha Mama*, and drank the rest in one go. The coca leaf and wine rituals were repeated twice more, by which time the alcohol was beginning to take effect and I didn't feel quite as bad about the prospect of dispatching one of the herd that was now mooching around the corral watching our strange ceremony.

Donato replaced his wine glass on the table and wiped his hands on a cloth. 'Now we select the llama,' he said. 'The best way to catch one,' he told me as he circled the animals, arms outstretched, 'is to grab it by the ears.' And so saying, he launched himself across one of the creature's backs, seized its ears, and hung on for dear life as the llama bucked and kicked at its captor. Dust flew everywhere as the llama struggled, and its companions pushed and shoved to make way for the tussle. Zahel and I were on top of the chosen animal in a flash and forced it to the ground. It was strong. I had a good grip, my hands full of its thick fur, but it wriggled, writhed and kicked viciously. 'That is good,' panted Donato, still clinging to its ears. Felicia was on hand to offer a rope and Donato set about tying the legs of the sacrificial beast.

As soon as we had it under some sort of control, Felicia started offering coca leaves to us all and we sprinkled them on the ground around the llama, again calling to *Pacha Mama* to make this a good time. I think by this time the llama had realized that while all his mates might be able to expect a good time, the phrase wasn't going to apply to him, so with a Herculean effort it managed to stand again, despite the truss around its legs, and we all had to abandon the coca leaf procedure to sit on it again.

More coca leaves hit the ground, followed by a round of pisco. By this time I was glad of the opportunity to spill some of the firewater before upending the glass down my throat. Felicia was busy twisting more bits of coloured wool into the fleece of the chosen beast and produced a needle with which she gave the llama a couple more 'earrings' to go with the pair it already had.

'The llama must be dressed well for its journey to the spirits,' Donato explained as he delved into his pocket and produced another plastic bag. This one contained brightly coloured confetti and we all sprinkled some on to the llama's back. It felt particularly strange for me since the last time I'd done this was at a non-llama friend's wedding.

Momentarily, the llama was calm, quietly taking in all the fuss being made over it. Meanwhile, its fellow llamas all around the compound had cleared a respectful distance around their compatriot. They were totally unconcerned, and a couple of them began to mate about a metre from the sacrificial beast. At that point, the distance didn't seem quite so respectful, but I decided there was a certain symmetry in the conception of one llama taking place right next to another that was about to be dispatched.

Decorated and dressed in its Sunday best to meet the gods, we hauled the chosen llama towards the corral entrance where Zahel sat on it. Despite the herd's apparent lack of concern, I had been uneasy at the thought of killing one of their number right in front of them. It was a relief when Donato pulled the willowy tree trunks away from the entrance, ushered the herd out and prepared to do the job in camera.

We manoeuvred the sacrificial animal to the entrance and, still holding the beast in the dust, lined up on one side. This was to make way for its soul to fly to the sun when the body was dispatched.

Felicia produced a knife, which Donato sharpened on a handy stone. He knelt on the animal's neck and it gave a final vain struggle as the blade sliced across its throat. A spurt of blood splashed across my face. I saw green bile and was almost overcome by the foul stench as the animal continued with its last fight. Donato was poking the knife deeper into the gaping hole in the animal's neck as the blood poured out, aiming to sever the spine as he'd explained to me beforehand. This would cut any sense of feeling so that the animal would not die too painfully. But now that he was actually doing it, I had my doubts. The llama was still putting up quite a fight. It made me realize that if anyone ever cut my throat I wouldn't die instantly. The llama didn't.

Like the ceremony that had led up to this moment, the wielding of the knife was all very matter-of-fact and mechanical. Donato rolled the llama over onto its back and cut into its chest. There was a huge cavity in front of me, deep and dark, like a hole in the ground. The blood inside wasn't red; it was a dirty clay-type colour.

Having been in namby-pamby, I like nice furry animals mode up to this point, my perspective changed the instant the knife sank into the animal's torso. As soon as Donato cut into the chest, it looked like meat and I no longer felt that I was caught up in a murder. It seemed more like I was participating in the proper management of the herd, and anyway, I was hungry.

The heart was huge and still pumping in the cavity, despite the fact that the animal was dead. Then Donato squeezed it, cut it out and put it on a white enamel plate held by Felicia. The heart continued to beat as it lay on the plate and we all had to sprinkle more coca leaves ceremoniously over it.

Covered in sticky leaves, the heart was taken up the stony hillside to a small fire and placed there to have more leaves sprinkled on it. As wisps of smoke carried the llama's soul towards the sun, we all had to shake hands and hug each other as the final part of the ritual.

Then we set about skinning the carcass.

T W O

By any standards, Collahuasi is a huge operation. More than US$3 billion have gone into getting it up and running as the world's fourth largest copper mine. Being situated in the middle of nowhere, some 4,500 metres up in the Andes, meant building everything from scratch. A new power line had to be constructed and 14 wells sunk to supply the mine's water requirements. Six thousand workers were involved in creating a purpose-built town to service the mine, but before they could start work there was the small matter of putting up somewhere for these workers to live. They built fuel-oil storage depots and maintenance shops, office buildings and operational buildings, laboratories, warehouses, a hospital, and a truck shop. Oh, and a permanent camp for 1,800 employees. A new pipeline takes copper concentrate down to a whole new port facility on the coast, along with a new 220-kilometre road that links Collahuasi to the Pan-American Highway. I'd followed the new road briefly on my journey up from the llama killing field the previous day. The mining engineers are confident that Collahuasi has a lot of copper. The mine has a projected life of 100 years.

The guy who escorted me around, Luis, drove a brand-new red Toyota pickup with the code number 007 on the door. It summed up

Collahuasi perfectly. The whole place was like a James Bond film set. My accommodation was better than a five-star hotel, with a bed slightly smaller than a football field and a lounge where I was served with cheese and biscuits before dinner. The rooms splayed off in four wings from a central atrium that housed video rooms and Internet connection sites. Each of the four glass wings looked in and down on to a lush interior garden transported straight from the humid tropics.

Outside the ultra-modern, hi-tech man-made sanctuary, Collahuasi operates on a different scale to the real world. Just beside the opencast pit, gigantic crushing plants grind solid rock into mincemeat at a rate of 6,000 tonnes every hour. They are supplied by dumper trucks that looked like boys' toys from afar, but up close, turn out to run on wheels taller than a two-storey house. Inside the pit, 60 tonnes of aggregate are shovelled into the trucks in just a couple of scoops by cranes the size of small skyscrapers. Twenty-four hours a day, every day for 365 days a year, the miners at Collahuasi are gradually inverting a mountain into one of the world's biggest holes in the ground. Soon, there will be one less Ande on the skyline of northern Chile.

The very first thing I had to do when I arrived was to submit myself to a medical check-up at the mine's hospital. A doctor led me into a sparkling clean ward stuffed full of gadgets to take my pulse and to measure my blood pressure and blood oxygen content. My pulse was 100, normal for such an altitude, the doctor said, but my blood oxygen content was low at 78 per cent. 'How do you feel?' the doctor asked. 'All right,' I told him, 'other than a lot of farting.'

He ignored my attempt at levity and told me to take some deep breaths. I watched as the blood oxygen monitor rose to 85 per cent. 'You're fine,' he told me, 'but come back if you feel any effects of the altitude.' I was relieved, because the mine has a strict policy of flying you down to the coast if you show signs of ill health.

Because Collahuasi is one of the highest mines in the world, considerable amounts of time and money have been invested in ensuring a safe and healthy working environment. The walls of the hospital and the accommodation block were plastered with brightly coloured posters with bar charts and tables depicting their safety record. There hadn't been an accident at the mine for more than six weeks.

The company running Collahuasi has undertaken extensive research into the effects of working at high altitude. One of the outcomes of this research was the building of the accommodation, canteen and hospital somewhat farther away from the mine than originally planned. This was to reduce the altitude of the camp, which is at 3,800 metres (700 metres lower than the mine), an altitude at which most people experience relatively few problems. Several specific working practices had also been adopted to help employees further to cope with working in the mountains, including the shift system worked by most, which was seven days on, seven days off.

But even so, Luis told me as he drove me out to the pit one morning in his red Toyota, he still felt poorly for a day or two when he first arrived for his seven-day shift. Luis lived down on the coast, in the city of Iquique, when he wasn't working, and felt the effects most when he flew to work in the company aeroplane. 'It takes just 45 minutes,' he told me, 'which is fast to rise 3,800 metres. I always go white and get headaches for the first two days,' he said, 'but it's not so bad if I drive up, which takes three hours.'

Luis was a former naval officer who was rather officious and liked standing to attention and directing the mine traffic whenever I wanted to stop and take photographs from the side of the road. Herds of wild vicuña, a smaller, rare cousin of the llama that lives at altitudes where the air is too thin for most mammals to lead a normal life, wandered the area around the mine.

Since Luis had a barrel of a chest and looked as if he could jog up from the coast if he wanted to, I took seriously his comments on the effects of working at altitude. Some say that the Chilean character is partly moulded by the constant battle waged against the country's inhospitable environment, a wild land of untamed wilderness and mountains typified by this high-elevation desert. Here at Collahuasi, human ingenuity had created its own little oasis, an outpost of comfort designed to defy all that Nature could throw at it. All, that is, except the altitude.

Luis was not the only person to complain of headaches and minor nausea when they arrived for work, and it came as no surprise to me when I learned that the mining company was experimenting with pumping oxygen into some of the bedrooms in an effort to sort out this final challenge. I wondered for a while whether perhaps I had been assigned one of these rooms because, other than a slight difficulty in getting off to sleep at night, I continued to feel few effects from my high-altitude abode (even my farting had subsided to a normal rate). Until, that is, I spent 20 minutes one evening trying to find my wash bag that had apparently completely disappeared from the basin in my bathroom. I couldn't believe that the chambermaid had pinched it, but it took me an eternity to realize that the mirror above the basin was also a cupboard. I opened it to find my things all neatly laid out and ready for use. Trouble with concentration is supposedly another sign of altitude. I had stopped farting and started to lose my mind.

There was a definite sense of community about Collahuasi and I wondered whether it was the isolation that engendered it. Whenever I passed anyone in the camp or at the mine itself, I was met with a cheerful '*Hola*' or '*Buenas Dias*', and everyone seemed comfortable and at ease. It wasn't all James Bond, I discovered in time, since alcohol was totally banned and there were very few women (even my chambermaid was a man), but the workers enjoyed rates of pay that were significantly higher than the national average and while on site, the food and luxurious accommodation were supplied free of charge by the company.

Luis told me that 99 per cent of the workers were Chilean, so it was a fluke that I met one of the few employees who wasn't. I did so on my first morning at Collahuasi. I had just missed the early rush, which started at 7.30 in the morning in time for the shift change at the mine, and there were few people around as I hovered at the self-service canteen trying to decide which of the numerous food stations I should approach for my breakfast. Startled by an English voice behind me asking if I needed any help, I turned to see a man in a white coat and caterer's cap who offered to show me what was on offer.

'You don't sound particularly Chilean,' I ventured as he led me past the juice dispensers. 'No,' the man replied, 'I'm from Wakefield, Yorkshire.'

Being in such a remote spot, in a faraway country, I was prepared for many types of surprise, but not one that emanated from so close to home. I didn't want to blurt out anything so inane as, 'What are you doing here?', but that was the only thing that came to mind. He told me he was the catering manager. Dazed, I selected breakfast and took my tray to a table. Some moments later, the man from Wakefield, Yorkshire came over and sat down. He asked what brought me to Collahuasi and I told him. Recovering somewhat, I introduced myself.

'My name's Graham,' the man said, 'but everyone calls me Paul.'

'Why?' I heard myself say. Altitude sickness and inanity clearly went hand in hand. 'Because Chileans can't pronounce the name Graham.' I shoved a piece of toast into my mouth to stop me saying anything mindless in response to that.

Paul was married to a Chilean and had been working in the country for over ten years, though not all at this mine, which had only been in production for three. The company he worked for, based in Santiago, was responsible for all the catering, he told me. I complimented him on the canteen's food as I drew a plate of fried eggs towards me. With knife and fork poised over the yellow yokes, and my mouth watering, Graham said, 'Oh, that's not very sensible at this altitude.' This was getting beyond a joke.

'What's wrong?' I asked. 'Fatty foods aren't a good idea on your first days up here,' he told me. 'You shouldn't be eating butter either,' he said, pointing to my toast.

Deflated, I put down my knife and fork.

'What should I have for breakfast?' I asked, probably a little too aggressively.

'Well tea is better than coffee.' He nodded at the cup of black coffee by my elbow. 'And you need to drink lots of other fluids. Plenty of water and juice. You should eat light things, like fruit. Jelly is also excellent food for high altitude. It's nourishing and gives you plenty of fluid.'

'Looks like I'd better go round another time and start again,' I said irritably. 'That's fine,' Paul said. 'Go round as many times as you like.'

It must have been a measure of the minor shock I still felt at having just met a Yorkshireman in a remote copper mine in the Andes that I went back to the food stations and selected a healthy high-altitude breakfast of jelly, fruit, tea and juice. Back at the table, Paul smiled and told me I'd feel much better for it. Unconvinced, I drew the plate of jelly towards me. It made me feel like a recalcitrant schoolboy.

'Can you drink the water here?' I asked Paul. He said it was fine, since it came straight from the mountains, 'but it smells a bit of sulphur,' he added. 'It reminds me of Harrogate Baths.'

I detected just a hint of homesickness, so I asked Paul if there was anything he missed from home. Out came a list that included pork pies, fish and chips, and most of all cricket. 'I have cable TV in my room, but you only ever get brief highlights of the cricket,' he lamented. 'I think that's what I miss the most.'

His comments seemed strangely appropriate given his white coat and hat. Paul could easily have been an off-duty umpire chatting over breakfast before taking the field for the day. He said he worked ten days on and ten days off. The facilities were excellent, he said: games rooms with ping pong and pool, video games, a sports hall, Internet connections, TV in most of the rooms, but they all became boring after a while. 'You must have seen cable TV,' he said, 'you watch for more than a day or two and you just do your nut.' 'So how do you relax?' I asked him. 'I work,' he said. 'Like everyone else, I have 12-

hour shifts, but I often work 14 or 15 hours because otherwise there's nothing else to do.'

Among the many surprises Paul sprang on me that first morning was the pronouncement that going down from high altitude could be as injurious to health as going up. He told me several times to drink a lot of water when I came to descend from Collahuasi towards Arica on the coast. Indeed, as he wandered off to check on the food stations and pass the time of day with the few stragglers still turning up for breakfast, or an early lunch, his last parting comment to me was, 'Don't forget, drink lots of water.'

Even without Paul's words, I was intent on sinking several bottles of mineral water the morning Zahel and I left the mine and headed for the coast. The reason was that I needed it to rehydrate after a particularly foolish attempt at machismo the evening before. For reasons best known to my inner psyche, I had talked my way into the mine's five-a-side football team for a friendly match against the local border police. I kidded myself that this was because I was so confident about being unaffected by the altitude that I felt some kind of perverse need to test myself. Conversely, of course, some might say that my choice of test was complete proof of the fact that the altitude had indeed had an effect – on my judgement – and a serious one at that. The football match completed the full set of effects, physical to go with the mental, it nearly killed me.

That's not quite true. I was pleasantly surprised at how long I actually lasted. The big problem was breathing. I just couldn't get enough oxygen into my lungs. The rest of me felt OK, physically my muscles and things kept going, but I had to stop because I just couldn't breathe properly. At one point, while I was bent double outside the opposition goalmouth, the border guards' goalie put his hand on my shoulder and told me to take deep breaths, rather than the quick, feeble pants that I had opted for, as the best way to get more air into my lungs. I stopped panting and took deep gulps instead, which did indeed seem to get more precious oxygen into my body. But only for a short time, and soon I was bent double again, desperately trying to satisfy my body's needs. There was no option but to bow out gracefully and lie down on the ground.

Once I had got my breath back and the game was over, I challenged our centre forward, who was half Indian and had told me he'd been born at some altitude, to a 'hold-your-breath' competition. Children born on the Altiplano are supposed to have a greater lung capacity than those born at sea level. This guy was small and stocky, and a very skilful striker, and his chest looked like it probably contained a specially enhanced set of lungs.

There are no prizes for guessing who won. While we both managed quite happily for what seemed like a minute or two, our centre forward still looked supremely unconcerned when I finally gave up, gasping. The second prize was a few slugs of pure oxygen from the bottle that Luis had wisely brought along with him to the match. I had always wanted to have a go on neat oxygen, but it was rather disappointing. It didn't taste of very much and actually I'm not quite sure if it made any difference to me. Oxygen or not, I still felt as if I'd been run over by a truck.

So, I felt somewhat deflated as we sailed down the fresh tarmac road towards the coast. From the rolling high plateau with quite a lot of grass on it and a fair number of llamas wandering around giving us idiotic looks as we passed, we sped through a zone of more vegetation with lots of blue lupins by the roadside. Large rolling dunes, fixed in suspended animation by salt, took over while the plant life disappeared as we descended further. Warning signs about sand on the road began to appear while I was pouring water down my throat and my ears began to pop.

Most of the Atacama Desert lies in a central valley that runs north–south parallel to the coast, bordered on the Pacific side by a low range of coastal hills and to the east by the Andes themselves. The uplift of the Andes, formed in this zone where two of the Earth's great crustal plates collide, gives rise to one of the greatest altitudinal contrasts found on the planet. Over a distance of less than 300 kilometres, the Andean peaks up to 6,000 metres above sea level plummet down to the Peru–Chile trench deep in the ocean floor just off the coast at 7,600 metres below sea level.

The rise of the Andes is one of the reasons the Atacama is so dry. South America's mountainous backbone provides an effective barrier to any moist air from the Amazon Basin, casting a 'rain shadow' across Chile's northern coastline. Another central reason for the area's aridity is the existence of a cold ocean current that runs most of the length of South America's Pacific coast. The Humboldt Current brings cold water from the Antarctic, and this cold water prevents evaporation from the ocean surface, so limiting the amount of moisture in the atmosphere that can fall as rain.

The Atacama is not only one of the world's driest deserts; it is also almost certainly one of the oldest. It has been extremely dry for about ten million years, since the rain-shadow effect of the Andes and the drying presence of the cold Humboldt Current have been in place. Extreme aridity also helps to explain the presence in the Atacama of vast quantities of salt. This central valley contains probably the most famous and important nitrate deposits in the world, locally known as *caliche*, a Quechua word for salt. This sodium nitrate is more soluble in water than other materials common to the Earth's crust and is only so plentiful because the climate is so dry. That night, our first in the Atacama proper, we camped on the ancient crust of a dry salt lake that had been planted with Tamarugo trees, one of the few plants that can thrive on the saline surface, before forging on northward towards Arica.

Life in the driest desert on Earth is a question of grabbing opportunities. Permanent settlement for people is only possible where you can find a reliable source of water. Since rainfall is so sporadic in the Atacama, the only dependable supplies of water come from the Andes, reaching the desert either along surface rivers or as underground water found in aquifers. On occasion, where the incentives are big enough, people have built pipelines to maintain towns without their own natural water supplies. In most cases in northern Chile, the incentive has been the nitrate deposits, but once the nitrate has been worked out, the settlements have been abandoned. As we made our way up the Atacama's central valley, we passed a string of derelict nitrate towns, cast-off shells left to wither slowly in the desert sun.

Parts of this desert were, in fact, inhabited for nearly ten thousand years. At a few choice spots in the coastal hills, where brackish water could be found in subterranean springs, the Chinchorro people eked out a living based on the abundant marine life fed by the Humboldt Current. They traded with other cultures established in the Andes, but the commercial traffic of those ancient times had to cross the inhospitable Atacama. Those trade routes probably made use of the valleys dissecting the desert, and evidence of these early highways can still be seen today in huge pictures, drawn with carefully laid patterns of stones on the valley sides, perfectly preserved thanks to millennia of near-zero rainfall. Archaeologists debate the significance of the stick men, animals and intricate designs. Were they icons put up to appease their gods, or desert road signs for weary travellers indicating the way to the coast? Or maybe the Chinchorro simply liked doodling on a very large scale?

We crossed a series of *pampas* on the last leg of our journey to Arica, extraordinarily flat, gravel-strewn plateaus where not even cacti could find enough water to survive. Then all of a sudden (wham!) we would come across these yawning gashes in the flat terrain, dramatic, steep sand-covered slopes plunging down to lush green valley bottoms.

In the last valley we came to before the Peruvian border sat Arica, the driest city on Earth.

THREE

It had been difficult to know what to expect from the world's driest settlement. Dry was always going to be the least tangible of all the extremes. Hot, cold and wet would be in-your-face climates, immediately obvious as soon as I stepped out of the front door. I was ready for physical pain in temperatures of plus or minus 40°C (104°F to -40°F), and I knew that I'd be permanently wet in a place that could boast nearly 12 metres of rainfall on average in a year. But dry was not so palpable. OK, I was in a desert, but it wasn't even a very hot desert. The Humboldt Current takes care of that. Temperatures in the Atacama are lower than anywhere else in the region of the Tropic of Capricorn or in any other of the world's deserts at the same latitude.

Arica simply isn't a parched, scorching place full of dust and mirages. In fact, it has a very pleasant climate. It is completely devoid of rain, but always enjoys a soft sea breeze, which gives rise to luxuriant vegetation with landscapes of abundant palm trees and other tropical plants. The city has several sandy beaches and promotes itself as a tourist resort. The average temperature during the year is 20°C (64°F). The local authorities have dubbed it the 'city of eternal spring'.

And despite the lack of rain, water did not appear to be a problem. As we drove into town, we passed lush green public parks full of municipal workers dressed in blue overalls watering the gardens liberally with their hoses. These guys were even wearing wellington boots. In my hotel room, there were no notices on the door saying 'water is precious, please conserve it', as there had been up on the Puna de Atacama. Damn it, my bathroom even had a bath.

I learned later that the city gets its water from a variety of sources. There are underground supplies and the San José River that flows through the heart of town, the latter being rather salty, so they have to desalinate its water. But Arica *is* actually worried about supplies. The groundwater level has been declining for some time and the authorities have experimented with the recycling of sewage water. There is even a plan to pipe the stuff from the highlands in nearby Peru. Water is a problem in Arica; it's just that no one seems to have told its inhabitants yet.

Nevertheless, it is still the driest inhabited place on Earth. When you add up all the water that comes from the atmosphere as precipitation – not just rain, but fog, dew, mist, hail and snow, though they don't get snow in Arica – it comes out at less than a millimetre of water on average each year. Arica's annual average total precipitation is just 0.8 mm (0.03 inches). Rainfall is almost unknown here, and when a freak storm does produce some, it usually comes in small amounts. The 10 mm (0.4 inches) of rain that fell at Arica on one day in January 1918 accounted for almost a third of the total precipitation during the first half of the twentieth century.

My first stop therefore, after I'd settled into my hotel, was the meteorological station. I jumped into a taxi and sped out to the airport where it was located. I wanted to meet the man who presided over the driest station in the world.

Situated on the floodplain of the San José River, the city is hemmed in all around on the landward side by the barren coastal hills. To the south, these steep, sand-covered slopes rise abruptly, almost straight from the ocean, leaving just a strip of land 100 metres or so in width. It's room enough to put up a few hotels and restaurants beside the beach and a highway to get to them, but not much else. The slopes themselves are useless for anything other than as giant advertising hoardings. Mimicking the ancient geoglyphs of the Chinchorro, local taxi firms and radio stations, as well as a familiar international fizzy-drinks company, had scrawled their names and numbers across the hillsides.

The road we followed to the airport, which is 15 kilometres outside the city, led north, where Nature had left a kilometre or so of flat land behind Las Machas beach before the hills began. We sped round the bay along the coast and, nearing the airport, hit a diversion. The driver told me it had rained heavily inland the previous month, sending huge volumes of water down towards the coast. Large chunks of land in town next to the San José River had simply disappeared, and out here, to the north of town, the river had washed away the bridge to the airport. That's the thing about rainfall in deserts. It doesn't happen very often, but when it does it can be very destructive. Little water percolates into the ground and the flow of any rivers increases dramatically for short periods. Engineers who build bridges and other structures in deserts have to cater for these rare flash floods, but in this case it seemed that the engineers had got their sums wrong. The army had put up an emergency bridge that we rattled over to reach the airport.

Aldo Espindola looked too cool to be Arica's meteorological observer. Unlike your average English male weather buff, (think of the weather bulletins on the BBC), he wore a well-pressed, white sleeveless shirt, beautifully polished shoes, and trousers with a crease that looked as if they would draw blood if you ran your finger down them. His complexion brimmed with vitality beneath his slicked-back hair and reflective sunglasses. He looked like a Chilean version of Tony Curtis, but the mild surprise I got when I met him was nothing to what was to come.

We walked out of his office at the small regional airport and moved over to the compound containing the meteorological instruments. I moved towards the rain guage and asked him how often he checked it. 'Every six hours,' he told me.

The pluviometer was a standard piece of apparatus, a white cylindrical funnel stuck on a pole at about chest height. In the bottom of the metal funnel a hole allows any water to drip into a metal bottle stored below. 'And how often do you find something inside?' I asked. 'At least once a day,' Aldo started to say, which stopped me in my tracks. 'I find bird shit in the funnel,' he continued, smiling as I let out a sigh of relief.

Now at the rain gauge, I opened the metal door to take out the bottle. 'When was the last time that you found some water in here?' I asked him. 'You can find a bit of drizzle every now and then, in January and February, but there is no rain,' he said. 'No rain at all?' I tipped the metal bottle upside down over my hand. A little dust fell out, and a dead fly. 'Absolutely no rain.' Aldo was very definite about that.

'What about fog?' I asked. Fog is pretty common on the Atacama coast, about the only reliable form of precipitation it gets, but there was no fog here either, he told me. 'But they get some in Arica,' Aldo added. That stopped me in my tracks again. From the airport, we could see the city across the bay.

'They *do* get fog in the city?' I asked, just for confirmation. All the climatology books on the region I'd read said otherwise. 'Yes,' Aldo said, 'because of the hills. There are no hills here, so no fog. And Arica gets some rain too.'

I wasn't reeling from this revelation, but I did find it disturbing. It's not uncommon for towns and cities to have their official meteorological stations some distance from the actual settlement. But in this case, the short 15 kilometres between Arica and its airport made a significant difference. Here at the airport, source of the meteorological data that gave Arica the record as the world's driest inhabited place, Aldo was telling me that he recorded no rain and no fog. But across the bay, in the actual city, they had both. In minimal amounts, no doubt, but nonetheless, they got some.

Disturbed as I was by this information, it was nothing compared to what came next. I was still pondering what Aldo had told me, speaking almost to myself. 'So, is Arica the driest place on Earth because the meteorological station is out here and the city is over there?' 'I don't think so,' Aldo said. His remark was so conversational that I almost missed it.

'Pardon?'

'I don't think so,' Aldo said again. 'There are drier places in Chile.'

I just looked at him.

'In the interior of the Atacama Desert, down the coast, inland from Antofagasta, it is drier than here. It is the Domeyko region. That is the driest place in Chile.'

My mind was racing. 'But does anyone live in that region?'

'It is a desert, but there are some villages there,' he said.

I stood with my mouth open. My legs felt weak. If anyone else had told me this, I'd have laughed it off, but when the official meteorological observer in the world's driest inhabited place tells you he thinks there are drier places, you have to listen.

'Would any of these villages have meteorological stations?' I asked cautiously. Even if any one of these villages was drier, I was thinking to myself, they would have to have some data to prove it.

'Perhaps,' Aldo said simply.

It looked like maybe my journey wasn't yet over.

It was a peculiar feeling. I'd only just arrived in the place that represented the culmination of my journey, the city I'd come to Chile to see, and already I was itching to leave. If what Aldo had told me was right, and there were villages further down the coast and inland that were drier than Arica, and had meteorological records to prove it, I might have a coup on my hands. It wasn't every day that I got the chance to overturn an established world record. I was eager to start searching for a new driest inhabited place in the world.

But, before I quit Arica, there was one place I definitely wanted to visit: the San Miguel de Azapa museum of Arica's University of Tarapacá, where they kept some of the world's oldest mummies. The Atacama's long history of aridity, combined with the widespread presence of salt, represent near perfect conditions for preservation. But down on the coast, archaeologists have also found numerous burial sites containing ritually preserved human bodies, and a lot of them are now in the San Miguel de Azapa museum.

The Chinchorro, as the group who occupied the northern coast of Chile are known, settled around Arica and further south around 9,000 years ago. Where these people came from remains a matter for debate. Some suggest they crossed the Andes from the Amazon Basin, others think they may have moved down the Andes from the north of Colombia.

Whatever their origins, the Chinchorro developed a simple lifestyle on the arid coastline based on fishing, hunting and gathering of the plentiful wildlife of the Pacific Ocean. They fashioned fishhooks from bone, shell, cactus spines and copper, and wove nets using cotton and fibres from a tree that grew in nearby riverbeds. Stone spearheads were carved to make harpoons so that they could hunt sea lions, and animal ribs were employed to gather shellfish. Their way of life has been pieced together from remains found in archaeological sites at Chinchorro camps of round dwellings built with wooden posts covered in mats, hides and branches. Seemingly, these people moved their homes with the seasons, migrating inland to valley bottoms and oases.

All this, the presence of a culture that thrived in what is seemingly such a hostile environment, is extraordinary enough. But more remarkable still is the fact that the Chinchorro also practised mummification. Ritually preserving the dead is often thought to be the domain of more complex societies, who supposedly had more time to indulge in such rites. Civilizations such as the ancient Egyptians, and the Incas (who didn't emerge in South America until 1000 AD), were into the practice of mummification when they weren't managing fantastic feats of construction like the pyramids and Machu Picchu. Simple societies with mobile lifestyles, like the Chinchorro, weren't supposed to have the time or energy to indulge in such things.

But indulge they did, and in a big way. The San Miguel de Azapa museum was full of mummies. Calogero Santoro, professor of archaeology at the University of Taparacá, showed me around a back room of the museum that contained row upon row of glass cases raised up on legs to waist height. It looked like a mortuary, which it was, only for people who died thousands of years ago. Yet these bodies weren't wrapped in white bandages like the mummies of ancient Egypt or a Hammer horror film. Most of the Chinchorro specimens were recognizable as human forms, but had been transformed to look more like life-sized dolls. Faces were covered by flat clay death masks, their features reduced to minimalist noses and mouths. Limbs and torsos, unnaturally straight and wooden-looking, were also encased in clay, often braced with sticks and, in some cases, clothed in rush matting. The sex of the individuals was only discernable by stylized breasts, small fistfuls of clay attached to their upper bodies. Dead people of all ages were on show, adults, adolescents and tiny babies that really did look like dolls.

The mummification process was elaborate and must have been very time-consuming. 'Each one of these bodies,' Calogero Santoro told me, 'has had the flesh removed. Then sticks were bound to the bones and the body covered in an ash paste.' All the vital organs had been taken out and the skeletons reassembled. Muscles were re-created with thin bundles of wild reeds and sea grasses. Then, incredibly, the body was 'reupholstered' with its own skin, which must have been carefully removed and set aside. Any gaps were filled with sea lion skin before the outer covering of ash paste and clay was applied.

Another interesting aspect of the Chinchorro mummies was that they were usually found buried collectively, in groups of distinct sex and age. 'We think this means that the basic unit of Chinchorro culture was rooted in a group of individuals,' Calogero said. 'Perhaps the concept of one person did not exist.'

Needless to say, we can only guess at the reasons for this sophisticated procedure. Was it to prepare the dead for an unknown fate, or to allow them to play a new role in their coastal community? We know that the Incas worshipped the mummified remains of their forebears, because missionaries working in Peru after the Spanish conquest recorded their disapproval of religious ceremonies in which Inca lords were publicly displayed, dressed in fine robes, and given cups of corn beer to drink. For the Incas, death marked not so much the end of life, but a transition of the soul, which needed help to enter the afterlife. In exchange for such hospitality, the dead would mediate with the gods on behalf of the living to ensure fertility and good crops. The Incas were the last in a long line of Andean peoples to preserve the remains of their ancestors, a line that began with the Chinchorro.

But what we do know is that the coastal Chinchorro must have experienced some fundamental changes to their culture around 3,000 years ago (the oldest mummy prepared by humans has been dated at 7,050 years old), because the doll-like mummies disappeared and bodies began to be interred as individuals.

Calogero led me through a door from the mortuary for the long dead into a laboratory where four more recent bodies were lined up sitting in trays awaiting examination and dating. Sitting they almost literally were, because these corpses had all been buried in a foetal position. They were more recognizable than the dolls as unadulterated human forms since they had been preserved not by artificial mummification but by the natural aridity and salt of the Atacama. The state of preservation was incredible, although Calogero deduced from the woven clothing the bodies were wrapped in that they were several thousand years old. These people had their hair, toenails and teeth. The skin was parched and stretched taut across their bones, but the sinews on their feet were clearly visible. Even the fingerprints on the hands were unmistakable. Dryness had robbed the faces of eyes and noses, but otherwise the features were totally recognizable. It was only the unaffected hair in plaits that lent their expressions an alien air.

'The conditions in the Atacama are ideal for preservation,' Calogero said. 'The oldest naturally preserved Chinchorro specimen we've found has been dated at 7,020 years before Christ. But, if a human body was buried in the sand today, it would look like this in a few months.' He paused. 'We are always getting phone calls from people telling us of new bodies,' he added, indicating several rows of shelves behind us lined with innumerable human heads, some just skulls, but many with desiccated skin like the full bodies in front of me.

If this level of preservation occurred so fast, I wondered if some of the bodies were more recent, victims of General Pinochet's purges, the disappeared whose bodies were supposed to have been dumped in the desert during the 1970s and 80s.

Calogero nodded. 'Sadly, not all are so old,' he told me. 'The preserved body of someone who died a few decades ago looks very similar to these. On first inspection, before we date them, it is only the clothes that allow us to guess at their age.'

As I was leaving, Calogero pointed out another, much smaller human form perched on a shelf beneath a line of heads. It was the body of a small baby, chubby and with tiny fingers. The skin was brown and soft to look at. I couldn't help but be reminded of a dried fruit. 'How old is this one?' I asked. 'About 2,500 years,' Calogero replied. 'We think it was probably killed by strangulation,' he added. 'Here you can still see the marks.' He pointed to a linear smudge on the baby's stretched neck. 'It might have been one of twins. Andean peoples were suspicious of twins.' In a sense, that didn't seem so different from the reasons put forward to excuse political murders in the modern era.

When I left the laboratory and walked out into the bright sunlight in the museum's lush garden, I was feeling strange. I had found being waist deep in dead people rather off-putting after a while, but I was also disappointed in how quickly I had begun to talk about the bodies as if they were artefacts rather than real individuals who had died a long time ago. I had asked Calogero how old the baby was, but the little boy had clearly been less than a year old when he died. He'd just been dead for 2,500 years.

Despite my unconscious attempt to distance myself from the dead people on show in the museum, I realized the following day that I could never make it as an archaeologist. I had travelled out of Arica down the coast to a spot near the fishing village of Caleta Camarones. It was a site Calogero had told me about, where the museum staff had found numerous Chinchorro bodies.

I enlisted a ten-year-old boy from the village to show me where I should be looking. In a world-weary tone that was far beyond his years, he told me that of course he knew where the mummies were. Would he show me, I asked. 'Well I haven't got anything else to do,' he replied.

He led me up and along a dirt track cut high into the precipitous sand-covered cliffs that plunged down into an aquamarine sea. As we walked round the headland, I asked him what he was going to be when he grew up. 'I'm going to be a doctor,' he replied confidently. 'I'm going to study,' he added, 'but if I'm unlucky I'll just be a fisherman.'

We walked on in silence, me pausing on occasion to jot down some notes about the coastline. In the distance, I could see some small fishing boats bobbing up and down by a short jetty. As we neared the spot, the boy looked at me quizzically and said, 'You look like a tourist, but you're not are you?' 'Not really,' I told him. 'I'm writing a book.'

He nodded knowledgeably, as if he'd had a few itinerant authors through here and was still trying to decide whether or not he approved of them. If he didn't make it as a doctor, I thought, perhaps he could become a publisher.

'There,' he said, pointing to a place about 3 metres above the track.

I looked in the direction he was pointing, but couldn't see anything. It was just a sandy slope with a few stones. In fact, I wasn't quite sure what I was supposed to be looking for. I couldn't believe that it would be anything as dramatic as a mummified foot sticking out of the sand. I saw what I thought was a black stick about 40 centimetres long, then a piece of cloth, more like an old rag really, but of the same texture as those I'd seen in the museum.

'Ah yes,' I said, 'is it a piece of clothing?'

The small boy gave me his world-weary sigh.

'No,' he said, scrambling half-way up the slope towards the spot that he'd indicated and pointing again, 'it's some feet.'

I started to climb up the slope myself, but slipped back in the sand. I had the spot in my focus now. Most of a sun-dried foot pointed upwards, its toenails clearly visible as such across the horizontal black stick that I had already seen. Only the black stick was nothing of the sort. It was a human shinbone and at its end was another partially buried foot. As on the specimens in the museum, the desiccated skin was perfectly preserved, although the sun had turned its colour to that of an over-ripe banana. Just beneath the sands must have lain another mummy, waiting to be excavated and taken to the laboratory for examination.

After my junior guide had taken his leave, I wandered up and down the track alone, passing the mummified legs several times, trying to get to grips with what seemed like an open-air wholesalers for Chinchorro cultural artefacts. The more I looked, the more I saw. Not further bodies, but fragments of cloth, and hair, and pieces of bone that looked distinctly human to my untrained eye. Calogero had told me it was a rich site, but I hadn't expected to see for myself in quite such graphic detail. Apparently, the museum hadn't got the resources to excavate the site properly and had been trying to educate the locals to view the slope as a sort of open-air museum, a place to come and look, but not to rob. Grave robbers have already spoiled many such sites in this part of the world.

The museum had done a good job, it seemed. I could easily have imagined the small boy digging up the legs that he'd showed me, so that he could start his human anatomy classes early. But such a thought could not have been further from his mind.

On my final walk past the legs, on my way back towards the village, I caught sight of a round object almost totally buried in the sand. It was dark brown, rather smaller than a CD, but slightly spherical in shape. It looked just like the top of a buried coconut. I stopped. It couldn't be a coconut, I thought to myself, because there are no coconuts here.

I moved closer to my find that, like the legs, was located a couple of metres above the track. Perching precariously on the shifting sand, I picked up a flat stone from the slope and carefully dug a small amount of sand from the side of the round object. The sand slid away, revealing a little more and leaving a circle of salty residue, like a water-mark from a receding lake, on the curved object. The portion I had uncovered was a slightly lighter brown than the top circle.

I used my stone to move some more sand from the other side. The curve started to straighten out, revealing the beginnings of a flatter surface turned out to sea and towards me. I dug again. More sand slid down past my knees. The flatter bit continued. My stomach tightened. With a couple more scoops from my stone, the beginnings of two symmetrical elongated bumps appeared across the bottom of the flat part.

I hesitated, but moved more scoops of sand with my stone to reveal the tops of two eye sockets staring blindly out towards me.

For a minute or so, I just looked at my find, not quite knowing what to do. I felt bad inside, like a grave robber myself. Then I carefully scooped sand back around the skull until just the dark brown top bit was visible as it had been when I'd first seen it. I decided to ring Calogero that night and tell him of my discovery. I'd been right; it wasn't a coconut.

F O U R

The cold Humboldt Current is a two-edged sword running most of the length of South America's Pacific coastline. It is largely responsible for the presence of the world's longest stretch of desert and semi-desert that extends for more than 3,500 kilometres from southern Ecuador, through Peru to the Atacama of northern Chile. But at the same time, this cold expanse of water plays host to some of the richest marine life in any ocean. The reason for this lies in the current's twin sources. On the one hand is water brought up from the Southern Ocean that surrounds the Antarctic, but this flow is complemented by water from deep down near the ocean floor. This deep upwelling water is also cold, because it starts so far from the sun's warming rays, but it is rich in nutrients from the seabed too, so it supports a diverse array of marine life.

The Chinchorro people relied on this fertility, and the ocean's riches still provide some of Chile's major exports today. I got a glimpse of the abundance of life beneath the waters when I stopped off on my way down the coast towards the area that Aldo, the meteorologist, had pointed me towards as the driest area in Chile. Mejillones used to be an important port for nitrate export, but is now just a workmanlike fishing village with a narrow sandy beach populated mainly by pelicans and gulls. Three large sea lions wallowed in the shallow waters that lapped at the stanchions of the sturdy jetty and more pelicans, standing in groups, occupied some of the many small boats bobbing at anchor in the water.

I got talking with a swarthy fisherman named Rodrigo who told me he caught octopus when he could, since octopus could be sold at the best price. He was only allowed to catch them for six months of the year due to a partial ban introduced to preserve stocks, and the rest of the time he collected seaweed. He surprised me when he asked if I'd like to come along with him that morning.

We motored out for an hour or so towards the arid headland, Rodrigo at the helm of his small red boat. When we reached a rocky promontory, he cut the outboard motor and took up the oars as his two friends, Enrique and Adolphe, pulled on their wet suits. Rodrigo said he would stay in the boat so I could use his wet suit if I wanted to.

While Enrique dived with the aid of a lengthy yellow tube connected to an antiquated air pump in the boat, Adolphe and I donned snorkels. We each held long metal hooks to pull the octopus from their rocky lairs.

It was exhausting work. The rocks lay 6 or 7 metres below the surface and it was the best I could do to dive to that depth, let alone stay down long enough to survey the crags for our prey. After an hour or so, Enrique and Adolphe had bagged 15 purple octopuses. All I had managed was one brief grapple. After I resurfaced, gasping for air, I dived again to resume the tussle, but couldn't find the same crag. The only thing I caught was half a dozen sea urchin spines in my hand.

Picking out the spines with a safety pin gave me something to do as we chugged our way back to port past a dead coastline on which nothing lived except a few seabirds, and even they only stayed long enough to have a shit and then fly on. Rocky islets, handy resting places for huge numbers of sea lions that barked at me mockingly, were also topped with seabirds and plastered with their white droppings. Before the Atacama's sodium nitrate deposits were exported to Europe and North America as fertilizer, bird droppings amassed over hundreds of years along this arid coast served the same purpose. Guano from Peru and Chile was big business in the 1800s and Mejillones had originally been founded as a base for guano-gatherers.

The vast numbers of birds on this coast, attracted by the enormous fish reserves, had built up guano deposits 40 metres deep in some places. The lack of rain meant that it was never washed away and the dry atmosphere prevented the nitrate in the droppings from evaporating, so maintaining its effectiveness. All the locals had to do was scrape the shit off the cliffs and sell it to rich farmers on other continents. Guano was just one in a long line of marine riches fed by the Humboldt Current. The distinction between barren desert and fecund ocean could not have been more stark. The coastal cliffs mark it like the cut of a knife. About the only thing that links the two is their salinity.

Although the Humboldt Current is a central reason for the lack of rainfall along the Atacama coast, it does produce some precipitation, in the form of fog. In the late afternoon, moisture-laden air from far out over the Pacific Ocean moves in towards the coast and is cooled as it passes over the colder Humboldt waters. As the air cools, its capacity for holding moisture is decreased. When it reaches the coastline, the air is forced to rise up the coastal hills, cooling further until the moisture in the air condenses out as fog. This fog occurs all along the coastline of northern Chile, where it is known as *camanchaca*, and on the desert coast of Peru where they call it *garua*. *Camanchacas* roll in off the Pacific around 200 days every year, so although the amount of water they hold is small, they are a frequent and regular phenomenon.

Ecologically, this recurring, if limited, supply of water, is important. Dotted along the coastline are small pockets of vegetation known as *lomas* that survive solely on *camanchaca* moisture. These plants exist in terrestrial islands, sort of fog oases, separated by hyperarid habitat where virtually no vegetation exists. Many of them are so finely adapted to the fog water that they are found nowhere else on Earth.

People, too, have latched on to the importance of fog as a source of water in this desert. Archaeologists think that the Chinchorro set up their camps in *lomas* areas, taking advantage of the plants and associated animals to supplement their marine diet. Some even think that the Chinchorro collected water where the fog droplets condensed on flat cliff faces.

At Chungungo, a modern successor to the Chinchorro idea has been developed. High on the hillside overlooking the small fishing village, an array of huge nets has been set up to catch the *camanchaca* as it races in off the ocean. Droplets of fog condense on the mesh and the water drips down into a plastic trough. The trough acts just like a gutter, channelling the collected water down through a pipe to a reservoir near the village, about 6 kilometres away.

Pablo Osses, a geographer at the Catholic University in Santiago who was involved in the fog collection system at Chungungo, drove me up the hillside to look at the nets. About 30 of them were spread across the hilltop, each stretched between two posts like an oversized volleyball net. The idea had been born when one of his team had noticed fog condensing on the leaves of eucalyptus trees growing at the crest of the hill, he told me. The design of the nets was the result of considerable experimentation to hit on the best materials and the optimum size of net. These were made of polypropylene, which didn't absorb the droplets like traditional fishing nets, but allowed them to drip down to the gutters below. The technology was fantastically simple, straightforward to construct and easily maintained. The nets didn't need any power, they just sat there and did their job of harvesting the fog water.

The system had been born of necessity. For several decades, Chungungo was supplied with water from a nearby iron mine, just over the crest of the hill. But when the mine closed down, tankers had to be hired to bring in the water by road. The water they brought was often of dubious quality because the trucks were also used to carry other liquids that left residues in the tanks, contaminating the water being delivered to the village. Sometimes the trucks broke down and simply didn't arrive. The people of Chungungo had to live with a limited supply of poor quality freshwater for about 20 years.

In the early 1990s, when 100 fog-collecting nets were strung across the hillside, each harvesting an incredible 170 litres of water a day, Chungungo was able to dispense with the truck service. Residents were able to double their consumption from about 15 litres per person per day to more than 30 litres. The nets provided water for everything. People drank fog water, washed with it, and even had enough to water their gardens. Some started to grow vegetables among their flowers.

Although the fog didn't roll in off the ocean every day, there was usually enough in the reservoir to tide the village over. A system of flags was introduced to let villagers know how much they had in store. A green flag meant that supplies were plentiful, yellow indicated that people should think before using it, and a red flag was raised when supplies were low and water should only be used for essential purposes until the next fog bank came in. Even so, the fog collectors were still more reliable than the trucks.

For the first time, Chungungo was no longer reliant on outsiders for water. The villagers had an inexpensive, sustainable supply system that they ran themselves. It sounded perfect, but it wasn't quite.

When we reached the top of the hillside, Pablo walked over to a net and showed me the problem. 'You see,' he said, tugging one of the thin metal cords that held the giant green nets in place like horizontal sails facing out to sea, 'this is too loose. The nets must be kept taut to catch the fog most efficiently.' The metal cable had rusted and become slack. 'The problem here is that no one is interested in maintenance.' He looked up at the lines of nets marching across the slope. There were gaps in the lines where nets had fallen. Elsewhere, posts that had once held nets stood pointing to the skies ready to do their fog catching duty, but their nets had disappeared.

'In 1992 there were 100 nets here,' Pablo said. 'They were enough to supply all the village's needs. But now there are just 30 left. It is not enough.' Because no one had bothered to look after the fog collectors, the village had started to receive tankers again to supplement the fog water supplies. Pablo couldn't understand it. The maintenance wasn't a difficult job. Tightening a few cables, clearing eucalyptus leaves from the plastic gutters occasionally, checking the nets for holes, these weren't arduous tasks, but if no one did them, the system was stuffed.

I found it difficult to comprehend too, but it wasn't a totally unfamiliar story to me. I'd seen many development projects like this, simple, clever ideas that worked technically but foundered on people's inability to keep them going, or disinterest in doing so. This wasn't rural Africa, where well-meaning white foreigners don't always get the social side of their projects right. The villagers down in Chungungo weren't rich, but they all wore shoes and had enough to eat. Pablo was certainly well meaning, but he wasn't a foreigner. Yet still the problems were similar. The fog collectors were a brilliant technical solution to the village's water-supply problem but unless the villagers could be encouraged or cajoled into participating, the system simply wasn't going to work.

I'd gleaned a few clues as to why earlier that day when I'd sat in on a meeting of Chungungo's Water Committee. It was a pretty little village with dirt roads and houses painted in bright primary colours. On the breeze-block wall beside the committee's building, someone had daubed a slogan that read: '*Queremos una solucion definitiva de agua para Chungungo*' (We want a definite solution to Chungungo's water problem). It wasn't the sort of village where you'd expect to find graffiti.

A dozen people sat round the small hall. Although getting their water from both the fog collectors and trucks didn't really seem to be a problem that I could see, it was a shame that the fog-collecting nets weren't being properly maintained since it was a good project and had been proven to work. But in the wider scheme of things, did it really matter as long as Chungungo was getting enough water? Then someone pointed out that the trucks were paid for by the government, as part of a drought relief scheme, and Chungungo couldn't rely on deliveries forever. The drought relief budget might be cut at almost any time. It wasn't a long-term solution to the problem. So why weren't they maintaining the nets up on the hillside? I wondered to myself. The solution to their problem lay in their own hands. The answer to the quandary slowly became clear.

Everyone paid a water rate to the government, and the amount they paid was the same irrespective of where the water came from. If they received all of their water by truck, they paid the same. If all the water came from the fog collectors, as it had done a few years previously, they paid the same. If Chungungo's water came from both trucks and nets, the rate was the same. No one had an incentive to fix the nets because it made no difference to the amount they paid.

The debate continued. It was clear that most people preferred in principle to have their own fog water. It was a more reliable source than the trucks, and some said it tasted better, but no one was willing to take on the responsibility of maintaining the nets.

Pablo and I left the meeting as someone was suggesting that the fog collectors could become a tourist attraction for the village. It had become more difficult for everyone to support themselves by fishing. Tourism would bring new jobs to the village. The idea struck me as a red herring. The fact remained that until someone took responsibility for those nets, the problem would continue.

A solution seemed obvious to me. Why not get the government to waive the water charge if Chungungo supplied themselves from the nets, I asked Pablo. 'They won't do it,' he said sadly. So why not ask the government to put Chungungo's water rates into a special account and use the money to pay someone to maintain the nets?

That way they would save the money used to pay for the water trucks and create a job too. 'The sums don't work out,' Pablo replied, 'and besides, no one in government is really interested. Chungungo is too small a place to bother with.'

There is a woman who lives a few doors down from me at home in Oxford. I don't know her very well but we always exchange greetings when we pass on the street and, without fail, her cheery hello is always followed by a comment on the weather. 'Hello Nick, colder today.' Or 'Hello Nick, it looks like it's brightening up.' British people are obsessed with the weather in a way that few other races are. Our constantly variable atmospheric conditions provide a perennial topic of conversation and TV weathermen are national heroes. It's not like that in northern Chile. The weather is more or less the same every day of the year, so there's not a lot to comment on. 'Hello Pedro, dry again today,' wanes after the first rainless month.

But ask a Chilean when it last rained and you start something. Motoring back to Mejillones in the boat after my unsuccessful sortie into the octopus fishing business, I put the question to Rodrigo. 'There was rain in 1982,' he said. 'It was an El Niño year. There were very few fish and lots of the sea lions died.' El Niño is the name given to the phenomenon that occurs every few years in the Pacific when the Humboldt Current fails, the waters are warmer than usual, most of the fish disappear – killed off by the warm temperatures and the lack of nutrients upwelling from the seabed – and the weather gets uppity. El Niño kicks in around Christmas time; the name means little boy or Christ child. There was a really severe El Niño phase in 1982/83.

'It rained in Antofagasta in 1992,' Enrique chipped in as he peeled off his wetsuit. Rodrigo nodded. 'Yes, there were mudslides, 120 people died. But the last time it rained here was in 1999.'

Enrique looked at him with a frown on his face. '1999? Are you sure?' he asked. Adolphe looked puzzled too. Neither of them was convinced. 'Yes, 1999,' Rodrigo continued. 'It rained for about ten minutes. Don't you remember? I think it was in January.' But neither Adolphe nor Enrique could remember and the three of them argued about it for the next quarter of an hour.

While fog is a frequent visitor to the coast, sometimes penetrating up to 50 kilometres inland, rain is almost unheard of. Beyond the fog belt, the exceptional rainfall event is virtually the only precipitation they get, and this is why Aldo, the Arica meteorologist, had told me to go inland to look for a drier place.

By a curious turn of events, the first two days of my journey through the interior of the Atacama, in search of a new driest inhabited place on Earth, I spent with the Chilean army. I met with a climatologist in Antofagasta, a tough city that looked as if it worked hard for a living, and he told me about a large area of desert where no one went except the army. 'Go and talk to them,' he suggested, 'they know more about that area than anyone else.'

The seventh regiment commandos had their base near the seashore where flocks of pelicans roamed and fierce breakers rolled in from the Pacific to crash against the rocks. I'd been a bit uneasy about consulting the army. Chile was no longer under military rule, but by all accounts these guys had kept the country on a pretty short leash during the Pinochet years. But when the commanding officer had to turn down the salsa music in his office so that we could hear each other speaking, I felt a little less nervous about seeking their advice.

After half an hour in his office, I'd been invited along on the next visit the commandos were making to what they considered to be the very driest part of the Atacama, an area known as the Plain of Patience. The name made it sound as if it might be a rather relaxing trip, but I was under no illusions. The commandos go to the Plain of Patience for desert survival training. My initial thoughts on the offer were clouded by a sense of curiosity. So far, I'd seen little of the rigours of the Atacama. All the towns I'd passed through were protected from the harsh realities of desert life by their water supplies.

Getting a dose of the real thing might be interesting, I thought.

Well, of course it was interesting, but even more so it was also bloody hard work.

The Chilean army is proud of its desert survival skills. Back in the late nineteenth century, they were involved in a conflict with Bolivia and Peru over part of the Atacama Desert. It was a struggle for power and influence over the Pacific coast of South America based on control of the thriving guano and nitrate industries. Some call it the War of the Pacific. I prefer the alternative: the Fertilizer War.

Today, Bolivia is a landlocked nation. Until 1884, it had a coastline on the Pacific, but that territory was surrendered to Chile in the truce that ended the fighting. Bolivia didn't have much option, because Chile had occupied the Bolivian coastal region (today's Antofagasta province) easily before moving on to deal with the more powerful Peru. Chile did pretty well out of the conflict with its northern neighbour too, securing Arica amongst other places. But it could have been much worse for Peru because Chilean forces occupied Lima, the Peruvian capital, for three years before withdrawing when a peace treaty was negotiated.

No one had really expected the Chilean army to be able to reach Lima because there was so much desert in the way. The Chileans couldn't do it, the Peruvians thought, because they wouldn't be able to carry enough water. It is said that the army managed this extraordinary feat by leaving all the metal objects they carried with them out in the open each night. In the mornings, they would be covered in dew, and the soldiers would lick their rifles and shovels clean before setting out to march each day.

I didn't get to carry a rifle on my survival exercise, but it wouldn't have been much good as a water source because modern Chilean commandos' rifles are encased in plastic so that they don't get too hot to hold during the day. But the commandos still harvest dew. It's just that they use plastic sheets to do it nowadays.

The one thing that anyone who has spent any time in a desert will tell you is to take lots of water. It's simply the main thing you need, and you need lots of it because deserts are very dry places. I have made several journeys through the Sahara and Gobi Deserts and I know that a good supply of water is essential. A person can survive for many days without food, but without water you simply don't last long. Ten litres a day per person is a sensible average to take. The ground rules for the two-day course were outlined to me by the commando instructor, a man a little younger than me whose name was Zeus, pronounced *Zé-ous* in Spanish. Each day, he told me, I had one meal to eat and 1 litre of water to drink.

The rules began as soon as I pitched up at the commando barracks in Antofagasta at 8 o'clock sharp. I climbed into the back of a large lorry with six men from the lower ranks and off we set for the Plain of Patience. The higher ranks led the way in relative style in a pickup. The journey took eight hours and the wooden benches in the back of the truck were very hard. As soon as we'd unloaded our packs, and camouflaged the truck with netting, we set off for a march. It was quarter to five and the sun was very low, but still scorching hot. I could feel it burning my face even with sun protection factor 35 on.

The lack of water and food I was mentally prepared for, but the marching was something else. It was curious, because when I'd been thinking over the option of spending two days in the Atacama on a commando desert survival course, I hadn't considered marching. This was stupid of me, I know, but I hadn't got further than visions of digging holes in the ground to harvest dew, and maybe catching a few lizards for breakfast.

But armies are made for marching and that's what we did. I was thankful that Zeus called a halt after about an hour. We had reached a gentle hillside littered with stones, not unlike all the other gentle hillsides we had just spent the last hour marching across. Zeus knelt down and scraped the stones away from the surface with his small spade, dug a few preliminary shovelfuls of dirt, and announced that this was where we would set up camp. 'The ground is easy to dig,' he told me. 'We don't sleep in tents because they would be easily seen by the enemy. We try to blend into the landscape.'

After eight hours sitting on a hard bench in the back of an uncomfortable lorry and another hour marching across stony ground with a heavy pack on your back, about the last thing you want to do is dig a hole in the ground. But the idea of going to sleep was an attractive one, so I set to. Zeus and I spent 40 minutes digging our two-man hole, about 30 centimetres deep. We stuck a green plastic tarpaulin over the top and secured it at the edges with soil to keep it in place. Then, one at a time, we eased our way in through the flap left at one end and settled down for a short rest. Short was the operative word. To conserve energy and water, we would mainly be sleeping during the day. Night was the time for proper marching.

So less than two hours later, Zeus woke me with a dig in the ribs and we marched again. The sun had disappeared and all around me shadowy commandos were checking their weapons. Now that it was night-time, in one way the marching was easier because I wasn't so hot. But in quite a significant way it was more difficult, that way being that I couldn't see a bloody thing. A march on a parade ground at night would have been one thing. Marching across a rough and stony desert landscape was quite another. I slipped and stumbled, the pack growing heavier on my back.

We marched in silence, Zeus communicating with his men by means of low whistling, so I couldn't grumble. I also couldn't afford to slow down because I had to keep close enough to see Zeus' feet otherwise I'd be lost in seconds. Every now and again, my stomach put in a rumbling complaint, having not received any nourishment since 7 o'clock that morning. I was also getting thirsty, not having drunk a drop of water since breakfast. To add to my worries, I began to feel just a bit breathless. The Plain of Patience lies at an altitude of 2,500 metres. On top of all this, my pack was seemingly tightening around my shoulders, stopping the flow of blood to my fingers.

After 40 minutes, I made my way to within whispering distance of Zeus to tell him about my pack and bloodless fingers. I wondered whether the pack's strap needed some readjustment. When I explained my predicament, he just laughed.

Fifty-five minutes after leaving our sleeping holes, Zeus called a halt. 'We rest for five minutes every hour,' he told me in a whisper. I hadn't been able to see the dozen commandos around me for the last hour, but they emerged from the dark and made a circle, all facing out. I saw one of them unhook the strap over his water bottle and take a swig. Momentarily, this made me feel better since I'd made a promise to myself not to be the first one to drink. Happily, I raised my own water bottle to my lips and took a sip of beautiful water.

We marched some more. Zeus found me to explain how he knew where we were going, pointing out the Southern Cross that he was navigating by, bright and sparkling in the clear night sky. With something other than stumbling to concentrate on, I almost felt good about being out in the desert with a group of commandos, but the high only lasted for a few minutes.

Then, 30 minutes into the second hour of marching, things got significantly better. I was just beginning to have serious doubts about lasting the night when the moon came up. It was quite extraordinary. I don't think I'd ever seen it rise before. Really fast to begin with, it just popped up from behind the mountains. Then it just sat there, clear of the skyline, not quite full but completely surreal. The light it shone was remarkably bright and all the commandos around me suddenly became visible and took on very long shadows. I allowed myself another drink in celebration.

But Zeus didn't like it. 'Too much light,' he complained in a whisper. 'This would be bad for a night march in battlefield conditions because we would be clearly visible to the enemy.' As far as I was concerned, it was brilliant because at last I could see where I was going. 'We are also walking too fast,' Zeus continued, 'we make too much noise walking at this pace. It should be much slower, which

*Pipeline carrying water from the Andes, across the world's
driest desert, to the city of Antofagasta on the coast.*

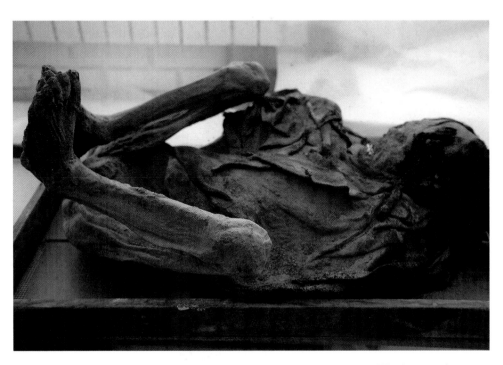

*Chinchorro mummy in Arica's San Miguel de Azapa museum. The Atacama's
minimal rainfall and abundant salt are ideal conditions for preservation.*

ABOVE
Sea lions off the
Atacama coast enjoying
the fertile waters of the
Humboldt current.

LEFT
Watering a public park in
Arica – suspiciously lush
and green for the driest
inhabited place on Earth.

Fog-collecting nets set to catch the camanchaca
as it races across the hillside above Chungungo.

Ancient geoglyphs in the Atacama – icons to appease the gods? Desert road
signs pointing the way to the coast? Or maybe just giant Chinchorro doodles?

LEFT
Apparently unaffected by the lack of food and water, Zeus disappears over a ridge in the Plain of Patience.

BELOW
The author getting to know the least active rain gauge on the planet at Quillagua.

A world-weary ten-year-old points out a pair of Chinchorro legs in the open-air mummy museum near Caleta Camarones.

takes a lot more effort. We'll do it later.' Oh good, I thought to myself.

When we stopped for our five-minute break just before 11 o'clock, I felt very tired indeed. The soles of my feet hurt a lot, and my legs ached all over. My shoulders hurt because the rucksack was too heavy, and my blood had given up even trying to reach the ends of my fingers. My pulse was racing like a maniac's and my breathlessness was getting to be a habit.

The next hour was the worst. For the first time, I began to feel thirsty. I think it was partly the altitude because I couldn't get enough oxygen and I had to breathe through my mouth. I caught myself panting and my tongue, well my tongue started to ache if you can imagine such a thing. The relentless marching began to mess with my mind. When trudging across a dry river channel, I swear I heard flowing water. I was getting hallucinations of the ears.

I kept reminding myself that my body wasn't actually designed for this sort of behaviour. It was designed for a sedentary lifestyle, writing at home in the mid-latitudes with lots of water and food available. My tiredness started to make me stumble much more often that I had been a few hours before, but I didn't actually fall over. One of the real commandos did though, which made me feel much better. Perhaps I was not the only one feeling rough, I thought to myself.

Thankfully, at midnight, Zeus called a halt. 'We'll sleep now,' he told me. I asked him how far he thought we'd marched. 'About 12 kilometres,' he said. I wasn't surprised I was feeling bad. I couldn't remember the last time I'd walked 12 kilometres anywhere, let alone at 2,500 metres altitude, in the middle of the night, carrying a 10-tonne pack, with no food and just a few sips of water, across the driest desert in the world.

FIVE

We checked our dew collectors at 6 o'clock the following morning. They were shallow pits we'd dug in the dirt the previous evening and covered with plastic sheeting. A canteen was placed below the middle of the sheet, weighed down with a stone and punctured with a few holes. A small gulp of water sat in the canteen.

Not wanting to be thought a complete novice in desert survival, I had also dug a second hole that I'd peed in before covering in plastic. This one did not have holes punctured in the sheet because while water condenses on the top of the dew-collecting sheet and dribbles down to the holes, it condenses on the underside of the sheet when urine evaporates. It was with some satisfaction that I noted my urine recycling had produced a little more water than the dew system. The water in my canteen didn't look like urine. I smelt it. It didn't smell like urine. I put the canteen to my lips. It didn't taste like urine either.

'What about some breakfast?' Zeus asked as I put down my canteen. 'Bacon, eggs, hot coffee?' He suggested with a broad smile. I couldn't believe my ears. It sounded as if, having survived the midnight march, I was to be rewarded. My one and only meal was going to be a proper one. Despite having not eaten for 26 hours, I didn't actually feel hungry, but saliva started to flow in my mouth when Zeus mentioned breakfast.

Eagerly, I followed the commandos as we marched across the arid landscape towards where we'd left the vehicles the previous evening. I was feeling much better for having had a few hours sleep and was egged on by the prospect of something serious to eat.

More fool me. Breakfast it was, but both bacon and eggs were conspicuous by their absence. Breakfast on a Chilean commando desert survival course was a sort of maize paste made from toasted flour mixed with a lot of sugar and a bit of water. It tasted like glue, but I ate it anyway.

I didn't finish the course. Despite the general principle that survival in the desert with minimal food and water means you sleep during the day and do things at night, Zeus explained that sometimes daytime marching was a necessity. So we were going to do some of that too.

It wasn't as bad as during the night in that we didn't have to wear our packs and at least I could see, but the down side was that it was very hot. Physically, I think I could have kept going, but after the first two hours my mind was telling me otherwise. The commandos just kept walking because that was their job, but in my case I was able to ask myself why I was doing it. I had come out here with these guys to see what it was like when it got really very dry and you get weak from lack of inputs. I thought I'd seen that by now. I felt like shit. I couldn't see the point of doing any more. So I stopped.

I resumed my quest for a town or village that was drier than Arica instead, since this was what I was really here for. It wasn't on the Plain of Patience because no one lived there, but Zeus recommended I try the area to the north-west. I consulted my map and plumped for a chain of settlements strung out along a road that ran inland from Antofagasta.

The map I was using was accurate. There was a string of towns along this road, but I'd made the false assumption that where there was a town there would be people, some of whom may be taking meteorological readings. Not so in this part of Chile. The towns were all abandoned.

There was a signpost to the first one I came to along Ruta Nacional 25. It said Oficina Concepción. But Oficina Concepción was no more. It was just a collection of crumbling walls and deserted streets, discarded shells of buildings that had once been useful but were no longer. Faded signs on adobe walls indicated where people had once queued at the bank or come to drown their sorrows at a bar.

The trail of abandonment continued, town after sorry town, rejected and left to crumble in the dust. Their populations had absconded and their few trees left to fend for themselves, most now just skeletal outlines against a barren horizon. I came across a cemetery, forlorn and abandoned beside the road, line upon line of crude wooden crosses in the sun-baked ground, their crosspieces creaking in the desert wind. Most of the graves had long since been neglected, but a solitary red plastic rose, though faded pink in the Atacama sun, offered a secluded splash of colour to the sun-bleached wood and dun-coloured sand.

'Office' was the curious name given to these mining camp towns, industrial settlements created with the sole purpose of excavating sodium nitrate for sale as fertilizer. The name was a reference to the offices of the purchasing agents who bought everything mined within a certain radius. At the height of the nitrate boom, there were more than 300 industrial and housing installations dedicated to the extraction and exploitation of this mineral in the world's driest desert.

The salt of the Atacama became known as white gold and it turned the barren north into a new California. The white gold boom blossomed between 1880 and 1914. In 1913, Chile supplied 90 per cent of the world's total volume of nitrogenous fertilizers. But the First World War crisis and the development in Germany of synthetic nitrate spelt the beginning of the end of the boom. Half the *oficinas* were closed. Most of the rest gave up during the world economic crisis of 1929.

Today, there is just one left. I had almost given up hope of finding it when I reached the welcoming arch over the road into María Elena. Its founding year, 1926, was imprinted at one end of the arch, the year 2000 on the other, the entrance to a town of more than 7,000 people living in a 1920s timewarp.

A faded air of grandeur pervaded the whole settlement, with its wide dirt streets and grand *teatro* sporting life-sized stuccoed miners on its sturdy walls. The theatre's construction had been financed by Metro Goldwyn Mayer no less, an MGM picture palace in the middle of the desert, put up for the miners to watch the latest Hollywood releases in an era when world-renowned artists came to South America only to perform in the *oficinas*.

In the hostel where I stayed they had lost all the keys to the rooms. There was no point in fitting new locks, the woman on the desk told me, because no one was sure how much longer María Elena would continue. Rumour had it that the town would be closed the following year. I got talking with the cleaning ladies one morning, and they expressed dismay at the prospect. Two of the four women had been born here, and they had nowhere else to go. These women emitted a palpable sense of pride in their town, and leaving or not they still polished the parquet floors until they sparkled every morning.

Elsewhere, though, I detected a feeling of resignation. Although it was nearly Easter, no one had taken down the Christmas decorations hanging above the town's one small supermarket, appropriately named *El Salitre* (The Saltpetre).

I asked the chief administrator of the mine if the rumours I'd heard of the town's imminent demise were true. Marco was a cheerful, swarthy figure with short grey, kinky hair and dark glasses. He sat in his office pulling on a Kent cigarette, dressed in a short-sleeved shirt with the logo of the mining company on its pocket.

'Those rumours have been circulating for ten years or more,' he told me. He sighed, 'I honestly don't know whether they are true or not,' he added, in a tone that convinced me of his sincerity.

Marco's office was a friendly mess. His wide desk, which looked as if it dated from the 1920s, was swamped with mining reports and correspondence that only just left room for a large computer. The shelf behind Marco's head was lined with photographs of his family and the walls with old prints of English hunting scenes. María Elena had been established by a British company, he told me. The town's layout had been based on the Union Jack, with streets radiating out from the central park to mimic the flag, some with English names like Calle Wilcox and Calle Edwards. The British had run the mine for a dozen years before selling out to a local company.

When I told Marco of my quest, and posed the question about meteorological data, his reaction was immediate and positive. He leapt out of his chair and dug deep into another pile of papers that swamped an auxiliary table to one side of his office.

'Here!' he cried with glee, and thumped five bound volumes onto the desk in front of me. I opened the top one and leafed through its pages. Typed tables of wind speeds, temperature, relative humidity and numerous other variables cascaded before my eyes. I turned to the next green folder and flicked through that. My heart started racing. It was certainly the sort of thing I'd been after.

As I looked through the five-volume report, Marco gave me a brief run-down of his personal history. 'I was born near here,' he said. 'There's no doubt that it's the driest part of Chile. The only green thing I ever saw before I left here was an army uniform.'

I was only half listening. The report I had in my hands detailed the climatology of the region surrounding the *Salar de Atacama*. It had a wealth of detail, but as far as I could make out, the area it covered did not include María Elena. The *Salar de Atacama* was some distance away to the east. I found a map. María Elena was marked. I flicked through the contents pages of each volume, but couldn't see any reference to the town. The nearest place with data seemed to be a place called Coya Sur, but it was only a few kilometres from María Elena.

'The last rain we had here was in 1992,' Marco was saying. 'It caused chaos. Roads were washed away, the electricity was cut, houses were flooded. Rain is unusual here, so nothing is designed to cope with it.'

I had found rainfall averages for the meteorological stations mentioned in the report. They were all low, but none lower than Arica. I was now looking for data from Coya Sur. The cleaning ladies I'd spoken to in my hostel had mentioned the same 1992 storm. They had laughed on remembering it. Then one of them became serious and said that it was the same year that General Pinochet had come to visit. 'The rain washed his footsteps away,' she added.

I had found some stuff from Coya Sur, but the data was incomplete. I didn't seem to be getting anywhere. 'There doesn't appear to be any data from María Elena itself,' I said to Marco.

'I have that here,' he replied, turning to face his computer. My heart missed another beat. Marco opened the Excel program on his computer and started flicking up all sorts of graphs of various meteorological phenomena that he said were for María Elena. I looked closely at the screen. At the bottom of each graph, the station stated was again Coya Sur.

'Where is Coya Sur exactly,' I asked.

'It's the mine itself,' Marco said. 'It's where the meteorological station is.' It was another situation like Arica, the observing station being a few kilometres out of town.

'How long have they been taking measurements there?' I asked.

Marco paused, his finger on his computer mouse. 'About five years, I think,' he answered. 'Wait, I have it here.' He clicked and another chart came up labelled *Cantidad agua caida*. It was indeed the precipitation record. The chart was blank but for a single line. In the last five years, Coya Sur had recorded one rainfall event. A small note in a box arrowed from the peak said it had occurred on 15 May 2000, when 0.9 mm of precipitation had fallen at 3 o'clock in the morning 'I remember that one,' Marco said pointing to the screen.

'Lots of people were scared because they see rain so rarely. Everyone woke up to watch. It was very exciting.'

But it was no good to me. Most climatologists say that 30 years of data is the minimum required to define a climate. Five years was simply not enough. I knew that a 30-year run was what I was after.

I was feeling deflated when I left Marco's office. He had given me the five-volume report to take away and read, but I already knew that it didn't contain what I was after. Marco had suggested I go and ask the town's mayor if he could help me, although I wasn't very confident that I'd get anywhere.

But I found the office of the mayor, another kindly man who was equally eager to help. He confirmed that there was no meteorological station in María Elena.

'Although this place was founded in 1926,' he told me, 'up until 20 years ago, it was a private town, run by the mining company. My post was only created 20 years ago, when a municipal authority was established.' He looked at me seriously. 'The authorities in Antofagasta don't really care about this place,' he said. 'They assumed that the mining company would take the meteorological readings, so they didn't set up their own government station. In fact, the mine only began making observations five years ago.'

'Antofagasta decided to establish a station in Quillagua instead,' he went on, 'a small village of only 200 inhabitants. They simply ignored this town of nearly 8,000 people. Other towns have stations,' he said sadly, 'Sierra Gorda, Baquedano, but nothing in María Elena.'

'And how old were these other stations', I asked. Between 30 and 40 years old, he told me. I asked him how I might get to look at their records. The mayor said they came within his jurisdiction, but that the records would be held in Antofagasta. He said he'd telephone and ask for them to be sent. 'Someone is coming up from Antofagasta tomorrow,' he told me, 'I can ask them to bring what records they have.'

I returned to the mayor's office the following afternoon, and true to his word the mayor handed me a thick plastic folder full of records. They covered the three stations he had mentioned, Sierra Gorda, Baquedano, and Quillagua. A covering letter on government notepaper, from the director general of the *Direccion General de Aguas – ii Region*, detailed the data enclosed. Sierra Gorda's records dated from 1974, Baquedano's from 1963 and Quillagua's from 1969. I flicked through the report as the mayor continued his somewhat sorry tale of neglect from the previous day.

'I hope you find what you are looking for there,' he told me. 'It would be good for this area if it were to get the record of driest place on Earth because our government prefers to forget this region.' María Elena was the last of 300 saltpetre mining towns and the region represented a pivotal part of Chilean history, he said. 'Fortunes were made here,' he told me, but the region was now being consigned to the rubbish dump of history.

I had already flicked through the records for Sierra Gorda and Baquedano. The data were just exactly what I had been searching for, annual precipitation totals since records began. Unfortunately, Sierra Gorda's station had been running for less than 30 years, so it wouldn't be able to lay claim to the record. The data for Baquedano covered a sufficient length of time, but I saw immediately that they had received too much rain to make a bid to rival Arica as the driest town on Earth. Quillagua, however, was a different story. The records looked good. The rainfall amounts were very small. I couldn't wait to get out of the office and look more closely at the data in my hand. I thanked the mayor for his help, and promised to let him know the results of my investigation. He wished me luck, and told me again how good it would be for his region if it were to hold the driest place on Earth title. 'It would put the spotlight back on a forgotten part of Chile,' he said.

Back in the hostel, I settled down to look more closely at what the mayor had given me. The covering letter was important, because it certified that the stations I had data for were official government installations, and thus their readings could be assumed to be reliable. I quickly looked again at the records for Sierra Gorda and Baquedano confirming that they had no chance of beating Arica as the world's driest inhabited place.

Then I turned to Quillagua. The records started with annual summary sheets of precipitation by month. The top page started at 1998 and continued to part way through 2001. Every monthly summary box on the grid had a dot in, the sign for no rain according to the key at the bottom of the page. The amount of precipitation was zero for all these years.

I turned the page. The next one covered the years from 1982 to 1997. The last time it had rained in Quillagua was in 1992, nearly a decade before, when 1 mm had been recorded in May. I assumed it was the same event that had washed away General Pinochet's footsteps after his visit to María Elena.

Other than this entry, all the other years showed rows of dots for zero rainfall, except for 1984 when 0.4 mm of rain had been recorded in June and 0.2 mm in October of that year. Quillagua was certainly a very dry place. That was just three rainfall days since 1982. I turned to the next page.

Rainfall-wise, this page continued in the same vein. Absolutely no rain had been recorded at Quillagua in the years 1969 to 1981. But there was a problem. The record was blank between March 1975 and May 1978. I flicked through the rest of the sheets. There were annual summaries by month that showed the recordings for every day. Sheet after sheet was blank, indicating no rain. I came across the sheets for 1984 and 1992. These confirmed that the three rainfall events I'd picked up in the annual summaries were indeed just three separate events. Since 1969, it had rained three times in Quillagua. On 7 June 1984, 30 September in the same year, and on 28 May 1992. Except, that is, for the missing years. There were daily summary sheets for 1975 and 1978, but each had just a few months of recordings. There were simply no sheets at all for 1976 or 1977.

Mildly perturbed at the missing years, I nonetheless decided to add up what I'd got. The records began in June 1969, so I started with the first complete year: 1970. Over the period 1970 to 2000, 31 years, I had 27 years of data once I had omitted the years that were missing. In 27 years, Quillagua had recorded a grand total of 1.6 mm (0.06 inches) in precipitation. The average annual amount therefore was 0.06 mm (0.002 inches). I did the sum again. There was no question. Quillagua's average annual precipitation was 0.06 mm. I flicked through my notebook to get the figure for Arica, although I knew it already. It was 0.8 mm (0.03 inches), a whole order of magnitude larger.

A mixture of glory and pain came over me. Quillagua definitely looked like a drier place. And not just a bit drier but a whole order of magnitude drier. But the record was still only for 27 years, not the magic 30 years, and it wasn't continuous. So close to the record, and yet so far, it seemed.

It was curious because I had never really seriously believed that I'd find records to prove a place was drier than Arica, despite what people had been telling me since I had arrived on the Atacama coast. But now that I had, and come so close to proving Aldo, the Arica meteorologist, right, I felt a tremendous sense of disappointment, a sense of being robbed.

I put my calculator to one side and flicked through the pages of the plastic-covered book of records again. Perhaps this was the 'one small problem' that Don Cecilio, the soothsayer in San Pedro, had seen in the coca leaves. I stopped. A page I hadn't seen before lay open in front of me. It was another annual summary sheet for Quillagua, covering the years 1963-1972. All of the years had the familiar black dot in the month boxes, indicating no rain.

I flicked back to the start. Quillagua was only supposed to have started its readings in 1969. I compared the new sheet I'd just found with the previous one. Both were headed Quillagua. The only difference was in the latitude and longitude marked at the top. It seemed that meteorological readings had been taken in the village prior to 1969. Someone had started in 1963, but at a different site. It is not unusual for meteorological stations to be moved, and it seemed from the slightly different latitudes and longitudes, each different by just one minute, that the instruments had been moved from one side of the village to the other.

I did my sums again. This time I had 33 years of data, from 1964, the first full year of the pre-1969 readings, to 2000. The rainfall total was still the same: 1.6 mm (0.06 inches). The average this time came out even lower: 0.05 mm (0.002 inches) a year.

I could hardly contain myself. There was still the problem of the missing years, but now I had 33 years to average from and Quillagua was still an order of magnitude lower than Arica. The missing years remained a fly in the ointment, but I was 70 per cent sure that I had found a new driest place on Earth.

Quillagua was about 90 kilometres north of María Elena, straight up Ruta Nacional 5. The Atacama was unrelentingly barren for every kilometre in the desert sun. About 15 minutes from Quillagua I passed some geoglyphs of human forms on a hillside, and then, as the road took a slight rise, I caught my first glimpse of the town that I hoped to make the new record-holder. It was a sliver of green tucked into a deep valley slit into the wilderness.

It was a sleepy little village with a leafy main square, one side of which was bordered by old car tyres, half buried and painted bright colours. The meteorological station was in the grounds of the small school, closed today because it was Sunday. The padlock on the gate to the instrument compound was open and I walked in to take a look at what I reckoned was probably the least active rain gauge on the planet. It was of the same cylindrical white metal design as that at Arica airport. After I'd peeked inside and seen just a slight deposit of red dust, I bent over and kissed it.

After my return to the UK, I contacted the World Meteorological Organization and the *Guinness Book of Records*. Both were interested in my claim to have found a new driest place on Earth. The *Guinness Book of Records* wanted confirmation from the World Meteorological Organization before they would think about including Quillagua in their next edition, and the WMO said they could only look into the matter if the Chilean authorities could confirm my inkling that Quillagua was a drier place than Arica. I contacted the Chilean meteorological authority and put my findings to them. Then I waited.

A few weeks later, a fax came through from the *Direccion Meteorologica de Chile*. In addition to a brief covering letter, there was a page marked *Certificado*. The certificate said that after looking at the respective records, the Chilean meteorological authority confirmed that Quillagua was a drier place than Arica and that the meteorological station at Quillagua was the driest in Chile.

It was official. I'd found a new driest place on Earth.

HOTTEST
Dallol
Ethiopia

ONE

'What is the purpose of your trip to Region Number Two?' the man asked from behind his chipped wooden desk. His voice sounded perplexed, laced with a hint of suspicion.

'I want to visit Dallol, the hottest town on Earth,' I told him.

'I see,' he replied slowly, his speed of delivery implying quite the opposite.

Flyblown letters and lists embossed with official-looking purple stamps, all in Amharic, were pinned to the notice board behind him. He ran his gaze over a pile of similar papers on the desk in front of him and then looked at me.

'Wouldn't you rather visit some of our other regions?' he asked, adopting a more positive tone. 'All are more interesting and comfortable than the Afar region.' He proceeded to list some of Ethiopia's conventional tourist sites, places where I could see ancient rock-hewn churches, spectacular landscapes and amazing wildlife, all from the security of modern hotels and safari lodges.

I told him that I might try to take in some of these sites after my trip, but that my heart was set on visiting Dallol. The man surveyed the papers in front of him a second time, then shrugged, scribbled his signature across the bottom of my permit, and handed it to me across his desk. I folded the paper, put it in my pocket and shook the man's hand. As I turned to leave, he said, 'Good luck, and be careful.' I was halfway out of the door to his office when he added finally, I think more to himself than to me, 'I hope they don't kill you.'

It was thus with a feeling of some anxiety that I spent my first few days in Addis Ababa traipsing round various government departments collecting documents giving me official permission to venture into the land of the Afars. My nervousness was not eased by any of the bureaucrats I had dealings with, all of whom obviously considered my venture to be foolhardy in the extreme.

My journey to the world's hottest inhabited place had been the most difficult to plan of all my trips to the world's climatological extremes. The main obstacle had been a distinct lack of information about the record-holding town of Dallol and its surrounds. The Danakil Desert appeared to be one of the least explored and least understood deserts anywhere on the planet, and I got an immediate inkling as to why from what little material I did find on the place. Situated at the northern end of the East African Rift Valley at its junction with the Red Sea, it was an area of vast salt flats, bubbling hot springs and active volcanoes belching smoke and sulphurous fumes. A friend in Australia sent me a quotation from Ladislas Farago in 1936: 'The desert of Danakil is a part of the world that the Creator must have fashioned when he was in a bad mood.' My friend said she thought this charming little quote summed it up rather well.

The Danakil's few inhabitants, the Afar, have developed a lifestyle based on animal husbandry and nomadism to cope with this harsh environment and have also become renowned for their ferocious protection of the few resources the region has to offer. It seemed to me that if there is a hell, the Danakil is situated on its roof. The place sounded like a burning inferno inhabited by demons.

In truth, it was the demonic Afar, rather than the hellhole they lived in, that most exercised my mind as I left the office clutching my

permit and emerged on to one of Addis Ababa's nondescript highways. A hot desert I could cope with, having visited several in my
academic line of work, quite apart from enduring the commandos'
survival course in the Atacama. But by all accounts, the Afar did not
welcome outsiders into their fiery wilderness. In fact, to say that the
Afar don't encourage visitors gives a somewhat misleading impression
of their legendary lack of hospitality. It is more accurate to say that
they actively discourage them. And their favoured method of active
discouragement is castration.

The two most comprehensive accounts of the Afar that I had laid
my hands on agreed on this. Both were written by British explorers
and published during the 1930s. In 1933, Wilfred Thesiger travelled
the length of the Awash River to its bitter end in Lake Assal, reputed
to be the saltiest body of water in the world and the lowest point in
Africa. Five years before him, Ludovico Nesbitt, a mining engineer
and a member of an English family long settled in Italy, had traversed
the entire Danakil Desert from the Awash to Asmara, in present-day
Eritrea. Both men presented accounts of their journeys to the Royal
Geographical Society in London which were subsequently published
in the Society's journal. The fact that both men had returned to tell
their tales was a significant achievement in itself. All previous expedi-
tions into the Danakil by white men had been, without exception,
massacred by the unsociable Afar.

And it wasn't just white men who had previously failed to penetrate
the Danakil. Although notionally a part of Ethiopia, the Afar had never
been effectively subdued by the Highland Ethiopians. As I was to
discover, the Afar are still very much a law unto themselves, and I rather
suspect that it was this fact that had been uppermost in the bureaucrat's
mind when he had tried to dissuade me from my quest. As my blue
Lada taxi chugged its way through the mid-morning exhaust fumes,
and my driver drew my attention to a notable local landmark, Addis
Ababa's first set of traffic lights, I could still see the look of genuine
concern on the face of the man behind the chipped desk.

The Afar castrated their victims by means of a very long knife known as a *jile*. The blade was about 50 centimetres long, with one bend in it, rather like the shape of a boomerang, and sharp on both sides. If the operation could be conducted while the victim was still alive, so much the better, but for obvious reasons most of the injured parties had to be killed first. The Afars' motive for castration and murder was variously justified on harshly objective grounds – as a logical reaction to their region's aridity: a newcomer would necessarily have to drink some of the scarce water available, jeopardizing the survival of all native inhabitants – and also for cultural reasons.

Thesiger pointed out that until he has killed someone, an Afar man is called a woman and is not allowed to marry. But it doesn't stop there. An Afar's great ambition is to collect more trophies than his neighbour, since a man's prowess is rated according to the number of his kills. A system of decorations has evolved to indicate the castration count. Not until he has killed can a man wear a coloured loincloth, or a comb or feather in his hair. After two executions, a chap can split his ears, but the most common method of denoting kills is to attach a brass-bound leather thong to the knife or rifle, one for each trophy taken. Ten kills gives a man the right to wear a coveted iron bracelet. Indication of a man's competence in this matter even follows him to the grave. A line of stones stood upright before his memorial gives notice of his achievements to posterity.

In the matter of castration, Thesiger and Nesbitt held opposing views on just one issue. Nesbitt claimed that it was also customary for an Afar to display the testicles of a victim either in his hut or around his neck, while Thesiger stated that he never saw any such thing. The trophy would be displayed around the village, Thesiger maintained, but it was then thrown away. It seemed like a very minor point of disagreement to me.

Addis Ababa means 'New Flower', but at first sight Ethiopia's capital doesn't live up to its name. Neither character, nor charm, are words that come to mind when proceeding along the city's wide boulevards, some straddled by monumental communist arches proclaiming the struggle of the people, superfluous reminders of the country's Soviet-inspired Marxist-Leninist regime that had been overthrown ten years previously.

Ethiopia's communist government was just the most recent twist in the history of a state that has been on the world scene for more than 2,000 years. The country's name is derived from the Greek, meaning 'land of the burnt-faced people', and the ancient Greeks held Ethiopia in high regard. In the *Odyssey*, Homer states that Poseidon attended an Ethiopian festival where he accepted a mass sacrifice of cattle and sheep in his honour. The kingdom of Ethiopia traditionally dates back to the tenth century BC, when it was founded by Menelik I, Solomon's first son (supposedly by the Queen of Sheba). The first recorded kingdom, however, grew up around the city of Axum in the first century AD. Either way, Ethiopia is one of the world's oldest countries, and it is unique among African nations in never having been colonized by Europeans. In fact, while European powers were scrambling for power in Africa in the late nineteenth century, Ethiopia was still busy building her own empire, and continued to annex areas on her southern borders well into the twentieth century. Italy had a go at setting up shop in Ethiopia in 1895, but retired with a bloody nose after the battle of Adowa, the following year. The Italians tried again in the late 1930s, when Mussolini fancied an African colony, and actually managed to occupy parts of the country for a brief five-year period before being kicked out during the Second World War.

So, for all intents and purposes, Ethiopia remains relatively untouched by European influence, a few Marxist monuments and clapped-out Soviet motor cars notwithstanding. These reminders of Eastern Europe have been augmented in more recent times with a few equivalents from the West, like T-shirts adorned with the faces of Liverpool footballer Michael Owen and Kate Winslet in her *Titanic* role. But in many respects, the country has followed its own path into the twenty-first century, retaining its ancient home-grown Christian church which dates back 1,600 years, its own alphabet, and its own calendar and system for measuring time. Although the city of Addis is distinctly unremarkable, these other aspects combined to give me a feeling of moving in some sort of parallel universe.

Actually, Ethiopia has not yet reached the twenty-first century. All my permits for travel into the Afar 'Region Number Two', as today's government insists on calling it, were dated 1993, a year that began in what I know as September 2000 according to the Gregorian calendar now used in the West. The calendar used in Ethiopia is divided into 12 months of 30 days each, plus a 'thirteenth month' of five days (or six days during a leap year). Hence Ethiopia's tourism slogan claiming: 'Thirteen Months of Sunshine'. The Ethiopian calendar is now about seven years and eight months 'behind' the calendar I am accustomed to.

More troublesome to my everyday existence, however, was Ethiopian daily time. The days begin at sunrise, which is always considered to be one o'clock. On several occasions, I managed to miss appointments by assuming the times given were according to the Western system. Converting one to another was enough to give me a brain haemorrhage. On one occasion I turned up for an 8.30 meeting just after breakfast, only to be told that the appointment wasn't until after lunch. Somehow, 8.30 was supposed to mean 2.30 in the afternoon.

It wasn't just time that was disconcertingly different in Ethiopia. Space, too, was viewed rather differently. Getting from place to place in my Lada taxi was manageable just so long as I knew the name of the building I was aiming for. An actual address, in the British sense of the word, was less commonly used. For postal purposes, Ethiopians have PO boxes rather than door-to-door deliveries, a fact probably not unrelated to the almost complete lack of street names. At first, I put down the absence of name plaques on the thoroughfares to bureaucratic inefficiency, but after several enquiries as to how I should refer to particular roads, it became clear to me that most streets simply didn't have names.

As a geographer, this alternative approach to spatial referencing should have been interesting to me, but when combined with continual thoughts of imminent emasculation, the lack of recognizable frames of reference for both time and space resulted in a surreal effect. Some time ago, I had a session in a sensory deprivation tank in Oxford. It was an enclosed bath of warm, salty water in which you lie floating in darkness for an hour or so in order to relax. The first five minutes after the lid was closed, shutting out all light, I found to be anything but relaxing. They were disturbing in the extreme, and the effects of my first day in Addis Ababa were not dissimilar. Here I was, in the capital city of an ancient African civilization, meandering along a street with no name, six hours adrift and seven years previously, pondering the impending demise of my most valuable of masculine assets.

Consequently, I've no idea what time it was when I wandered into a small shack covered by a blue tarpaulin in an unknown location somewhere in the Ethiopian capital. Beer was being served and it was just what I needed. I sat down on a low wooden bench and ordered a Castel, one of the local brews. I soon got talking to some of the men sat around me, Addis professionals taking their ease after a hard day's work. I was in the company of a young journalist, very smart in his suit and tie, an older man who happened to work for the British Council, and a rather dishevelled figure of indeterminate age in an open-necked white shirt.

'I studied law at university in Moscow,' he told me apropos of nothing. 'Many Ethiopians used to study there during the time of the Derg, but not so many now.' The Derg was the Amharic name for the former Marxist government, a regime that had been associated with widespread repression and curfews in its later years. I thought to myself that my new lawyer friend had probably been well out of it in Moscow, since radical students had borne the brunt of the Derg's oppression. Had drinking dens like this one been open during those years I wondered aloud. The question was largely stonewalled. The journalist chose the moment to sup his beer. The British Council man took an interest in something going on at another table.

'Those were different times,' the lawyer told me. It seemed like an appropriate time to change the subject, so tentatively I raised the topic of the Danakil.

'It is a desert area,' the journalist told me.

'Home of the Afar,' the British Council man chipped in, his attention now refocused on our discussion, 'Moslems who claim to be descendants of Noah's son, Ham.'

'They say it is the hottest place in the world,' the Moscow lawyer announced, 'for me this is a good enough reason for not going there.' I told him that this was precisely the reason for my interest. I was intending to visit the Danakil, to make a trip to Dallol, the world's hottest town.

'Is it not hot enough for you here?' The lawyer giggled. Addis had indeed been warm, despite being more than 2,400 metres above sea level. 'No,' I told him, 'I want to go to the place where it gets no hotter.'

'An interesting thought,' mumbled the lawyer into his beer, 'but you should take care, the Afar are not civilized people like us Highlanders.'

There was a pause in the conversation as a man appeared asking if we wanted more beer. We did, though not all of us needed it.

'A beer, a beer, my kingdom for a beer,' declared the lawyer with a broad grin on his face. I returned to the subject of the Afar, and asked the assembled drinkers whether there was any truth in what I'd read about their penchant for castrating foreigners. The lawyer was draining his beer glass and I saw his red eyes bulge as he heard my question. He almost choked on the last drops of his beer as the others burst into laughter. The journalist reached out to slap him on the back.

The man from the British Council was the first to regain his composure. 'When were these accounts written?' he asked. 'In the 1930s,' I told him. He nodded. 'These are just historical stories,' he declared, 'it's not like that any more. Such behaviour is very rare nowadays.'

'Ethiopia is not a land of savages,' the lawyer stated, mildly contradicting his earlier remark about the Afar not being civilized.

Our next round of beers arrived. The lawyer pounced on his and gulped half of it down in one. 'The Afar are a proud and independent people,' the British Council man continued. 'Their women are beautiful and bare-breasted, but don't even think about touching them. I wouldn't advise that you so insult an Afar, but even if you do, he won't castrate you ...' This pronouncement was a cue for more laughter and I almost breathed a sigh of relief, but caught myself just in time '...he'll just shoot you instead,' the British Council man continued.

Although my questions had been a source of some mirth at the pot house ('It's called a pot house because it's where you drink pots of beer,' the journalist had explained), my new-found friends seemed to have taken a shine to me, and after a couple more pots, they suggested I accompany them to their next destination.

'It's an *azmari beit*,' the British Council man told me. 'There you will see some of our culture.'

'Yes,' said the lawyer, 'and considering where you're going, a dose of *iskista* is just what you need.' This latter comment was met with another gale of laughter as we tumbled out of the pot house into the late evening sunshine. My enquiries as to the meaning of the joke were met with a chorus of, 'You will see,' and it wasn't long before I divined the lawyer's meaning.

An *azmari beit* is literally a place of *azmaris*, an *azmari* being a peculiarly Ethiopian phenomenon, sort of a cross between a stand-up comedian and a sharp-tongued folk singer, usually accompanied by a one-stringed fiddle with a diamond-shaped soundbox covered with goatskin. In centuries past, *azmaris* were a caste of wandering Amhara minstrels who made up topical songs. Some were assigned to the courts of sovereigns, much like European jesters, but they also performed religious functions, celebrating liturgies and officiating at certain ceremonies.

Their repertoire gradually became more secular, singing love poetry and eventually inventing humorous or satirical verse in which they poked bawdy fun at anyone and everyone, but particularly prominent figures of the times. The *azmaris* are often described as cultural scapegoats, held in contempt by the heavily Christian society at large, yet at the same time admired for their ability to create music that embodies emotional and physical intoxication. *Azmaris* helped maintain morale during the Italian occupation in the 1930s, and so potent a force were they that many were executed by the Italians as a result. They were not well thought of during the time of the Derg, either, and many of the Addis alcohol dens like the one we entered were closed down during that time.

My friends led me through a gate in a breeze-block wall, across a muddy forecourt, and into a small, dark room inside a concrete house. A fug hit me as I walked in to see low benches around the walls hung with coloured drapes and wicker baskets. An assortment of men were sitting comfortably behind low round tables laden with beer bottles, ashtrays and glasses. Their eyes were all fixed on a young woman dressed in a long white flowing robe with an embroidered strip down the front. Her singing, to the accompaniment of a man also dressed in white, playing a one-stringed fiddle, brought forth occasional gales of laughter.

We ducked past the *azmari* to the short bar in one corner of the room, got beers and found seats. The woman performing gave a loud and piercing whistle while breathing in as I passed, which made me jump, much to the amusement of all present.

'This woman is called Zewditou Yohannès,' the British Council man said in my ear. 'She is quite famous and has toured in Europe. Her style is specific to Addis. It is known as *bolel*, which is an Amharic word for car exhaust fumes.' I could see the parallel between her rapid-fire combustible delivery and the put-put of my Lada taxi.

Azmari performances are often interspersed with *iskista*, a traditional Ethiopian dance involving shaking shoulders and heaving chests. It was the heaving chests that had provoked such laughter among my friends on leaving the pot house, because at this particular *azmari beit*, they belonged to several rather well-endowed and very beautiful young women. As Zewditou Yohannès closed her session, a dancer took the floor accompanied by another fiddler and a man on a bongo drum.

Her dancing was decidedly interactive, the woman shaking her stuff directly in front of various members of the audience, who were at liberty to stand up and dance in kind with the performer. Being the only white man in the *azmari beit* made me an obvious target, and it wasn't long before I was on my feet facing an impossibly attractive woman doing extraordinary things with her shoulders, shaking and thrusting her head as if her neck were made of jelly on springs, and performing a range of gravity-defying tricks with her ample bosom.

After ten minutes of my trying my best to keep up with the erotic *iskista* gyrations and gymnastics, I left the floor to a hearty round of applause. The small room had become sauna-like, and I was sweating like a pig.

'The heat must be good preparation for the Danakil,' I shouted above the hubbub to the lawyer, whose smiling eyes were shining even redder than before.

'No, the Danakil will be much hotter than this,' he shouted back, 'but *iskista* is good preparation of a different kind. You must get these feelings out of your system before venturing into the Danakil.' The lawyer stooped to take a drink from his beer bottle, then he started laughing and slapped me on the back. 'Enjoy it while you can! It's like the condemned man eating a hearty breakfast, is it not?'

I told him it was probably a very apt simile.

TWO

Ethiopia may have developed in a parallel universe, but the country has still managed to acquire a penchant for paperwork that would be the envy of the most ardent Western bureaucrat. This meant that in addition to my permits from the central government in Addis Ababa, I also needed to obtain similar documents from the Afar regional government. This was a bore because I had to go out of my way to get them. Asayita, the regional capital, is at the southern end of the Danakil depression, while Dallol is up north, and there is no recognized route along the length of the desert between them.

Although Addis is a capital city, it isn't sealed off from the rural economy it represents. Donkeys laden with firewood mix with the Ladas and lorries on the streets, while chickens and goats root among the debris along the pavements. But just beyond the city's outskirts, the countryside begins in earnest, circular mud huts with perfectly conical rush roofs sitting in a sea of neat fields tilled by men walking patiently behind pairs of oxen.

The road between Nazareth and Awash was lined with heaps of charcoal packaged for sale in sacks that had originally contained food aid, and Awash itself was the last town where horses, pulling two-wheeled carts like chariots along the dusty roads, were the main form of transport. After crossing the Awash River that Thesiger had followed, at a bridge guarded by two stone lions and four real soldiers, the appearance of camels and donkey carts marked the beginning of a different environment. As we'd descended from the Highlands, we had been driving up a temperature gradient. The bushy savannah had all but disappeared as we entered the lowland oven. I put my hand out of the window of the truck into an airflow as hot as a hairdryer.

We continued north, along a good tarmac road that led to Djibouti, Ethiopia's main port after it lost its coastline to Eritrean independence and a senseless two-year war with its former northern region left Ethiopia with no access to Eritrean harbours. A constant flow of articulated lorries trundled goods back and forth to the Red Sea coast. We passed through wildlife reserves where oryx stood motionless beneath the rare trees and a huge vulture surveyed our passing from the roadside. The occasional warthog trotted nonchalantly across the road in front of us.

The sun was setting as we turned off the highway towards Asayita, the battered signpost and dirt track belying its importance as a regional capital. An extended family of baboons cleared the way through a green patch of low trees and thorn bushes fed by a spring, and we motored the final leg of the ten-hour drive across a lifeless salt plain accompanied by the last remnants of huge dust devils. Darkness had fallen by the time we saw the silhouette of the town against the sky.

Ethiopian time still had a trick up its sleeve. Entering Asayita was like driving back into the Middle Ages. Despite being in the middle of an arid wilderness, the town was closed off at night, and the driver had to brake hard to avoid bursting through a motley chain strung low across the track. Beside it was a sentry box with a guard who approached carrying a Kalashnikov slung casually over his shoulder. After checking our credentials, he lowered the chain and we drove into a shadowy world of adobe and stick houses. Street lights sprung up haphazardly along the rough track, but none appeared to have been blessed with electricity. Flickering candles and burning braziers did their best to ward off the darkness, affording brief glimpses of children playing in the dust. Further into town, dated Western pop music was pumping from battery-powered cassette players as breeze-block buildings took over where the huts left off. Our progress along the streets was slowed by a throng of strollers taking the torrid evening air along with a small battalion of goats. Our vehicle was met with curious glances, but whether this was because we were arriving after sunset or simply because it was a truck, I couldn't tell. Certainly, other motor vehicles were conspicuous by their absence.

I made a mistake at the Lem Hotel, situated, I discovered the following morning, just a stone's throw from the huge town square, a rough patch of stones and goats that encircled an odd-looking monument about 5 metres high in bright sheet metal with some sort of coat of arms at the top. Faced with the choice of a very basic box room, or one of the beds lined up outside in the courtyard, I plumped for a room. My reckoning was based partly on thoughts of security, but was clinched by the presence of a ceiling fan that, miraculously, was working, despite the apparent lack of electricity elsewhere in the town. For an hour or two, the fan did a passable job of carving the stifling atmosphere into chunks of hot air that buffeted my weary torso. But when even the Lem's electricity gave out sometime during the night, I was left to stew in a motionless sauna, all the courtyard beds having been taken by those more familiar than me with the ways of Asayita.

When I awoke at 5.45 in the morning, the temperature was perfect. It lasted until about 8 o'clock by which time my thermometer was registering 36°C (97°F) in the shade and outside it was already too hot for the flies. They had all taken refuge in my room instead. Breakfast consisted of a piece of bread and a refreshing glass of tea, followed by an ice-cold Coca-Cola that gave me the strange sensation of feeling like a human sieve. As I poured the caramel-coloured liquid down my gullet, it almost instantly seeped out through every pore in my body.

In the morning light, Asayita looked less medieval and more like a seedy frontier town. But its streets were busy with men in sarongs going about their business, a bicycle repairman hard at work on a puncture and a couple of shoeshine boys awaiting their first customers of the day. Opposite the Lem Hotel, a donkey cart was making its morning delivery of beer to a building with red walls and yellow shutters, which turned out to be a brothel. Small kiosks were opening to ply their trade of cigarettes and household goods, while larger shops revealed row upon row of brightly coloured sarongs. Curiously, every other establishment appeared to be a hairdressing salon.

I crossed the desolate wastes of the town square to shrieks of '*Farang, farang*' from innumerable small children who seemed positively ecstatic at the sight of a white man in their midst. I knew the meaning of the word from the pages of Nesbitt, who had been similarly harangued more than 70 years before. But while the children's delight was endearing, I was mildly perturbed by the implication that little had changed in the Danakil in more than half a century. A few moments later, however, I was berated with the more contemporary exclamation of, 'You! Money!'

The upside of having to make this side trip to Asayita to trawl round regional government offices was that it also gave me the opportunity to make contact with the Afar Pastoralist Development Association, a non-governmental organization that I'd heard of while still in Britain. Their office, if office it could be called, was in a compound a short walk from the town's central square on the opposite side from my hotel.

Nomadic pastoralists like the Afar tend to inhabit the fringes of modern societies, and governments in most parts of the world have a propensity to view these kinds of people as a bit of a nuisance. Often overlooking the fact that their nomadic lifestyle is one adopted out of necessity, mobility being the ideal response to an environment that offers few and rather unpredictable resources, much of the 'help' offered to nomads comes in the form of encouraging them to settle.

From a benevolent viewpoint, getting nomads to put down roots and stay put means it is much easier to provide them with education, health and other services. Conversely, critics argue that settlement makes control and taxation of these people more straightforward.

Once in a while, however, somebody tries to meet the nomads' needs on their own terms, and the Afar Pastoralist Development Association was one such body. Valerie Browning, who ran the organization with her husband, explained to me that they had started with primary health care, not by building a clinic but by training health workers who could go out into the desert and visit families where they camped.

'Putting up a clinic is bloody useless for people constantly on the move,' Valerie told me in her straightforward manner. She was a no-nonsense woman, well over 4 feet tall, with the constitution and energy of someone much larger. 'The Afars' whole life is centred around their livestock and the animals have to be kept moving to find grazing, so health-care workers have to move with them.'

Valerie was not what I'd expected. She was an Australian who had happened upon the Afar nearly ten years before, married one, and taken up residence. Her association had also established an education programme, teaching Afar people to read and write. 'The rural Afar are 98 per cent illiterate in this country,' Valerie announced. 'Mind you, their language was only first written down in the 1970s.' Consequently, numerous aspects of grammar were yet to be agreed upon, quite apart from the fact that there were very few books in Afar. Like many other nomadic peoples, they have a strong tradition of storytelling and the Afar Pastoralist Development Association had begun to send out fieldworkers to collect stories and oral histories and write them down.

Latterly, Valerie's team had also been involved in women's issues and veterinary training. 'Next we want to go into marketing. The Afar are useless businessmen because they have no experience of a cash economy. They're always being ripped off. When they come into town to sell a sheep or goat in exchange for grain, the merchants sit around all day and refuse to talk to them. The Afar gets nervous because he has to get grain so his wife can make bread. By the evening, he's at his wits' end. And that's when the merchant pounces. The Afar never gets a fair price for his animals.'

The merchants were all Highlanders, Valerie told me, and Asayita was essentially a Highlanders' town. This surprised me. I'd thought that I'd arrived in the Danakil, but obviously I hadn't really quite yet.

'Look around you,' she exclaimed, 'the majority of shops and businesses you see here are owned by Highlanders. And it's not just animals they're here for. The Danakil is full of salt and other minerals – they're all after a piece of the action. They want to suck the Afar dry.' She made the Afar sound like a people under threat, but with Valerie the one-woman whirlwind on their side, I felt as if they had a chance.

A couple of days later, my regional government permit in hand, I was sitting in a Land Cruiser, on my way to an Afar community some-where a bit further north of Asayita. Valerie was taking two women who had recently completed a health-care course back to their families, and had asked if I'd wanted to come along. 'It'll give you a chance to see what the Afar are really like,' she had told me.

The offer had come not long after I'd tentatively broached the subject of castration with her. Valerie's response was fairly unequivocal.

'Total nonsense,' she scoffed. 'I'd like to get my hands on that Mr Thesiger; most of what he wrote was bullshit.' Afar men often carried the long curved *jile* knife, she said, but it was for ceremonial purposes only. 'It's part of the coming of age thing. At the age of ten, a boy gets a stick. At 18, he gets a knife. When he's 21, a fully grown man, he can have a gun.'

'But this whole castration business is all Highland propaganda,' Valerie continued. She had dark hair and a pointy little chin and eyes made to read your inner thoughts with. They were burning with indignation as she said this. 'Highlanders hate the Afar, because they're scared of them. But castration, huh, the Afar were never like that. They have a tradition of hospitality to foreigners, not hostility.'

Coming after the comments on the matter from my friends in the pot house in Addis Ababa, Valerie's definitive dismissal brought me further mental relief. But even she left me with an element of doubt when she added a little later, 'It's the Oromo who castrate their enemies, not the Afar.' I sensed, perhaps, an element of displacement here, of one group blaming another. Nobody had actually denied that this sort of behaviour took place, albeit perhaps less frequently than in times past.

We were continuing on the Djibouti road. After slowly gaining altitude, passing burnt-out shells of tanks now stationed forever at points that were strategic during the civil war that led to the end of the Derg regime, we were now descending steeply through the Doobi Pass. The route was in a perpetual motion of trucks grinding their gears as they struggled up the hairpin bends laden with goods from Djibouti. Earlier, we had passed through a couple of settlements, long lines of brightly painted wooden shacks, whose raison d'être was to service the passing truck drivers with food and drink. Sweat had drenched the shirt on my back. The heat was still and palpable.

The dramatic drop of the Doobi Pass gave hazy views of flat salt pans shimmering in the afternoon heat at the foot of towering volcanic peaks. Valerie pointed out the rift valley pinnacles and reeled off their Afar names: Pregnant Mountain, Children's Mountain. The pass itself featured in one of the stories told to youngsters by their mothers. 'They say that Auntie Doobi eats small children,' Valerie told me with a provocative smile.

My mention of the castration 'myth', as Valerie called it, was obviously still bothering her, and she proceeded to give me some more details on the tolerance of Afar culture. Even when disputes arose among themselves, violence was the very last resort, she told me. 'They're not like the Somalis, who seem to solve everything with a gun,' she said. 'The Afar have clan judgements, not retribution. They have a very well developed system for dealing with disputes.

Everyone sits down before the elders and has their say. Evidence is given by witnesses, and there's even an official recorder who repeats what has been said and the elders say, "We have heard with our own ears," and then it's officially on the record. The process can continue for days.' Penalties usually came in the form of livestock being handed over by the guilty party, who also has to make a public apology for their misdemeanour. The only exception to this rule occurred in the case of murder, when retribution certainly was on the cards.

We had passed the turn-off to Djibouti and were continuing north-ward along the road that led to Assab, formerly one of Ethiopia's major ports but now cut off in Eritrea and no longer used for Ethiopian trade thanks to the war between the two countries that had ended only a few months before. Without the lifeblood of trade, the route had withered in the desert heat. There were gaping potholes, stretches where the tarmac had simply been worn bare and not replaced, along with sorry shells of former settlements that had died along with the road.

The closure of the border with Eritrea had been a disaster for the Afar both economically and socially. Afars live in neighbouring parts of Eritrea and Djibouti, and Assab was an Afar port. Ethiopian Afars had sold livestock to Assab traders for export to the Arabian penin-sula, but now everything had to be sold through Djibouti. But in 1998, the same year that the war with Eritrea started, Saudi Arabia imposed an import ban on livestock coming from Horn of Africa countries due to a suspected outbreak of Rift Valley Fever somewhere in the Horn. Sales to Djibouti exporters dried up and now Afars who wanted to sell their animals had to rely on Djibouti's domestic needs. Many Ethiopian Afars also had relatives in neighbouring Eritrea whom they had not seen for three years.

We turned off the dilapidated Assab road and our vehicle lurched its way across country. After an hour of listing and swerving to avoid thorn trees and small sand dunes, we came to a halt. 'From here, we walk,' Valerie announced. And walk we did, across a desolate land-scape, flat and tedious, hemmed in by great walls of rock thrust up along fault lines in the distance. All around us, towering columns of dust quivered upon the skyline, hovering momentarily like umbilical cords to the heavens before twisting away to set off for a race across the desert plain.

The community, when we came to it, was a group of half a dozen low, oval-shaped huts in a rock-strewn patch of desert. The huts consisted of a patchwork of palm mats covering stick frames. The rocks were everywhere, hot and black and hard to walk on. It wasn't the sort of spot that I'd have chosen to set up camp.

Goats wandered in and out between the huts sniffling at God knows what because there wasn't any vegetation for 200 metres in every direction. A camel sat unperturbed beside a rock enclosure covered in thorn branches that contained three baby goats bleating for all they were worth. A couple of small children sat among the rocks, not playing as I might have expected, but just sitting. Occasionally, the small girl, perhaps five years of age, would push away a goat that fancied a nibble at one of the rush mats that covered her hut.

From inside the hut, a woman's voice called a greeting above a constant grinding sound. She was squatting just inside the entrance pounding grain between two pieces of rock while simultaneously breast-feeding a tiny baby that clung precariously to her chest inside a brightly coloured dress. Behind her, the dirt floor of the hut was strewn with lengths of rope, encrusted wicker baskets and a rolled rush mat. Hanging from the stick frame were a couple of well-used wooden spoons and other cooking utensils. These nomads certainly seemed to have few personal possessions.

The woman wore a flower-patterned headscarf tied over a black veil and showed us some of her white teeth when she smiled. She didn't once cease her rhythmic grinding as she chatted away. Afars greet each other with a ritual of enquiries into the health of livestock followed by an exchange of news. As Valerie told me, news can consist of almost anything seen or heard since the parties last met. 'This woman,' said Valerie, indicating one of the health trainees, 'is telling her that she saw what looked like a stray camel by the road when we drove up. She's telling her the clan it belongs to, which she knew from its markings. It may not seem important, but the news will be passed on until it reaches the ears of someone from that clan. Information like this keeps these communities going. It's an extremely efficient intelligence-gathering system.'

I was grateful for the rest and partial shade of the hut as the news bulletins were exchanged. By the time they had been exhausted, the woman in the hut had finished grinding her grain and had proceeded to make a dough of the flour in a battered metal bowl. She handed her baby to the five-year-old girl and walked a short distance to a square hole in the ground lined with flat slabs of rock. At the bottom of the hole, perhaps 40 centimetres deep, were the smouldering ashes of a fire. She turned them over with a stick and fashioned four flat pancakes out of her dough, slapping each on to a side of the hole. Then she carefully covered the ground oven with more flat rocks and a piece of damp cloth.

While waiting for the bread to bake, the woman set about roasting and grinding coffee beans back at the entrance to the hut. By this time, we had been joined by three other women and the menfolk, and we all squatted round the hut on rush mats to be hypnotized by the delectable smell of the coffee beans roasting on a small metal pan. All the men carried stout sticks and wore Western-style T-shirts and sarongs that hung below the knee. To my relief, none of them wore a knife at his belt and only one carried an ancient Kalashnikov.

Once ground, the coffee was carefully put into a black pot, which was filled with water and sugar, and placed on the fire. Tiny cups were produced on a battered tray. After the head of the family blessed the coffee in a short ceremony as the sun sank towards the horizon, it was poured to accompany the flat bread still hot from the oven.

That evening, I was given the best mat to sleep on and one of the men produced a roll of material for a pillow. He also insisted on wrapping it with his headscarf as a pillowslip. The mat was laid in a patch largely cleared of stones and the other men settled down on their mats nearby to pray. Getting comfy for me meant moving a few more rocks from beneath my mat.

A cool, blustery wind blew up as the children played with sticks and an old tin can and the stars began to twinkle in the night sky. A three-quarter moon bathed the rocky scene in a wholesome brightness. The goats still pottered about sniffing at this and that, their pelts glistening in the moonlight. Before I settled down to sleep, I was offered a bowl of their warm milk to drink. As I drifted off into slumberland, I heard, far off, the howl of a jackal, but any thoughts of danger now that I was finally amongst the Afar could not have been further from my mind.

The next morning, the harsh reality of a nomad's life hit me square between the eyes. The women set off early to collect water and Valerie suggested we go with them. We took with us the goats, and four donkeys that I hadn't seen the previous day, because they all had to be watered. It was a three-hour walk.

'They're always walking, these Afar,' Valerie chirped as we picked our way over the stones away from the camp. 'I love walking. I could walk all day.' I didn't say that taking a 20-kilometre trek as soon as you get up in the morning wasn't exactly my idea of fun. It was 7 o'clock and I was sweating already.

'Why don't they set up camp a bit closer to the water?' I asked.

'Because the grazing's better here.'

As they walked, all the women were busy weaving mats from a wrap of rushes tied to the small of their backs. They never seemed to stop doing something. 'We did a survey and found that 80 per cent of the daily tasks are done by women,' Valerie told me. 'It's the women who do all the work in this society. The men do nothing by comparison. They just sit around and demand coffee.' I was beginning to think that perhaps the men had it right. An hour into our walk, as the sun had crept progressively higher in the sky and the temperature had risen accordingly, I decided that the reason the men lounged around all day was quite simple. They probably couldn't hack it as a woman.

The heat was becoming unbearable. We had crossed a cracked clay plain and were once more clambering over bloody rocks. Just picking my way through them took all my concentration and, weary as I was, the chances of slipping and turning an ankle were increasing all the time. But Valerie and the women just marched straight through the boulder field as if the rocks weren't there, and they were all wearing flip-flops. They also never stopped weaving, even once.

'The Afar are in love with goats and rocks,' Valerie announced as if she could read my mind. 'Goats are part of the family, and rocks they use to build compounds, as grinding stones, as pillows. They love rocks too much.' She could say that again.

Somehow, I managed to stay with them all the way to the waterhole, but it wasn't the sort of waterhole I'd been expecting. While trudging across the desert wastes, I'd conjured up images of a palm-fringed oasis of sparkling clean water with a sandy shore. I imagined shedding my sweat-sodden shirt, splashing the cool liquid on my chest and then just lying in the fresh waters for a lengthy period. More fool me.

I started to become suspicious when the last stretch was uphill. The hillside was, of course, covered in large rocks. 'I thought this was supposed to be a waterhole?' I asked Valerie, probably more aggressively than was entirely necessary.

'You'll see,' she said as she skipped between the boulders.

Short tufts of bright green grass sprouted every now and again between the rocks and the goats had spotted them immediately. Up above, I could make out what looked like cairns, large piles of stones marching along the top of the ridge. We stopped at the second one. 'Here we are,' announced Valerie, 'the waterhole.'

I didn't feel disappointed immediately. On the one hand, this was at least the end of the walk and, on the other hand, frustration was being temporarily averted by my mild curiosity as to where the water was. I moved round the side of the cairn, which I could now see was sealed between the stones with mud. A large oil drum appeared. It was full of water. Now I did feel let down. This was cheating. I was about to say so, but one of the women had finally stopped weaving her mat for long enough to kneel down beside the cairn and start pulling out some of the stones at its base. As I opened my mouth to voice my irritation, she leant back on her haunches to avoid wisps of steam that emerged from the hole. I shut my mouth, deciding instead to bend down for a closer look. The ground was hot beneath the hand I stretched out to balance myself. Not just sun-baked stone hot. This was too hot to touch hot, and the heat was coming from beneath the ground. The woman was pushing an old tin can on a rope into the hole she'd excavated. It fell a short distance inside the cairn and then I heard a splash.

I looked at Valerie. 'Steam harvesting,' she said, 'clever, huh?'

The women had poured water from the oil drum into a shallow metal tray and the goats had suddenly lost interest in the green tufts of grass and were lapping it up. Meanwhile, one woman was refilling the drum from the can that she was using to draw hot water from the cairn. It was steaming, too hot to drink. The oil drum was an intermediate cooling device.

The tufts of green grass indicated where hot steam could be found after a little digging, Valerie explained. A larger hole was dug immediately to one side of the mini-geyser and lined with thick mud. When the mud had dried, it sealed the hole so that it would act like a basin, and the cairn was built over it. Inside the cairn, the steam condensed on the inside of the rocks and dripped down into the basin. The process continued, and a water supply was maintained, as long as the steam kept seeping out of the stony ridge. In this tectonically active area of the Rift Valley, it would probably last forever, I thought. Valerie said that it was usually the cairn that failed before the steam. A well-built cairn lasted for about ten years.

THREE

Two of the warriors with the Afro hair leant against their Kalashnikovs and didn't say anything or look as if they wanted to say anything. Valerie's husband, Ishmael, sat cross-legged on a rush mat and watched the third warrior, whose name was Hayu Yassin, clean his knife in the trickle of water. I stood in the shade of a thorn tree, grateful for the light breeze. Hayu Yassin was a willowy figure with long fingers to match. He ran them up and down the flat of the blade until the last drop of sticky blood had been washed away.

The long *jile* knife had made short work of the kid. A quick swipe across the neck, and the job was done. But Hayu Yassin's weapon was far too big an instrument to skin the small goat with. He slipped it back into the sheath it his belt and wanted to borrow my Swiss Army knife instead. I handed it to him. He lopped off the feet and cast them aside, then made an incision from the neck, down the belly, to the tail.

'How long will it take to cook in the hot spring?' I asked. Ishmael uncrossed his legs and reclined on the mat, propping his head on his hand. 'Not long,' he said, '20 minutes, perhaps 30.' He had an aura of calm about him, and would probably have approached a wait of two days with the same relaxed manner. He'd just lie there, quiet and patient, like a leopard conserving energy in the desert heat. His peaceful demeanour was in total contrast to the tightly bundled energy of his wife, and the antithesis of what I'd been expecting of an Afar male.

The three warriors looked more like it. Each wore a *jile* and carried a Kalashnikov that never left his side. At night, the warrior wrapped up the length of white material that he wore over his shoulders like a shawl and used it as a pillow on his gun. But Hayu Yassin had proved to be an hospitable fellow and had agreed almost straight away to initiate me in some of the ways of an Afar warrior. His infectious smile suggested that he might quite enjoy it. His two associates had been less forthcoming. They had been moody ever since Ishmael and I had arrived, and despite all the assurances from Valerie and my friends from the pot house in Addis, I had been nervous about spending the night with them out in the wilds.

But my apprehension had almost completely evaporated after our initial conversation. Ishmael told me that their Afro hairstyles, reminiscent of the Jackson Five circa 1971 and then some, indicated that these guys herded cows. Consequently, I started out by enquiring after the health of their cattle. They were all doing nicely enough, it seemed. The grazing in this area was good. There was water here too. Hayu Yassin asked how my cows were, but I had to say that I didn't have any. That stopped the conversation in its tracks. The Afar cowboys were confused. They shot puzzled glances at my shorts and hat, and gave each other sidelong looks. One of them began to toy nervously with his gun.

I took off my hat and ran my fingers through my hair, just to give myself something to do. 'It's very hot here,' I said, playing for time. 'If I had hair like yours, I wouldn't need my hat. It must be a very effective sunshade.' As Ishmael translated this inane comment, the looks on all their faces changed.

'Yours is too short,' one of them said immediately, reaching over and tugging a lock of my hair just above my left ear. 'It's a funny texture too.' He returned his hand to his own head and gently tugged the ends of his fuzz with an expert twist of the wrist. The cowboy squatting next to him patted his Afro in a delicate way that I hadn't seen since my childhood. There was a dinner lady at my primary school who used constantly to do the same with her perm.

'You'd have to grow it for weeks,' Hayu Yassin told me.

'I guess I wouldn't make it as an Afar warrior then.'

Hayu Yassin cocked his head, looking at me. 'We could give you extensions,' he said thoughtfully, 'like the camelboys wear it.'

The others nodded their agreement. 'Then you'd have to grease it.'

'Grease it?'

'Yes, camelboys rub animal fat into their hair.'

And so it went on. I couldn't believe it. Here I was, finally face-to-face with some Afar warriors, supposedly amongst the most fear-some characters on the planet. These were the guys I'd lost sleep worrying about since before I'd even arrived in Ethiopia, the people who were meant to castrate you first and ask questions later. And all they were interested in was hairdressing. No wonder Valerie's survey of household tasks had found that they're all done by women. If these cowboys were anything to go by, the men are all too busy at the beauty salon. Hayu Yassin and his mates had spent two hours doing each other's hair that morning.

I had left Valerie with the Afar community at the steam cairns and returned to Asayita where Ishmael had suggested I might like to go and meet some real Afar men. We had found the cowboys at a spot not far from Asayita, within 15 kilometres of the Djibouti border. I was standing at a triple junction of splits in the Earth's surface, the point at which the Red Sea, the Gulf of Aden and the African Rift Valley all meet in a geologically classic intersection with angles between arm pairs approaching 120°. The first two separate Africa from Arabia, great rips in the crust formed as Arabia moved to the northeast to collide with Eurasia along the Zagros Mountains of Syria, Iraq, and Iran. The third, the African Rift, is the early stages of a tear in the continental crust, the beginnings of a north-eastern African splinter that in millions of years from now will form a new continental fragment.

These gargantuan tectonic forces have wrenched the crust apart, stretching and splitting the very stuff of the planet. Great blocks of rock have bent and buckled under the pressures, thrown up along fault lines like deformed children's building bricks strewn at random across the landscape. Molten magma, the blood of the Earth, has oozed up through the fractured gashes to form scabby lava flows and volcanoes.

The 'hot springs', as Ishmael called them, were scalding geysers, boiling pools of bubbling water heated by the restless Earth below. We had seen them from some distance, marked by billowing clouds of hot steam. Too large to enclose with a cairn, the resourceful Afar had dug a small channel from one of the pools, draining off a shallow stream of water. As it flowed away from the geyser, the water cooled enough to become drinkable.

They also used the geysers to cook in, and our boiled goat was sweet and succulent. We were joined for lunch by another warrior whose matted dreadlocks indicated that he was a camelboy. He walked up to us from out of nowhere, leant nonchalantly on his Kalashnikov, and asked if we'd seen any camels. He had lost his, apparently, and was looking for it. But he didn't appear to be too concerned. No doubt because he was confident that eventually some-one would tell him some news about a stray camel. Meanwhile, he certainly wasn't going to say no to a bit of boiled goat.

Our cowboys weren't particularly friendly towards the new arrival and I sensed an element of rivalry between cowboys and camelboys. But welcome or not, the camelboy stuck around all afternoon, mostly minding his own business.

Our afternoon's activities took a bit of time to get off the ground. All of the warriors fancied a nap after lunch, so we lounged a bit more beneath the thorn trees, the warriors lying on their firearms, while

I used my shoes as a pillow. I wasn't complaining because it was 2 o'clock and fiercely hot.

After an hour or so, the two less co-operative cowboys decided they wanted to go and chase ostriches. 'Is that some sort of initiation rite?' I wondered.

'No,' said Ishmael. 'They just want to get some of its feathers to put in their hair.' They stalked off, bare-chested, with determined looks on their faces.

Hayu Yassin opened his eyes long enough to ask where they were going and then closed them again, mumbling something to Ishmael.

'He says they won't catch any. Ostriches run too fast.'

Half an hour later, the two warriors reappeared, their torsos glistening with sweat. They weren't carrying any ostrich feathers.

First they said they would teach me how to shoot. We wandered out of the shade of the thorn trees and into the searing heat of the afternoon. We found a spot not far from one of the geysers, a couple of hundred metres from a huge long ridge which stuck up out of the otherwise very flat desert. 'Aim for that big rock,' Ishmael advised. Hayu Yassin released the safety catch on his AK-47 and handed the weapon to me. I knelt down and he pointed out the sights along the barrel of the gun.

The crack of the shot echoed loudly along the full length of the ridge. There was no indication of what I might have hit. After a couple more shots, neither of which appeared to have hit the big rock, I said thank you and handed the gun back to Hayu Yassin. He nodded, obviously unimpressed, and said something to Ishmael.

'He says at 4 birr a bullet, you owe him 12 birr.'

Wrestling was next. One of the surly warriors stepped up, for the first time displaying his ability to smile. I could tell that he fancied his chances of putting me firmly in my place. That place being in the dirt at his feet.

We set to. I have some very minor experience of wrestling, having done a bit at school and suffered a few bouts against

Mongolians, who are amongst the world's best. I could tell there was not much point in asking about rules, so I just looked at my opponent and we took hold of each other. Although the cowboy was obviously younger and fitter than me, and better accustomed to the staggering temperatures, I did have one thing on my side: my stature. I am quite short and squat, and a low centre of gravity is a great advantage in wrestling. This cowboy was probably 6 foot 5, although the five was mostly hair. Nevertheless, he was built like a string bean.

After my poor display at the shooting, he was also overconfident. We struggled for a while, and my opponent lost his self-satisfied smile. I think I could have put him down, but I didn't want to in front of his comrades because I thought he might take the loss of face rather badly. We agreed to a draw. Hayu Yassin slapped me on the back and the other two looked reluctantly impressed. I had clearly gone up a notch in their estimation.

When I had asked the warriors the previous day about manhood and how they proved themselves, they hadn't mentioned shooting or wrestling at all to begin with. I think this was because the true sense of my question had somehow got lost in translation. The initial response that came was about cow racing.

Each cowboy picks about ten of his best cows and drives them towards a line. Whoever crosses the line first is the winner, but it is the cow that gets the prize rather than the cowboy. The winning cow gets special treatment thereafter. She is treated like royalty: never being milked and always offered the best of the fodder.

After the confidence gained from our lengthy conversation about hairdos, I rephrased my question more boldly. 'I understand that in times past, a man's ability as a warrior was rated according to the number of men he killed,' I started, adding quickly, 'but this is not how it is today.' I held my breath until they all nodded.

'How, then, does a man prove himself nowadays?'

After a bit of thought, they all agreed on one thing: *Kor'so*. Then one of them added wrestling, which was often part of the *Kor'so*, and finally shooting.

'They don't shoot each other,' Ishmael explained. 'Guns are carried here because of the danger of Issa raiding parties. The Issa are the Afar's traditional ethnic rivals.'

'What is *Kor'so*?'

This appeared to be a difficult question for Ishmael to answer. 'It's an Afar game,' he said finally, 'perhaps like your football.' He paused. 'But actually nothing like football.'

That made things much clearer.

I was still none the wiser after my *Kor'so* training. I had tried in vain to ascertain some of the rules from Ishmael, but he just said that the rules were different in his day. It wasn't the same since they had changed them, he added. I got him to ask the warriors, but they just wanted to get on with training me. 'What's the point of the game?' I asked finally. 'In football you score goals. What's the equivalent in *Kor'so*?'

No one appeared to be able to answer that question either.

My training consisted of the three of us running up and down, using an orange for a ball. The warriors started to squabble over who should be holding the orange, but eventually Hayu Yassin took charge. He grabbed me by the wrist and led me off on a trot. After a few paces, Hayu Yassin did a little skip and leapt into the air, flailing his arms as if he was trying to take off. I tried to do the same and we trotted on. Then Hayu Yassin started to wave his arms furiously as he leapt still higher into the air and flung the orange down towards his feet with some force. The orange was instantly pulverised on the volcanic lava beneath our feet.

Hayu Yassin was smiling broadly and was clearly pretty pleased with his performance. He wandered back towards Ishmael.

'Is that it?' I shouted, sweat now pouring off my body as if I'd been standing under a hot shower.

'Now you must run away,' said Ishmael, 'as far as you can.'

After a few minutes rest, when it seemed that my training was at an end, I suggested we try the running away bit. Over 50 metres, I'm pretty fast, and none of the warriors could get close. I think my prowess improved a bit further in their eyes, because they asked if I wanted to take part in a real game of *Kor'so*.

Being still none the wiser as to how to play, I said yes.

The *Kor'so* match took place in a village not far from the Awash River. It was meant to start at 7.30 in the morning, European time, but it was past 10 o'clock when the cowboys finally showed up. They were riding a red pickup truck, along with a dozen or so of their cowboy friends. I could tell they were all cowboys because of their Afro hairdos. The surly one who had challenged me to the wrestling wore an ostrich feather stuck in his. It had probably taken him the last three hours getting the jaunty angle just right.

After my training session in the desert two days before, my cowboy friends had stung me for expenses, and now I saw what they'd spent their money on. Each one of them wore a brand new pair of patterned socks. Hayu Yassin came over and shook my hand when he clambered off the back of the pickup, but the other two studiously ignored me. The village had been out in force since I'd arrived three hours before, and I'd weathered the delighted shouts of '*Farang*, *farang*' from a small army of boys who had then settled down in a huge semi-circle to observe the *farang* wait and swat the occasional fly. Now that the warriors had appeared, there was a fresh atmosphere of excitement in the air, and many of the boys reassembled around the pickup. The cowboys strutted about in front of them with their Kalashnikovs over their shoulders.

Within a few minutes, two other pickups, also laden with warriors, drove on to the scene. Some of these new arrivals were camelboys, and I assumed that they were the other side, but when they all gathered round in a huge circle and began singing, I decided perhaps not.

'The opposition are on the other side of the fields,' Ishmael told me, pointing across a dozen fields, their maize plants now just a

Players marching in slow motion before the Kor'so *match
with enough lethal weapons to start a small war.*

The Afar are in love with goats and rocks.

Fearsome Afar warriors turn out to be more
interested in hairdressing than castration.

ABOVE
*Hayu Yassin (left) and his mate advising
the author to grow his hair longer.*

RIGHT
*An Afar woman prepares bread
for baking in her ground oven.*
(Dudu Douglas-Hamilton © Keo Films)

BELOW
*Assabolo, last watering point before the
salt lake and the* Gara *'fire wind'.*

Loading salt hacked from the crusty surface of the Danakil Depression. Bars of Danakil rock salt were used as a form of money in Ethiopia for more than 1,000 years.

Mr Bisrat surveys what's left of Dallol, the hottest town on Earth.

The camel caravan heads into the Danakil's burning inferno.

collection of straw-coloured stumps. Far off in the distance, I could make out another huge crowd of people.

The two teams were from different clans. It was the Kadabuda clan versus the Diramo. I was on the Kadabuda side. I pushed my way through the swarm of small boys and joined my teammates in the pre-match singing. We were stomping our feet in the dust and clapping to the beat of the song. As the pace quickened, we began jumping up and down on the spot. All around us, the boys were doing likewise with their sticks under their arms.

This continued for nearly an hour, and I had to retire from the warm-up because I could see that if I did it properly I'd be totally exhausted before the match even started.

At some invisible signal, my team's warm-up took on a different stance. The Kadabudas began to line up at the edge of the adjacent field facing the distant opposition. They were an awesome sight. Each man wore a brilliant white wrap around his shoulders, a brightly coloured diamond-patterned sarong, and, in most cases, fancy socks (Argyle was the most popular style) inside their plastic sandals. A huge *jile* was at every hip, and a Kalashnikov was held at shoulder-height in every man's right hand. They were still stomping their feet in an on-the-spot march.

'You should join them,' Ishmael whispered in my ear as I sat surveying the scene from the shade of a spreading thorn tree. 'I'll find you a gun.' He turned to an aged man beside him, one of the village elders, and asked him a question. The elder turned, grabbed the barrel of a Kalashnikov from the shoulder of a young man standing beside him, and handed it to me. The young man, who looked as if he had probably only just earned the right to carry a gun, stood open-mouthed. The elder cut him off with a few well-chosen words, and I joined the end of the Kadabuda line with the gun in my hand. There was a buzz of excitement in the crowd, all men and boys, since women were not allowed to watch a *Kor'so* match.

Gradually, our line started a very slow, rhythmic march across the fields. We kept our formation, a long, winding snake of warriors, with me bringing up the rear, led by none other than Hayu Yassin. One or two of our number let forth high-pitched shrieks as we snaked our way across the maize fields towards the Diramo team that had proceeded to do the same in the distance. Little by little, the two tribes meandered their ways closer together, until there must have been about 100 warriors, 50 or so on each side, doing their slow-motion marching almost side-by-side.

The combination of blood-curdling shrieks and the hypnotic rhythm of the marching lent the scene a sinister, almost supernatural quality. After losing my fear of the Afar, having witnessed at first hand their obsession with hairdressing and patterned socks, doubts were beginning to resurface in my mind. Maybe it was just the baking sun, but I began to understand what Thesiger and Nesbitt had meant about this wild and untamed country, inhabited by fearsome blood-thirsty tribes. I'd never seen so many lethal weapons all in one place. There were enough to start a small war.

We snaked our way off the fields and suddenly all my teammates disappeared. Ishmael came to my rescue and relieved me of my weapon. 'There is a problem,' he told me. 'The Diramo team have made a complaint. They want to know why the Kadabuda have a white man on their side.' I could see the elders going into a huddle beside one of the village huts.

Time passed. I had taken a temperature reading at 8 o'clock. It was 43°C (109°F). I didn't know what it was now, but after the slow-motion route march in the full sun I was feeling decidedly groggy. I sat down beneath a tree to wait for the outcome of the stewards' enquiry and was immediately surrounded by a seething mass of small boys seemingly fascinated by the way I drank water from a bottle.

Ishmael and another man tried to clear them with the aid of sticks, and succeeded in pushing them back a metre or two.

'They will sort it out,' Ishmael said, referring to the elders. But I have to say that I didn't really care. In fact, if they'd called the whole thing off, or declared that I was ineligible to play, I'd have been quite relieved. I'd been reduced to exhaustion just by the warm-up. Then Ishmael said something that snapped me out of my daze.

'Retribution is not allowed for injuries or deaths during a *Kor'so* match.'

I don't know what prompted him to say it, but all of a sudden my grogginess disappeared and my mind became crystal clear.

'Injuries? Deaths! People *die* playing this game?'

'Only rarely is someone killed. Usually it is just minor damage, like broken arms or legs. But when incurred during a *Kor'so* game, the injured party must wait until the next game for revenge.'

I just sat there with my mouth open. I closed it just in time to prevent a fly crawling in. It tried to creep up my nose instead. I brushed it away. The kids around us sensed some excitement, and were edging in again. Ishmael wielded his stick and they fell back once more.

'You did say "killed", didn't you, Ishmael?'

'Don't worry yourself. It is very rare.' Ishmael gave me what he seemed to think was a reassuring smile.

'Suddenly, I don't think I want to play.'

'I promise you, actual deaths are very rare nowadays.'

I couldn't believe I was having this conversation. I thought back to my training session, a seemingly innocuous little outing in the sun where the only casualty had been an orange. I couldn't understand how jumping up in the air and flapping your arms about could result in fatalities. But then I became suspicious when I remembered everyone's inability to tell me either the rules or the aim of the game. Perhaps inability was the wrong word. Maybe it had been reluctance.

'How are people killed playing *Kor'so*?'

'When you run away, maybe they all will catch you. When that happens, it can be quite dangerous.'

Then a quite horrific thought hit me. 'Do the players wear their knives on the pitch?'

'Oh no.'

'What about guns?'

'No.'

'So it's just when they catch you?'

'Yes.'

'You're sure about that?'

'Oh yes, quite sure.'

I decided then and there to play, if the elders let me, but I'd be very careful to run the other way whenever anyone looked like they might be caught.

The elders did let me play. By the time they did so, it must have been noon. The sun was so incredibly hot that I was afraid my brain was frying. I couldn't wear my hat for obvious reasons. Needless to say, I didn't last the whole game. Nothing like it, because it went on for more than two hours.

It was total chaos. The Kadabuda and Diramo teams appeared from nowhere, each man stripped down to just his sarong. Most of them were barefoot, but some had kept their socks on. Each team jogged out on to the maize fields and did a few warm-up dashes. I'm not sure when the game proper began, because it was never clear to me how the game was played. I couldn't work out who had the ball half the time, or even whether there was more than one ball. But I did see Hayu Yassin attempt to fly several times and launch the yellow tennis ball down towards his feet, which appeared to be the signal for everyone to run at great speed. Whenever this happened, I made sure I ran in the opposite direction.

Some players sprinted large distances, plunging across the drainage ditches that lined the edges of the fields, followed by 100 warriors charging at full pelt. On occasion, a man would thrust his hand up towards the sky, a salute met by a volley of Kalashnikov fire. I decided that perhaps this indicated a score, but I still wasn't sure just how they had done so.

After two and a half hours of playing and watching, I was none the wiser. But apparently, we won. And no one was killed.

FOUR

It was several days later that I arrived in Mekele. Most of that time had been spent just getting there, driving back up into the Highlands and skirting the Danakil on its western side. I had entered Tigray, or Region Number One, as it was called on government issue maps. It was no surprise that this, the most northern Ethiopian region, had been given the number one because Tigray was where most of the national government hailed from. It was the Tigray People's Liberation Front (or TPLF) who had kicked out the communist Derg regime back in 1991, with a bit of help from their Eritrean allies, and they weren't going to let anyone forget about it. Sepia posters of TPLF fighters dotted the streets of Mekele, a rapidly growing town that the national government had been pouring money into ever since.

New roads were being built, a brand new airport terminal was going up to replace the tin shed that had done the job previously, and virtually every street corner could boast at least one recently constructed building. But most domineering of the work-in-progress was a giant monument to the fighters who had died in the struggle against the Derg. It looked as if it was modelled loosely on the Olympic torch, with a giant ball where the flame should have been.

Still wreathed in wooden scaffolding, it subjugated the skyline from every direction. It was as high as a six-storey concrete apartment block and just slightly less attractive.

I had come to Mekele because this was the starting point for my journey to Dallol. The two towns are more or less linked by the constant flow of camel caravans carrying salt from the Danakil depression up here to the Highlands. This trade has been going on for many hundreds of years, and the salt was not merely a kitchen commodity. Bars of rock salt mined in the Danakil, which are commonly known by their Amharic name of *amole*, were used as a principal item of exchange in Ethiopia, instead of money, for more than a thousand years. The Italians are said to have found bank vaults stacked full of them when they invaded in the 1930s.

My plan was to join up with one of the caravans, since seemingly this was the only hope I had of reaching Dallol. But, by all accounts, this would not be a simple matter. Just turning up at Mekele's salt market and asking around for a passage to Dallol was not going to work, I'd been told by several people in Addis Ababa and Asayita. The Afar's usual suspicions of foreigners were writ large when it came to this jealously guarded age-old commerce.

Hence, my one hope of hooking up with a camel caravan lay in a man whose name I had been given by Valerie while in the southern parts of the Danakil. The man's name was Bisrat.

I met him at his office in the centre of town. He was younger than I'd expected and dressed in a manner that on first impression made me dubious as to his suitability for the task. He wore a three-piece, pinstripe suit in fashionable dark blue serge. A figure less likely to have acquaintances in the Afar salt-trading community was difficult to imagine. With his expertly trimmed short black hair, and round black-rimmed glasses, Mr Bisrat looked more like a City of London banker. But, as I was soon to discover, looks could be deceptive.

After we had exchanged pleasantries, I put my request to him. His answer was immediate. 'Yes sir,' he said definitely. 'Your proposed itinerary is familiar to me. I myself personally can take you there.'

'Great news. Thank you.'

'However!' Mr Bisrat added, holding his index finger in the air. 'It will be *tough*, Mr Nick.' He emphasized the word with a frown as his index finger disappeared into a clenched fist. 'But we can do it. We *will* do it, and it will be an *honour* for me to guide you.'

Quite apart from being a model of civility, his well-mannered charm a throwback to the old school of Abyssinian refinement, Mr Bisrat also transpired to be a master of disguises. The morning of our departure, he turned up in white chinos, a black leather jacket and a woollen scarf slung casually over his shoulder. His black brogues were so highly polished that I could see my reflection in them. He looked as if he had just had breakfast with a group of intellectuals at a fashionable café on the Parisian Left Bank.

On Mr Bisrat's advice, we had decided not to try and join a camel caravan here at Mekele, but to drive the first leg of our journey to Berahile, a town just inside the neighbouring Afar region. Berahile was on the salt caravan route and also had a large salt market, but more importantly for us, it was where Mr Bisrat had several contacts who, he was sure, could place us on a caravan departing for the Dallol salt flats.

The drive to Berahile took all day. Our departure from Mekele took us up to and across a limestone plateau. We passed villages of sturdy rock houses and small enclosures of prickly pears, but for the most part the landscape was cultivated, every slope carefully lined with neat stone terraces designed to prevent the soil from being washed away when the rainy season came. The principal crop here was barley, Mr Bisrat said, but wheat, sorghum and teff were also grown. Teff is a fine Highland grain, used to make Ethiopia's traditional *injera* bread, a flat, spongy concoction usually served as a sort of edible tablecloth: meat and vegetables being placed on top.

Here and there, we passed small plots of eucalyptus trees, striking in an almost treeless topography. They looked recently planted, and Mr Bisrat confirmed my impression. 'This area was formerly *covered* in trees,' he said, 'but the people have cut them down. It is a clear-cut case of *deforestation*, Mr Nick.'

There were still some trees left on the far side of the limestone plateau, on slopes generally too steep to cultivate. The tarmac road had become a dirt track that wound its way down through the plunging mountainsides towards the Danakil depression. Villages here clung precariously to the inclines, their dwellings made of logs laid upright to form structures reminiscent of North American Indian wigwams. As we descended, the fresh mountain air faded away and the atmosphere became heavier. The lush foliage of the upper slopes was replaced by grey-brown thorn trees which themselves faded from the scene in all but the dry valleys that were scored into the precipitous landscape.

Berahile was marked on my Michelin map that covered the whole of north-east Africa, but its inclusion must have been a close call because there couldn't have been more than a thousand people living there. I was reminded of a story told by Nesbitt about his meeting with an Afar Sultan. The Sultan had heard that Nesbitt was preparing a map of the territory he crossed and asked him if it was true that he was able to put all of the country on a piece of paper.

Differences between the Afars here and those I'd seen in the south of the Danakil were immediately noticeable. None of the men had Afro hair, few carried *jiles* on their belts, and not all of them wielded Kalashnikovs. Women and girls wore their hair in dozens of long thin plaits and necklaces of tiny beads in primary colours hung from every neck. Most of Berahile's small boys had shaven heads but for a Tintin-like quiff right above their foreheads. Nevertheless, they were equally delighted when they saw a *farang* in their midst.

The town itself consisted of a few stone buildings surrounded by oval, Afar palm-mat huts and stick dwellings like those we'd seen on our journey down, only these ones were square. They were dotted about the slightly higher ground that hemmed in a sizeable wadi. The open, dry riverbed, more than 100 metres across, was like a gaping hole in the middle of town, an area unsuitable for building on because the river flowed with water for a couple of months during the Highland rainy season.

The sun was getting low in the sky when we pulled into town and the wadi was filling up with caravans for the night. Long convoys of camels, tied to each other from neck to tail, appeared at a stately pace from down the wadi, led by an Afar with a stick held across his shoulders. Donkeys trotted along in pairs beside them, trying to keep up. Each beast had a load of salt blocks lashed to either side of its rump.

Our first stop in town was at a compound surrounded by a low stone wall. Inside a stick house, we met Beléa Ashoba, a wiry man of about 50 with thick hennaed hair above a high forehead and a bright orange goatee beard. 'This gentleman should be able to help us gain a position on a camel caravan,' Mr Bisrat told me. We removed our shoes and took up position on a rush mat as a dark-eyed woman took a kettle from the small fire in one corner of the hut and served tea in tiny cups. Her multitude of plaits had been interwoven at the sides of her head, giving her a basket-like frame around her face. She was handsome, but just this side of beautiful.

Beléa disappeared as we sipped our sweet tea. 'Does his red beard indicate he has made the *hajj*?' I wondered. Although the Afar are Moslems, it was the first time I'd seen a suggestion that any had made the pilgrimage to Mecca.

Mr Bisrat doubted I had now either. 'I think this is only for decoration,' he said. 'Beléa is on the lookout for a wife.' I was surprised that a man of his age wasn't already married.

'He is, he has two wives and 17 children. But he wants a third wife, a young one, who can give him more offspring.' Mr Bisrat made him sound like a one-man population explosion.

Beléa reappeared, shooing away the gaggle of kids that had gathered at the entrance to his home before joining us on the mat. He listened intently as Mr Bisrat explained the purpose of our visit.

The virile 50-year-old looked me over. 'The journey takes three days from here,' he told me. 'It is arduous, even for us. After a week on the caravan, a man and his camels need two weeks to recover.' He sipped his tea and stroked his goatee beard. 'But a destination that is far in the morning is close in the evening,' he smiled. 'You will have to be trained in how to handle a camel. Our preparations will take two days.'

'So we've made it, Mr Bisrat?' I asked as we left Beléa's compound some time later. 'Yes, Mr Nick, this is *fantastic* news. He will take us.'

Over the next two days, Mr Bisrat and I busied ourselves preparing for our trip. We visited Berahile's general store and bought Afar sarongs, which Mr Bisrat declared were more suitable attire than either my shorts or his chinos. Beléa seemed pleased with our decision, and he lent me a camelman's knife, much smaller than the *jile*, which he said would complete my outfit.

On Beléa's advice, I consulted the local medicine man on some of the dangers that I would have to face on the trip. He met me in Beléa's hut wearing a black and white cap and carrying some Arabic books under his arm. Like Beléa's, his hennaed beard was in the goatee style.

Snakes would be a serious problem, he told me, but he could prepare a charm that would protect me against them. I asked if he could also do me a side-order of protection against scorpions. He nodded sagely, flicking through his books. Then he took my name and that of my mother. This would entail a lot of hard work, he said. It would take him a day to prepare the charms and they would cost me 500 birr: 300 for the protection against snakes and 200 for the scorpions. Mr Bisrat knocked him down to 450 birr and we shook on the deal. I was surprised at the cost, nearly £40, but I'd be happy as long as this was the only time I'd be stung.

The following day, I was presented with a string of four small leather pouches, each scored across the centre with a cross and containing magical herbs and passages from the Koran. I should wear them around my neck at all times, the medicine man told me, inside my shirt so that no one should see.

The evening before our departure, I was introduced to the men who would accompany us to the Dallol salt flats and their camels that had just arrived in the dry riverbed after a few days of good grazing further up the valley. Osman, the chief camelman, gave me a brief rundown on the animals. Camels were kind and friendly creatures, he told me, and not to be feared. They should be treated with respect at all times. As long as I did so, a camel would follow me wherever I led it. There just remained the important commands for sitting and standing. To sit the camel down, I had to tug sharply downward on its rope while shouting, 'Dee, dee.' A recumbent camel could be made to stand by shouting, 'Ha.'

We left Berahile at 6 o'clock in the morning, having saddled the camels and loaded them with straw and goatskins full of water drawn the previous evening from the town's well in the middle of the riverbed. We followed the dry course of the Saba River, an imperial procession of about 30 camels with me at its head. Osman said he had never had a white man on his caravan before, so I could lead the way. He had been working the camel caravans since he was a boy, when he had to stand on a rock to load a sitting camel's hump. That was more than 25 years ago.

The pace was stately and unhurried, the lead camel perfectly pacing itself just behind my shoulder, so that the rope that hung loosely in my hand was never taut. It walked so silently on its big padded feet that for the first half-hour I was constantly turning my head to make sure it was still following me.

Camels are better adapted to life in the hot desert than almost any other mammal, having developed exceptional ways of dealing with the two overwhelming imperatives of keeping cool and conserving water. For many animals these are conflicting requirements. Sweating cools a body because as the moisture evaporates it takes heat with it. People start to sweat when the outside temperature rises above the normal body temperature of 37°C (98.6°F), but the camel has its own, unique body thermostat. It can raise its body temperature tolerance level by as much as 6°C (43°F) before perspiring, thereby conserving body fluids and avoiding unnecessary water loss.

Their highly efficient kidneys cut down the amount of water in their urine, also allowing the camel to drink salty water; while their dung comes out in perfectly formed pellets that are so dry they can be immediately used as fuel for a fire like barbecue briquettes. Camels are also unique among mammals in having red blood cells that are elliptical in shape, rather than the round ones that everyone else has. They prevent a camel's blood from thickening with a rise in temperature.

And even with all these amazing adaptations to cope with water shortages, a camel can also survive a water loss of up to 40 per cent of its body weight (human's can afford to lose less than 14 per cent before the situation becomes critical), and can go for at least a week in very high temperatures without drinking. Then, when they do find water, camels can guzzle huge quantities – up to 60 litres – in a matter of minutes.

It doesn't go straight into their humps, however, contrary to popular myth. The hump is not an emergency jerry can full of water so much as a larder where energy-rich fat is stored. This can be broken down in the body to produce energy, carbon dioxide and water, helping the camel to keep going for up to several months without food if necessary.

The human body is rather less well adapted, as I was finding to my cost. Even by 7 o'clock, the outside temperature was well above 37°C (98.6°F) judging by the gallons of sweat pouring out of my every pore. My shirt was drenched and my hair matted. Tipping water down my throat hardly seemed to make any difference. When I commented on the heat to Mr Bisrat, his reply was not encouraging.

'This is *nothing*, Mr Nick. The heat will only get hotter as we approach the salt lake. And we are still to confront the *Gara*, a wind so hot they call it the "fire wind". It is *terrible*, truly terrible.'

Two days into our trip, I was feeling significantly better. The distances we walked were not great, perhaps 20 kilometres or so at a time, and always in the early morning or in the evening. The heat of the day was passed resting up, in the shade of a thorn tree or beneath an overhang where the wadi cut through a solid rock face. Sweet tea was brewed on a camel-dung fire and hard crusty bread was produced from saddlebags to fill our bellies.

I had got the measure of my body's need for water and I was finally, it seemed, drinking at the same rate as I was sweating. On my first day, I hadn't been consuming enough, I decided, because just two hours into the walk I had reached the stage where I was almost constantly desperate for a pee, but whenever I tried to go nothing would come out. This was doubly annoying because each time I handed over the rope of the lead camel to Mr Bisrat, and stepped to one side of the trail to relieve myself, the camels would just pad on, and by the time I had given up trying, I was half-way down the caravan and had to run to reach the front.

On the second day, I drank more regularly and the continuous desire to pass water had receded. But I still did not appear to have got it right because I was always thirsty, even when my stomach felt bloated and stretched to its limits with so much water. I was drinking more water and half wondering whether I should be concerned about the feeling in my stomach, when we rounded the red sandstone walls of a canyon and came upon Assabolo.

Osman and his colleagues had broken into song, a haunting tune that ricocheted off the canyon walls. 'We travel together, we help each other, we arrive together. One heart, one love,' Mr Bisrat translated.

It wasn't much of a village, there being just half a dozen palm-mat huts scattered on a ridge above the canyon floor, but it was certainly a significant spot for camel caravaneers. I'd never seen so many camels. Groups of them, some unsaddled and munching straw, others saddled and waiting patiently to shed their loads, were scattered all across the stony canyon. Further in the distance, where the canyon widened and disappeared into cliff faces that were just outlines of rock etched on to the desert haze, still more camels sat and stood and wandered around doing what camels do when they aren't on caravan duty.

This was the last watering point before the salt lake, and all along the small brook that ran down the canyon men were busy filling goatskins before the final leg of their journey. I was relieved to be stopping because it was 11 o'clock and the heat was so intense I thought I could cut it into blocks and build a house with it.

Without thinking, I waded into the middle of the stream and lay down in the cool water, fully clothed and with my shoes on.

FIVE

We parked our camels beneath a 50-metre overhang just where the canyon was giving up and the stream had decided to spread wide for a change. The overhang provided us with some shade, but the camels didn't seem to mind the sun and just sat munching their straw in the midday heat. Fires were built. Tea was brewed. Our bread had run out so a couple of the guys in our caravan made some more. This they did by collecting some large rounded stones from the canyon floor and heating them in the fire while they added water to a sack of flour and kneaded some dough. When the rocks were hot, they carefully moulded dough round each one and returned them to the fire, watching and turning the big round loaves when they got singed on the underside. Still cool and refreshed after my dip in the stream, the smell of the baking bread was good enough to make me think that God was in his heaven and all was well in the world.

That thought was well and truly consigned to history by the time we hit the *Gara* 'fire wind'. Our lay-up had been shorter than on previous days since Osman wanted to make it to the last settlement, on the edge of the salt flats, by nightfall. It was 3 o'clock in the afternoon and the sun was still a fiery orb when we left Assabolo. We had spent the last hour beneath the overhang chewing *chat*, a mild narcotic leaf with little taste that Mr Bisrat said would fortify us against the *Gara*. Beléa blessed the sprigs of small green leaves before we ate them, and blessed each one of our party too.

'Now we must face the *Gara*,' Mr Bisrat said.

Hot, dry, often dusty winds are typical of many deserts. The south side of the Sahara has the Harmattan, while the Scirocco blows north over parts of the Mediterranean. In the Arabian Gulf, they have the Shamal; in India's Thar Desert they have the Loo, in southern California the Santa Ana. And in the Danakil, I now discovered, it's the *Gara*. Having never read about it in any geography book didn't make it any less real.

It tore into my clothing as soon as we reached the top of the ridge, jostling and shoving like a herd of invisible, wild beasts on the rampage. It was hot, and it was loud, and it was desiccating in the extreme. I could feel it sucking the moisture out of me as I struggled forward, frazzling the hairs on my arms. It was like opening the door to the oven on Sunday lunchtime at home to check on the chicken, and finding that the chicken has pulled a fast one and turned the tables. I was in the oven and doing very nicely. Just another 20 minutes and my skin would be crispy and brown.

Trying to hide behind one of the camels, which just continued to stroll along, supremely unconcerned, was impossible. It was as if the *Gara* knew this trick and had developed the ability to blow from every angle. I'd been right to think of the Danakil as a burning inferno, but its demons weren't the Afar, they were this fiery gale.

'It is a *battle*, Mr Nick,' Mr Bisrat shouted against the wind, 'a battle we must win if we are to reach Dallol.'

After two days of tramping along wadi bottoms, where the intermittent thorn bush, pool of water (sometimes alive with tiny frogs), and occasional stretches of flowing stream lent some colour to the pallid mountain backdrop, the stony plateau across which we had to fight against the *Gara* wind was a foretaste of what was to come. It was an unrelenting wasteland of rocky monotony that continued all the way to Hamad Ela.

Somehow, we had descended 2,000 metres since crossing the limestone plateau above Mekele. Other than on that first day, when the drive to Berahile had taken us plunging down from the Highlands, it had never seemed to me that we were getting any lower. But finally, here at the miners' camp on the edge of a desiccated salt lake that bottomed out at 100 metres below sea level, I got a sense of being on the edge of the bowels of the Earth.

Hamad Ela was unlike any other Afar settlement I'd yet seen, and not just because it sat in the unremitting tedium of flat rocky plateau one way and horizontal salt lake the other. The place was dirty and dishevelled. It had an unkempt air about it as if no one cared where they threw their rubbish or paused to relieve themselves. On first sight, I thought this might be because it was a miners' village. It was, after all, just a resting place for hardened salt-cutters who must have been so exhausted from their three-hour walk into the salt lake each day, four hours hacking with hatchets, and another three-hour walk home, that they simply had no energy left to keep the village clean and tidy. But then I saw that they lived not alone, but with their families. The women and kids didn't appear to be bothered about living in a rubbish tip either.

We were up with the sun the following morning, and all around us camels were being loaded for the final push into the salt lake. A meandering snake of the beasts was already curling away into the distance. I counted them as they disappeared into the saline wilderness, stopped at 100, and tried to extrapolate. There must have been a thousand camels in our caravan now.

The Highlands of Ethiopia and the Red Sea form a natural conclusion to Africa's mighty Sahara Desert on its eastern margin. Although this is where the Sahara proper terminates, its arid character is continued in a boomerang-shaped strip that outlines the promontory known as the Horn of Africa. This desert, the Danakil-Somali-Chalbi, is unusual climatologically in being on the eastern coast in tropical latitudes. Dallol is on roughly the same latitude as Bangkok, Manila and Guatemala City, all hot and wet places. The extreme aridity of the Danakil Desert is due mainly to the fact that the prevailing winds rarely blow from the ocean and thus there is little moisture in the atmosphere. During most months the winds are north-easterlies blowing from Arabia, source of the terrible *Gara*, and south-westerlies from central Africa. Clear desert skies mean that the sun's rays are unobstructed by clouds in warming the air to produce the world's highest mean annual temperature. All deserts record high temperatures for the same reason, but few others are as close to the equator, where the sun's angle in the sky is closest to its maximum.

Here, at the dry salt lake, we were fairly close to the Red Sea, and seas tend to have the effect of reducing temperature extremes. But Dallol's position on the edge of the Danakil depression, 75 metres below sea level in the Rift Valley, counteracts any marine influence. The temperature data recorded at Dallol yield an annual average value of 34.5°C (94°F). This makes Dallol the hottest place in the world.

But at 5.30 in the morning, when the sun was still low in the sky, it didn't seem such a bad place. We left the rocks behind on the outskirts of Hamad Ela and chocolate-coloured dirt led us into sticky mud that clung to my shoes, making the walk heavy going. Within an hour, the surface had become firmer. We trudged across a hard salt crust, cracked by the heat into great polygonal slabs. It was like walking over an endless expanse of dirty scabs on the Earth's surface.

Shimmering on the horizon, the head of the camel caravan was being absorbed into a mass of tiny figures. 'The mine, Mr Nick!' Mr Bisrat started skipping along beside his camel despite the rapidly rising temperature. 'We have almost reached our destination, source of the *white gold*. My heart is filled with joy, and for that I sincerely thank you.'

The 'mine' was a hive of activity. More than 100 men were hacking away at the white salt crust with hatchets, cutting it into their own polygons that were levered up and set aside, later to be shaped into neat slabs. They were just a bunch of guys in their sarongs and T-shirts and plastic sandals, but it so happened that they were working in the world's hottest desert. And what immensely hard, physical work it was in the sweltering heat. The time was just 8 o'clock and already the temperature had passed 45°C (113°F). Most of the cutters weren't even wearing hats. Their efforts made the labours of Hercules look like a stroll in the park.

'The cutters supply the shapers,' Mr Bisrat told me as we wandered in awe around a scene that must have changed little in a thousand years. 'Cutters may be Highlanders or Afars, but only Afars are allowed to shape.' We paused to observe a squatting figure who was carefully shaving a block into a rectangular slab, as Mr Bisrat untied the length of white material from around his waist and proceeded to wrap it round his head as protection against the sun. 'A cutter will cut perhaps 100 blocks in a day, and the money he receives depends on how many caravans arrive that day. More caravans and the price goes down.' The miners were approaching a seasonal boom time, because when the rainy season starts in the Highlands, in a week or two's time, the number of caravans would sharply decline. There were Afar caravans, like Osman's, and caravans run by Highlanders, but the Highlanders left off during the rainy season to help plant the fields.

All around us, camels were kneeling patiently on the hard salty crust, awaiting their loads. Each caravaneer tends to do business with the same shaper on every visit. Osman was talking to a wiry fellow bent double over his pile of shaped slabs. He was buying the slabs at a birr each, and would sell them for 4.50 birr at Berahile, Mr Bisrat told me. One man with eight camels might make £60 profit from his week in purgatory.

We paused beside a pile of slabs, neatly bound with rope, ready for loading. A man was crouched in the meagre shade thrown by the small tower, drinking tea from a blue plastic mug. The sun was getting to me, its reflection from the white salt starting to hurt my eyes, but something rather more serious was also on my mind.

'So where is Dallol, Mr Bisrat?' I asked cautiously. He looked puzzled. 'Here, all around you. This area is known as Dallol, Mr Nick.'

It was my turn to be perplexed. There had obviously been a bit of geographical confusion. When I'd asked Mr Bisrat if he could take me to Dallol, I'd had a more specific place in mind. I didn't know what exactly to expect, but it had to be a permanent settlement of some kind to have the record of hottest inhabited place on Earth. It was clear that no one lived here, and Mr Bisrat had already explained that the cutters and shapers walked out from Hamad Ela to work every day. 'Dallol is a salt mine,' I said (I knew that much), 'but also a village or a town, or something. People live there.'

Mr Bisrat looked blank and mystified in equal measure. 'I have not heard of such a place, but we can ask,' he suggested.

He enquired after the man crouched beside us drinking his tea, who gave us a vacant look. Nearby, half a dozen other men were squatting in the salt chewing rounded hunks of hard bread that had been made using the hot stones technique. Here we were in luck. One of the men pulled the corner of what looked like a woollen blanket that was wrapped around his head, out from his forehead to shade his eyes, and pointed in a direction.

'He says it's about 15 kilometres north of here,' Mr Bisrat translated.

We set off with three camels carrying water, to cross the hottest desert in the world during the hottest time of the day, leaving the cutters and shapers digging away to eternity, mining a resource that was never going to run out. Geologists estimate that the salt is 5 kilometres thick in some places.

Dallol's claim to be the world's hottest inhabited place is based on records of air temperature measured during the 1960s by an American mineral prospecting company. While they were investigating Dallol's potash reserves, the Ralph M. Parsons Company set up a meteorological station at their base camp on the summit of a salt dome that sat at 79 metres below sea level. Here they recorded maximum and minimum temperatures between 1960 and 1966. With some gaps in the record, temperature readings were taken for about six years in total. The results of their findings were written up in the *Meteorological Magazine* of 1967. They showed that over the period of six years, the annual mean of the daily maximum temperature recorded at Dallol was 41°C (106°F) and the annual mean of the daily minimum was 28°C (82°F). Averaging these figures gives a mean daily value of 34.5°C (94°F), making Dallol the hottest place on Earth. During the period of observation, at least one day with a temperature above 38°C (100°F) was reported every month while some days the thermometer never sank below 30°C (86°F).

The record at Dallol is unusual in climatological circles for being so short. For the most part, climatologists require at least 30 years of data to define a climate. But comparing Dallol's short record with longer runs of data from other hot places suggests that the six-year values for Dallol are unlikely to be different from the long-term average by even as much as 1°F in any month. So the record stands.

But Dallol doesn't. It was a dead place and looked as if it had been for some time. We came upon it looming like a forgotten soul out of a quite astonishing landscape. The salt here took on bizarre and extraordinary shapes, one moment rising up in great towers from the plain, the next plunging into chasms so deep they might have been passageways to the very centre of the Earth. The colours, too, were otherworldly, bright lemon yellows and vibrant oranges screaming for attention in the dun-coloured topography. Bubbling springs gently gurgled from the summit of these flamboyant mounds, slowing adding sulphurous deposits to the age-old conical growths. The outrageous colours continued at their bases, splashed like primeval paint across the knobbly terrain where other saline springs burbled at the surface.

Elsewhere, the fusion of salts that had once attracted the Ralph M. Parsons Company was alternately as brittle as a biscuit and as rigid and sharp as shards of toughened glass. The salty crust had begun its job of reclaiming the base camp, because that was all it had ever been, just a couple of disintegrating streets that were too small even to be called a village. Rusty tin drums and salt-rotten wooden beams led the way past the decomposed skeleton of a Land Rover. Iron girders crumbled underfoot as Mr Bisrat and I clambered in silence over the debris of a failed frontier colony. Remnants of breeze-block walls stood solid and defiant, but dwellings made of what looked like local stone were crumbling back into the dust from whence they came.

I didn't feel elated at finally being in Dallol, just strange. The sense of desolation sat up and hit me hard across the face, and it hurt. This place was weird, seriously weird. It was clear to me that no one was meant conquer an environment like this one, where the Earth's crust was still in turmoil and primordial elements bubbled from the ground. It was as if Mother Nature allowed visitors but permanent settlement was actively discouraged. It was just too extreme. And somehow I still felt uneasy about even treading this primeval land.

Mineral prospecting companies have known about the salty treasures of Dallol since 1901, and like seven companies before him, Ralph M. Parsons had donned his poncho, buckled his gun belt and set forth with a cheroot between his teeth to see just how tough this Danakil Desert really was. The answer lay before me. Dallol must have been dead before it hit the ground.

And where did all this leave the record for the hottest inhabited place on Earth? I had to hand it to Hamad Ela, the scruffy miners' town that just clung to the edge of the Danakil depression. As Dallol showed too plainly, the salt flats were not a place to set up home. It was just for the hardiest day-trippers lured by the riches of white gold.

WETTEST

Mawsynram

India

ONE

I became an avid online reader of *The Times of India* in the weeks lead-
ing up to my departure for the subcontinent. The Indian monsoon
appeared to be well under way. Heavy rains were lashing the southern
state of Kerala, causing widespread floods in the lowlands and traffic
chaos in the highlands where landslips had cut off many roads. Power
lines and telephone lines were down all over the state. In the northern
city of Agra, where they were gearing up for potentially groundbreak-
ing talks between the Indian prime minister and Pakistani president,
the threat of disruption from Kashmiri separatists was not the only
problem faced by national security guards. The monsoon's first heavy
rains had left almost the entire city waterlogged. The flooding was
worse in the state of Orissa on the east coast. Several major rivers had
burst their banks and hundreds of thousands of people were fleeing
their homes in panic. The army and air force were on standby. The
state was gearing up for a full-scale monsoon emergency.

As yet, there had been no mention of rains in the north-east of
the country, where I was headed. The monsoon begins in southern
India and works its way north, so I assumed that either the rains were
yet to reach the north-east or that this area was so well adjusted to the

annual deluge that there was little to report. Mawsynram, the wettest inhabited place on Earth, receives nearly 12 metres of rain in an average year, and most of it arrives courtesy of the monsoon. A couple of months earlier, the India Meteorological Department's long-range monsoon forecast for 2001 indicated that they were expecting a normal rainfall year. Thirty-nine feet of water would be a staggering amount almost anywhere else in the world, but in Mawsynram it was just normal. Nothing to report there then.

Calcutta didn't appear to have had much rain at all. The streets were suspiciously dry as my taxi drove into town from Dum Dum Airport, but at least the air was heavy with moisture. Stepping out of the airport terminal had been like walking into a tropical greenhouse and a light sweat had immediately begun to ooze from every pore in my body. As the taxi swerved to avoid a small herd of cows, the only pedestrians on the dual carriageway at three in the morning, I decided that being damp was a state I was going to have to get used to. A month in India during the monsoon is like being locked in a sauna for four weeks.

And being India, you don't have the sauna to yourself. It is jam-packed full of other people. Arriving in the wee small hours of the morning had given me a totally misleading impression of Calcutta. By the time I emerged from my hotel to survey the streets just before lunch the following day, the city's full seething mass of humanity was out in force going about its daily business. Or at least, it was trying to. The roads were choked with yellow Ambassador taxis and buses bulging at the seams with human beings, three-wheeled auto-rickshaws and rickshaws pulled by wiry old men. But, for the most part, none of these vehicles was actually going anywhere. Their drivers just sat there and leant on their horns for a while until they realized that this was having absolutely no effect whatsoever, at which point they would turn off their engines and just sit. Streets remained gridlocked for tens of minutes at a time, which, judging by the patience of all concerned, was by no means unusual.

Unusual or not, it was frustrating. My mission that first morning was deliberately lightweight given the long flight from England. I had to get some passport photographs for my Bangladeshi visa application form. My plan was to travel overland from Calcutta to Mawsynram through the length of Bangladesh, a country virtually defined by its annual monsoonal floods. The aim was to pick up a few tips on how life is lived in a country as much known for its water as its land, before hitting the world's wettest place just north of Bangladesh in the Indian state of Meghalaya.

It wasn't far to the nearest photographer, the helpful man on the hotel reception desk told me, but I should go by taxi.

'Is it too far to walk?'

'Taxi is better sir,' he told me.

I jumped into a taxi and asked the driver if he knew the place.

'Most certainly sir,' he replied, but he answered before I'd finished the question, which made me think otherwise, so I got the doorman to give the driver directions. We set off at a stately pace for precisely ten seconds, the time it took to enter the traffic. Then we stopped and the driver switched off his engine. Twenty minutes later, he gunned the Ambassador into action again and we drove another few yards. After an hour, I could still see my hotel through the rear window, but we had managed to turn a corner. We were once more sitting in the gridlock. My driver turned to me. 'I am seeking further directions,' he said.

'But we haven't gone anywhere yet,' I started to say, although he had already jumped out of the cab. Reappearing from the mêlée a few minutes later, he announced that we had been going the wrong way for the last hour.

After another 30 minutes, we sat outside my hotel once more, now pointing in the opposite direction. I decided to pay off the driver and walk, despite his assurance that it was not long now. He was right in that respect. It took me two minutes to find the photographers on foot.

The Hindustan Ambassador is an Indian institution, nothing less than an early 1950s British Morris Oxford that has defied the passage of time and continues to be the most common motor vehicle on the streets of Calcutta. Since it was designed half a century ago, it is not surprising that the Ambassador is big, heavy and slow by contemporary standards. It is like driving a whale. Sometimes these cars would simply stop in the middle of the road, seemingly for a rest. Hence many of the traffic jams.

The following day, I decided that an auto-rickshaw would be a better way of negotiating Calcutta's insane traffic. Although its two-stoke engine sounds like a demented sewing machine, the three-wheeler is smaller and nimbler than the Ambassador and thus has a better chance of weaving a path through the frequent jams.

I made my way with Runa, my rather glamorous and highly efficient Bengali translator, through the streets of early morning Calcutta. People were still sleeping on the broken pavements beneath the awnings as horses and rooks nosed through the previous day's rubbish swept into neat piles in the gutters. We were off in search of fish for a dinner party to be thrown that evening by one of Runa's friends. The fish in question was known as hilsa, a monsoon speciality. Like salmon, the hilsa spends much of its life at sea but chooses to spawn in freshwater. During the monsoon, it swims up river estuaries to lay its eggs, and that's when the Bengalis catch it.

'Bengalis just love fish, but it has to be from a river,' Runa told me as we zipped along past a group of men washing at a gushing water pipe by the roadside. 'They look down on sea fish and anyone who eats them.' Our auto-rickshaw swerved overdramatically to avoid a gaping pothole in the road and abruptly veered back in the opposite direction to avoid a head-on collision with an on-coming tram. Runa carried on regardless, supremely unperturbed by our near-death experience. 'Hilsa is one of the absolute best. We are just crazy about hilsa. People eat it at lunch and dinner, and for those who can't afford to eat it twice in one day, they will leave the leftovers from dinner so that they can savour the smell at lunchtime.'

Our auto-rickshaw driver made an emergency stop outside the Kole fish market. Men tottered along the fetid pavement balancing world-record amounts of fish in baskets on their heads. Mini glaciers of ice wrapped in jute sacking were being manoeuvred off bicycles and onto ancient wooden trolleys. Ladies on the backs of lorries shovelled piles of sawdust, the bright yellow colour of building sand, into sacks, which were being carried into the cavernous market building. We followed one of the sawdust sacks inside.

The fish market was small but bursting with people. Runa led me up and down the aisles lined with men squatting beside baskets and bowls full of fish of every description. Every description, that is, except hilsa.

'The monsoon is late here, so there are not many hilsa yet,' Runa explained as she deftly elbowed her way through the crowd. 'We must try elsewhere.'

Half an hour later we found some in a nearby street market. It didn't look particularly spectacular to me – silvery coloured like a salmon, only slightly shorter – but it certainly went down well at the dinner party. Runa and I reverted to a faithful Ambassador for the short drive from my hotel that evening, passing, as we went, the income-tax office of the finance ministry marked by a bright neon sign that read, 'Pay your tax – hold your head high'.

I wore my best shirt for the occasion, though I was beginning to worry that I hadn't brought enough. I'd got through three on the first day alone, peeling them off as they became too soggy for comfort and hanging them up in my room to dry. But drying they weren't; they just hung there festering in the heavy atmosphere.

Runa was resplendent in a sparkling aquamarine sari, set off by silver ankle chains and toe rings. 'I wear these in honour of my father's evolution,' she said. 'He never let us wear silver, never. This was because the servants wore silver, you know. So we could wear gold only. It was gold or nothing. He was quite unyielding on the matter. Then one day he went to Delhi and came back with these anklets and toe rings. It was a sign of his evolution.'

A long sweeping staircase took us up to an apartment where you could play hopscotch on the Persian rugs adorning the white marble floors. High ceilings sported wooden beams painted white to go with the marble. The living room was slightly smaller than an aircraft hangar, its walls hung with an eclectic and unpleasant collection of paintings. Plush settees were arranged around a large glass-topped coffee table casually littered with enough silver ornaments to start a museum. Solid candlesticks stood on the mantelpiece above an ornate fireplace. Over in the far corner, a less formal zone judging by its population of wicker furniture, sat a black upright piano. Framed family portraits aligned along its top continued on across an assortment of classy looking sideboards that hung around the edges of the scene trying to be inconspicuous. Bearers in crisp white uniforms wafted in and out carrying drinks and the murmur of polite conversation could be heard above the buzz of the air-conditioning.

The hostess spotted Runa and me from across the room and started out towards us crying, 'Darling, how good of you to come!' Some minutes later we met, just south of the glass coffee table, and the woman smothered us both in kisses.

A drink was thrust into my hand and I was introduced to an interior decorator as 'a man interested in rain', while Runa was whisked off to the other side of the room. I told the interior decorator the reason for my visit and where I was heading.

'I don't know Meghalaya,' he told me, 'but I was at school in the north-east, at St Paul's in Darjeeling. It rains a lot up there too, you know. Used to rain for weeks on end; miserable place in the monsoon season.' He paused to sip his drink. He was well turned-out, with flowers on his blue corduroy shirt.

'And what about the clouds?' I asked. 'I understand Meghalaya literally means "Abode of the Clouds". Was it very cloudy in Darjeeling during the monsoon?'

'Funny you should ask that,' the decorator replied. 'I was unhappy at St Paul's to begin with, until I met a chum. I'll never forget what he said on our first meeting, it will always stick in my mind. He came up to me in the dormitory and said, "this is a place where the clouds come in through the windows."'

He smiled as he remembered the moment. 'And they did, by Jove. Floated right in through the windows and took up residence in the dorm. We wouldn't see the sun for weeks. But when it did appear, the school announced a sunshine holiday. Everyone got the day off to enjoy it.'

We had been joined by a bald and rather earnest arts correspondent for the Calcutta-based *Telegraph* newspaper who told me that the monsoon had been a great source of inspiration for poets and artists over the years. I sensed that this was a prelude to his instructing me at some length on the qualities of some of the poems concerned, but he continued in such a disinterested tone of voice, punctuated by that annoying cocktail-party trick of constantly looking over my shoulder to see whether there were more stimulating conversations to be had elsewhere, that I was not sorry when our hostess appeared across the horizon to give me her take on the monsoon season.

'Once the rains start, there's nothing for it but to stay in bed. It's the most delightful season if you like sleeping. I can stay in bed for days.'

When I turned round again, both the interior decorator and the bald arts correspondent had disappeared. A bearer had materialized in their place at my elbow to ask if he could get me another whisky. He said please, which made it sound as if I'd be doing him a favour by accepting. He also said that dinner was ready if I'd like to make my way to the buffet in the servery.

The hilsa had been steamed in a coating of Coleman's mustard and wrapped in small banana-leaf parcels. It was spectacularly good. I ate it listening to a police inspector as he gave me a synopsis of the conditions that could be expected in his city when the rains arrived. The drainage system often couldn't cope, he told me, and the water was knee-deep.

'Calcutta would grind to a halt in these circumstances if it weren't for rickshaw wallahs,' he went on. 'These fellows carry on working when none of the taxis or buses can get through. In actual fact, monsoon is their most profitable time of year. They can charge what they like because they are the only vehicles that can muddle through.' He was talking about the man-powered rickshaws, formerly found all over India, but now only in Calcutta. 'But this is dangerous work,' the inspector continued gravely, 'visual contact with the ground is impossible due to presence of water, and if municipal council has been deficient in replacing manhole covers, rickshaw wallah may suddenly disappear in unexpected manner.'

I asked the inspector whether there were any particularly seasonal crimes during the monsoon, a query that prompted what was likely to be a lengthy discourse about hilsa smuggling across the border from Bangladesh. But my companion was interrupted by a sudden shout of 'Oh my God!' from the other side of the room, an exclamation that briefly sounded as if it might warrant his professional attention. We both turned towards the incident, which had now dissolved into semi-hysterical laughter. Two labradors had entered the room, expressing their excitement with wagging tails that had sent several drinks flying from the glass coffee table. One of the dogs had then promptly peed on a rug. A bug-eyed fat man, who looked uncannily like a frog and had not moved from his position on one of the settees all evening, suggested that canine urine was probably very good for Persian rugs. It was at that point that the police inspector excused himself, judging the moment an appropriate one to leave.

The dinner-party talk of things monsoonal had certainly put me in the right frame of mind for my journey through Bangladesh to the world's wettest town, but the fact remained that the rains had yet to arrive in Calcutta and this was a disappointment. My daily perusal of the newspapers indicated that the monsoon was causing havoc just about everywhere else. Orissa, the state immediately to the south, was almost completely under water by this time. The papers carried photographs of sodden people pushing a few sorry possessions before them on makeshift rafts, up to their necks in water. But the best that Calcutta could offer was a 'few spells of light to moderate rain'.

It hardly even managed that. I got some gentle drizzle and on one occasion a minor shower, but it was all a far cry from the Biblical deluge I had mentally prepared myself for. The minor shower came when I was choosing an umbrella from Mohendra Dutt Grandsons Company, renowned umbrella makers, on Mahatma Ghandi Road. It had passed by the time I emerged to test my new umbrella beneath the elements. Nevertheless, after another day's shopping, I was fully equipped. I had a smart black umbrella, a blue plastic mac and a particularly unfashionable pair of moulded plastic sandals that Runa insisted were the best footwear for the monsoon. All I needed now was some serious rain.

TWO

We caught the train to Bangladesh. There were iron bars across the windows in my carriage and a public notice forbidding passengers from carrying explosive articles. It was just a local commuter service but Indian Railways were obviously taking no chances. The train didn't quite go all the way to the border since rail services between the two countries hadn't been running for 36 years. They were due to be resumed the following year, but while they were still laying the track, the end of the line for me was Bongaon Junction, a few kilometres from the border.

We took a taxi after leaving the train. The highway was straight and lined by huge trees with lime-green ferns clinging to their lower branches. Their thick trunks were dotted with dung pats drying in the sun, later to be prised off and burnt as fuel. Goats ran across the road between the bicycles pulling carts. Ducks and geese waddled through paddy fields that were an impossibly vibrant green; the sort of day-glow colour that I'd thought could only be achieved by scientists using synthetic chemicals with very long names.

Mixed in with the paddies were fields of jute plants. Their long thin stems, which grow to twice the height of a person, have no branches, a bit like bamboo but bushier at the top. Fibres from the stems' bark were draped across bridges and on makeshift frames prior to being turned into sisal string, ropes, cloth and sacking. On crossing the border, it became clear that the bicycle rickshaws in Bangladesh were more brightly painted than their Indian counterparts and that most Bangladeshi women wore headscarves. The full abruptness of the transition was brought home to me when I saw a cow being slaughtered by the roadside. I had left a Hindu world and entered an Islamic one. Other than that, paddy and jute fields looked much the same in Bangladesh as they had in India, although in Bangladesh they did seem to have more ducks in them. Bangladesh also had one other thing in common with its neighbour: it wasn't raining.

For the most part, Bangladesh is a country in just two dimensions. While other countries have mountains and hills and valleys and all sorts of sloping bits in between, Bangladesh is just flat. Not pancake flat, but river floodplain flat. It is made up of the ends of several of the world's major rivers, and a multitude of others besides, all flowing into the Bay of Bengal. The country does actually have a few hills, but they are tucked away down in the south-eastern corner, where no one really notices them. So the overwhelming impression of the place throughout my stay was one of flatness. Smooth, level, even, horizontal flatness. I suppose you could count the sky as a third dimension, but I wasn't going to do that until it did the decent thing by producing some rain.

It was lucky that there were some trees to break up the skyline; a task jointly shouldered by a quite phenomenal number of towering brick chimneys. I tend to associate chimneys as tall as a two- or three-storey house with industry, and therefore with cities, but these chimneys were in the countryside. And they weren't all gathered together in tall chimney zones either. They were spread out, dotted along roads and rivers wherever I went. Each one marked the site of a brick kiln, usually surrounded by neat walls of their produce. This multitude of rural kilns puzzled me for some time. I had seen a few brick houses, but nowhere near enough to absorb the output of so many manufacturers. Then I noticed that the forecourt of a petrol station we had pulled into was paved with red bricks. A little further on, the tarmac road from the border gave way to a brick surface.

Later still, I began to notice piles of bricks by the roadside. Squatting beside these piles were huddles of men and women, each usually hunched beneath the shade of an umbrella, busy demolishing bricks individually with the aid of a hammer. On one side of these brick slayers were perfectly good whole bricks, and on the other were fresh piles of small brick pieces. I'd never seen anything like it. The temptation was to ask Runa about it straight away, but I stopped and tried to work it out for myself. Try as I might, I just couldn't figure it. 'Runa ...' I began.

'There are no stones in Bangladesh,' she explained with devastating simplicity, 'so these people are making stones. They use them in construction and for filling potholes in the roads you know.'

And then it all became clear. The career of a brick breaker is intimately related to Bangladesh's status as a two-dimensional country. You might not consider it every day, but stones are actually pretty important raw materials. As Runa had said, they make up the foundations of solid buildings and underlay high streets and motorways the world over. Most countries have a ready supply of stones either quarried from rock faces or dredged from riverbeds. Rock faces presuppose hills of some description, so this is not an option in Bangladesh. But one thing it does have in abundance, not to say excess, I hear you say, is rivers. Right, but unfortunately from the stone point of view, all the stretches of river that flow through Bangladesh are at their wrong ends.

It is a well-known fact that rivers move lots of stuff from the land and dump it on to other bits of land and out to sea. It is also a fundamental principal of physical geography that as you move down a river from its source the average size of the material it carries gets smaller. This is partly because smaller bits can be carried further and partly because bigger bits – the boulders, rocks and stones – get ground down as they go. Either way, by the time you get to the end of a river all that tends to be left is fine-grained clay and silt. Hence, Bangladesh has a surfeit of mud, but no stones.

Some years ago, a friend invited me along on a weekend bird-watching trip. I wasn't converted, but for two days I was totally captivated. A whole new world had opened up before me at the end of a pair of binoculars and I have never looked at a bird again in quite the same light. In many ways, seeing Bangladesh's towering chimneys and its brick-breaking workforce had a similar effect. A two-dimensional country with no stones was a revelation to me. For about a day, I even forgave it for not raining.

But then I got to wondering. Using mud to make bricks that could be broken down to produce stones was a cunning way out of a serious deficit in the country's natural resource base, right enough, but why had no one thought of making smaller bricks in the first place? I consulted Runa on the matter. Her eyebrows became knitted for a moment, and then she said, 'breaking bricks employs a lot of people.' That wasn't the answer and we both knew it, but it would have to do until a better one came along.

Another thing that surprised me about the Bangladeshi landscape was the number of haystacks on view. Rounded, yellow and bulging, they sat in significant numbers beside every village. There wasn't any mysterious two-dimensional reason for them. The haystacks served the same purpose as they do in Europe; as a food store for livestock when grazing becomes scarce. What perplexed me initially was the implication that grazing would ever become scarce in such lusciously green terrain. Surely with so much water, Bangladesh was green all the time, I reasoned. And then it clicked. When the monsoon comes, most of Bangladesh disappears under water.

But the amount of water in Bangladesh is all relative. To me, it looked as if most of the country was submerged already. Everywhere

I went I was confronted with swirling brown rivers and ankle-deep paddy fields, but everywhere I went was with Runa, and she never stopped expressing surprise at how dry the country looked.

'It looks wet to me,' I told her.

'No, no. This is very dry.'

'How can you say that when everything's covered in water?'

'But this is July. There should be much *more* water.'

I simply hadn't yet become properly attuned to the two-dimensional mindset. What looked wet to me was actually dry.

And all over the country, villagers were gearing up for when it became wet. Men, women and children were out in the fields, busy ploughing with their oxen and planting tiny fluorescent rice seedlings ready for the monsoon crop. In the village of Harialgoup they were still waiting to harvest their jute because the crop was always best after it had been standing in water for a month.

Runa and I arrived there via a series of ferries that took us along the riverine highways and byways of rural Bangladesh. Every stretch of water carried an endless procession of water hyacinth clumps floating downriver in the murky waters as we passed fishing boats with huge nets, small ships laden with goods, and passenger craft of every size, transferring people back and forth. We caught fleeting glimpses of Ganges River dolphins leaping smoothly out of the water to disappear just as instantly without a splash. Virtually blind, because there's not much point in being able to see when you live in a muddy river all your life, the dolphins find their way using echolocation, building up sound pictures rather like bats who fly in the dark. Brahminy kites, flaked with golden orange like a Brahmin's robes, hovered in the skies above.

The people of Harialgoup were excited by the presence of a foreigner in their midst. The children were bashful, but responded to my smiles, while some of the men and boys got straight down to cases. They were intensely interested in my way of life.

'Do you eat rice?' asked a man with a headscarf tied around his forehead.

'Yes, but probably not as much as you. We also eat bread in my country,' I told him.

The next question came from a youth who was trying to grow a moustache. 'Do you eat fish in Japan?' he asked.

This threw me. I looked enquiringly at Runa who just shrugged. 'I do eat fish,' I told the assembled crowd, 'but I'm not from Japan, I'm English.'

This time it was the villagers' turn to be confused. They went into a huddle. A disagreement developed. Voices became raised. Some of the children were looking at me with renewed uncertainty. I began to think that a hasty retreat might become necessary. Either that or apply for a Japanese passport.

As Runa listened to the squabble a knowing smile appeared on her face. 'Some Japanese tourists came here two years ago,' she said. 'They were the first foreigners to visit the village, so they assume you must be from Japan as well.' With a flurry of hands and several shakes of her head, Runa put the record straight. Some of the men nodded knowingly; the boy with the nascent moustache just looked baffled.

With the question of my nationality settled, some of the villagers led me into the fields. They were alive with red dragonflies and tiny fire ants that administered surprisingly painful bites when I stood still for more than a few seconds. We walked in single file through the sumptuous green landscape, which the man with the headscarf tied around his forehead told me produced three rice crops a year. Keeping to the tiny raised paths between the paddies meant we all kept our feet dry, but when the rains came, everything I saw would be submerged beneath a metre or so of water.

'When do you think the rains will arrive?' I asked hopefully.

'He says, "The rain is nearly dressed,"' Runa translated. 'It is a Bengali phrase meaning it is almost ready to come out.' Perhaps there was some hope then, I thought to myself.

We had arrived at a spot where the paddy fields had stopped. We stood facing what might have been another field, with what looked like reeds growing in it. But here the water was obviously deeper because in the distance I could see people in low wooden boats punting their way through the reeds with long poles. It looked to me more like an inland lake, but I wasn't going to say as much.

The headscarf man said that the area was unusually dry for this time of year. I'd suspected that might be the case.

I asked what the people in boats were doing and the guy with the headscarf suggested we go and look. He pulled off his flip-flops and plunged into the knee-deep water.

Now I hadn't seriously been expecting to spend a month in the monsoon and not have to go wading through some fairly significant water bodies, and in preparation for just such an event I'd drawn up a short mental checklist of possible dangers I might encounter. High on the list were leeches, wriggly worm-like creatures that hang about in places like this waiting for some poor unsuspecting victim to appear and give them dinner. A leech latches on to any part of your anatomy and sucks blood. I'd been advised on the procedures for dealing with these unpleasant creatures by my sister's friend Alan. 'Don't pull them off,' he had said, 'because you'll probably only get the head, leaving the jaws in the bite, which could turn septic.' You have to rub them with salt or burn them off with a cigarette, he told me.

I wasn't looking forward to meeting a leech for the first time, but I had accepted it as inevitable. So while I removed my plastic sandals, I checked my shirt pocket for cigarettes and matches, and plunged in. Runa followed close behind, which impressed me. Given my initial assessment of her as a bit of a society girl, I'd thought that perhaps she would stay on dry terrain until I returned. She was obviously made of sterner stuff.

The water was delightfully cool and the mud oozed pleasantly between my toes, allowing me momentarily to forget the one particularly distressing aspect of the leech issue, as far as I was concerned, which was the fact that wading through water probably meant that I wouldn't be able to see any of the little bastards as they bore down on me for a free blood dinner.

Until, that is, the water got deeper. It was up to my crotch and we were still some way off from the boats when Alan's final piece of leech advice came back to me. 'Don't forget that they can get anywhere. You'll have to become intimate with someone to check each other's private parts.'

I stopped. 'Runa, are there leeches here?' I enquired, trying my best to make the question sound as nonchalant as possible. I held my breath as she relayed my query to the man in the headscarf.

'No'.

I enjoyed my wade much more after that. The boats turned out to be hollowed palm tree logs from which an assortment of boys and girls were busy gathering all sorts of edibles from the waters. Some of the small girls were collecting perfect white waterlillies called *shapla*, Bangladesh's national flower as Runa pointed out. Their long stalks were usually made into a marsala curry, but could also be eaten raw. They tasted a bit like celery. Others were collecting large snails or using short jute-stem rods to catch small fish the size of the children's hands. An older man, dressed in a thick pullover and wielding a rusty sickle, was cutting reeds. He was going to feed them to his cow, he told me.

Life in rural Bangladesh is well tuned to the monsoon, and, as I'd seen, the villagers were gearing up for the annual inundation. When the fields become submerged, many farmers turn their hand to fishing, either in the waterlogged fields or in the rivers. Others, however, fish full time and some of the fishermen of Harialgoup had a rather unusual way of doing it. I first became aware of their *modus operandi* when I heard a curious noise down on the riverbank. It was a cacophony of high-pitched screeching that sounded as if someone was frantically squeezing half a dozen of those annoying squeaky children's toys.

I followed the sound to a long wooden boat with a box-like cage at one end. The extraordinary sounds seemed to be emanating from the cage as a man in a white vest shoved small fish in through the bamboo slats. He opened the top of the cage and out jumped six otters. They scrambled over each other to slide eel-like into the water. Two of the otters wore harnesses attached to long ropes that were held by the man in the white vest. The others were apparently free, but none swam far from the boat. They all bobbed up and down by the shore, now with a lot less squeaking, looking enquiringly up at the man who held the ropes.

'They are fishing.' I turned to see Runa behind me and got her to ask the man in the white vest if I could watch. He invited me on board.

The man in the white vest, whose name was Ratan Hajra, used the otters to drive the fish into his net in a way similar to sheep farmers using dogs to herd sheep in Britain. He showed me how it was done. Once the otters were in the water, he and one of his crew unfurled a voluminous net over the full length of one side of the boat. The net was attached to a long pole at either end, which Ratan Hajra and his mate used to jig the net up and down in the water. At the same time, each man controlled the otters by manoeuvring another pole, to which the otters' leashes were now tied, with his foot. The co-ordination needed looked a bit like that old conundrum of rubbing your tummy with one hand while patting your head with the other. I tried it. It was more difficult.

Ratan Hajra trained the otters from an early age. It was only necessary to harness the two adults, he said, since the younger ones would just follow them in whatever they did, effectively being trained on the job. He and his crew of three, made up of a brother, a brother-in-law and a second cousin, had just returned from a lengthy fishing trip down in the Sundarbans, the world's largest area of mangrove swamps towards the coast on the deltas of the Ganges and Brahmaputra Rivers. They made reasonable money catching fish and selling it locally on a month-long trip like that, he told me, but he missed his family and it was sometimes dangerous work. There were tigers down there, he said, as well as crocodiles, snakes and pirates. Friends of his had been captured by pirates whose usual tactic was to hold one fisherman captive while the others were sent home to raise a ransom.

'I'd like to get out of otter fishing,' Ratan Hajra told me as he swept back a shock of slick black hair with his hand. His fingernails were painted red. 'Other jobs in the village are less well paid, but they are not so dangerous. One of my brothers runs a small shop. I could do that, or become a retail fish seller.'

With my inexpert help, our fishing trip had not been very successful. Ratan Hajra removed the lid from the cage and the otters leapt out of the water and streamed into it without any encouragement, curling up and nesting quite happily. We carried the cage ashore and fed the few fish we had caught to the otters through the bars.

Having seen the otter fishermen at work, I then got to see them at play. Ratan Hajra and his crew were off to play a game of hadudu. They led me away from the river, back towards the fields where a man had just finished marking out a small rectangular pitch in the mud with his hoe. It was about the size of a badminton court with a central dividing line and two other lines, rather like the tramlines on a tennis court, at either end. Two teams of men and youths were limbering up by the pitch, tying their *lungis* tightly up between their legs. A small crowd had gathered to watch the match. It was farmers vs. fishermen. Almost inevitably, I suppose, Ratan Hajra asked if I wanted to play on the fishermen's side.

Hadudu is the national game of Bangladesh. Its origins are obscure, but it has been traced back at least 4,000 years and some say it was originally meant to develop skills of self-defence, attack and counter-attack. Essentially the same game, with minor variations and under different names, is also played in India, Pakistan and much of the rest of Asia. Today it is a regular feature of the Asian Games. I'd never even heard of it.

It was like a cross between playground tag and rugby, with a bit of wrestling thrown in for good measure. Points were scored by touching or capturing the opposition players, and to add to the excitement, the person trying to score has to do it without drawing breath. The fishermen won the toss and one of our team stood at the halfway line where he drew a deep breath. As soon as he crossed into the farmers' half, he started to breathe out, chanting 'Hadudu, du, du, du ...' so that it was clear he wasn't taking a second breath. Slowly he neared the farmers, all stood behind their rear tramline. They weren't allowed to break ranks until our man had touched one of them. Once touched, the farmers' job was to prevent our man from scrambling back over the halfway line. If they did, the farmers got a point. If our man made it back, we scored. It was a game of tension until the touch was made, and then all hell broke loose as bodies were flung through the mud.

Hadudu played to Bangladesh's strengths. It didn't require any expensive equipment or large playing areas. All you needed was two teams and a lot of mud. The mud was glorious; gooey and sticky like black clotted cream. In no time at all, both teams had been reduced to unrecognizable swamp creatures. I hadn't enjoyed myself as much in years. As we made our way back into the village to wash, I was even rewarded with a light drizzle.

THREE

But the fact remained that it still hadn't started seriously raining yet. Runa and I caught a paddle steamer from near Harialgoup that took us all the way to Dhaka. The *Mahsud* was one of five original vessels, built in the 1920s by Garden Reach Workshop in Calcutta, that were known as rocket ships. Its first-class accommodation was done out in sturdy wooden panelling with thick jute carpets on the floors.

I visited the captain, a stocky little man with an engaging smile, on the bridge. He had virtually no hair on the top of his head but a noble set of grey whiskers flared almost horizontally out from his sturdy jaw. He gave me the, by now familiar, story of how dry the soggy paddies looked.

'When rains come, all these fields we are passing will be flooded,' he told me.

I asked him whether the *Mahsud* plied its route between Khulna and Dhaka throughout the monsoon. 'Oh yes,' he replied, 'we suspend the service for severe cyclones and tidal waves only.'

He had worked on the paddle steamers for more than 30 years, and I wondered which was the worst monsoon he had encountered. 'Nineteen ninety-six,' the captain answered without hesitation. He remembered it well, he told me, because there had been some tourists on board. 'They were visiting me here on the bridge, just like you are doing as we speak, and they are all taking their leave to procure some photography on the catwalk.' He pointed in front of him to the iron gangway that tapered away from the bridge along the roof of the ship towards the bow.

'But severe storm was brewing and strong wind was blowing already and I ordered them all below quick sharp.'

He had just had time to put down the anchors before the storm hit. It had blown the catwalk clean away.

The journey to Dhaka took 36 hours. When I stepped on to the quayside, the captain, accompanied by his chief purser, came ashore to say farewell.

'Which country are you coming from, please sir?' The purser asked me.

'England,' I told him.

'Oh England, yes sir, very fine country. And how have you found our country?' I said I had enjoyed myself very much and thought Bangladesh was a very beautiful place.

'I believe so, yes sir. It is very poor country, but very fine.'

Bangladesh was a fine country. It was green and lush and wet, but for me the only problem was that all the water was on the ground already. Just the occasional shower had disturbed the otherwise clear and bright weather on the paddle-steamer journey and we'd arrived in Dhaka in brilliant sunshine. The captain of the *Mahsud* had worried me the previous day on the bridge when I'd asked how long he thought I'd have to wait for some proper monsoonal rain. He had reckoned it would be another ten days before I'd see any.

Having not read any newspapers for nearly a week, I eagerly scanned the pages of the Bangladeshi press for reports of rain. My search was futile. There were regular stories about Dhaka's appalling air pollution, the worst in the world they said, and daily reports of attacks by armed thugs referred to as *dacoits*. One morning, the Bangladesh *Independent* carried a sad story on its front page about the murder of a rickshaw puller who had been stabbed to death by a fruit seller while haggling for a pineapple. The story ended with the declaration that, 'the name of the vendor could not be known.' But the closest I got to a water-related story was a cautionary piece about the sewer lines in the old city that had come under renewed threat of bursting because one of the pump stations had been inoperative for the past six months. The station, built with a loan from the World Bank, had developed problems soon after completion four years before. It desperately needed spare parts, but the Water and Sewage Authority couldn't afford them. The article pointed out that it was probably a disaster waiting to happen just as soon as the rains came, but it gave no indication as to when that might be.

I found an Internet café and logged on to *The Times of India* site. Here at least were some stories of rain. The floods in Kerala had eased, although the death toll had reached 89 since the onset of the monsoon. Orissa, meanwhile, was officially a disaster zone with all but one of the state's rivers flowing above their danger levels in several places. The Indian air force had begun to drop food parcels in remote areas. The number of people displaced by the floodwaters was put at 7.5 million.

With the start of the monsoon in Goa, local traffic police had appealed to vehicle drivers to exercise restraint while driving on slushy roads in an effort to reduce the usual rainy season peak in the accident rate. Among the instructions issued were the following: wear bright-coloured waterproof gloves and boots for better grip on brakes; put on headlights and don't use umbrellas; and keep to the middle of the road.

Even the Calcutta area had finally got a soaking. Two days of heavy showers had washed away 100 houses south of the city and damaged 70,000 acres of crops, while the whole of West Bengal was suffering power cuts because the coal was too wet to burn in the electricity generating stations. The monsoon was also blamed for power cuts in Delhi, something to do with underground cables getting wet, but as *The Times of India* leader put it, 'Blame it on the monsoon if every other excuse fails to hold water.'

The weather in Pakistan was even hitting the headlines in the Indian press. Southern parts of the country were being drenched by the heaviest monsoon rains in 50 years, but there was no mention of the situation in the north-east of India where I was going. The weather in Dhaka, meanwhile, continued bright and sunny.

A map on the India Meteorological Department's excellent website showed the full extent of my dilemma. India's north-eastern states had received a third less rainfall than normal since the notional beginning of the monsoon on 1 June. In the previous week just half the normal amount of rain had fallen. I scanned the daily satellite images of the subcontinent. Most of India and Pakistan was wreathed in thick rain-bearing cloud, but Bangladesh and the north-east of India were consistently clear.

I'd been through the full gamut of emotions, from amusement through frustration and annoyance to incredulity, since I'd arrived in Calcutta to be met with no rain. The situation was now becoming ridiculous. Here I was, halfway through my journey to the world's wettest place, during the monsoon's traditionally rainiest month, and all I'd seen was a bit of drizzle and a few half-hearted showers.

I was getting desperate. I spent a morning on the telephone in my hotel room ringing round meteorological centres in India and Bangladesh in search of positive news about the rains. The Bangladesh meteorological office gave me the forecast for Dhaka the following day. It was mostly going to be sunny.

'What about the day after tomorrow?'

'You must be ringing again tomorrow for that,' the man said rather impatiently.

I scoured the phone book and found a number for Dhaka's storm warning centre. I thought they might deal in longer-range forecasts, but after a couple of rings all I got was an answerphone with a message in Bengali. They had probably been given the day off to enjoy the sunshine. Dhaka's civil aviation authority meteorological office told me they weren't expecting any rain for at least three days, but beyond that they couldn't say.

I found some numbers for likely looking sources of information in India. First I rang the meteorological centre at Guwahati, the regional depository of weather data from Mawsynram, the record-holding wettest place, and other stations in Meghalaya, as well as the neighbouring state of Assam. The news wasn't good there either.

'We are expecting isolated thunder showers around Mawsynram,' a voice told me. Thunderstorms were something. At least there was some rain in the world's wettest village, but it wasn't the monsoon.

'What about monsoon rains?' I asked.

'Monsoon is yet to begin in north-east region,' the voice said.

'When will it start do you think?'

'This we cannot be saying.'

I had read a number of academic articles about the monsoon written by researchers at the Indian Institute of Tropical Meteorology in Pune, so I rang there. A Dr Nandargi told me that more than 100 years of monsoon records indicated that when Orissa received particularly heavy monsoonal rainfall, as it was now, India's north-east didn't.

'Historical records are showing this quite clearly,' he said. 'Low pressure zones move westward from Bay of Bengal over Orissa, but north-east region remains quite dry.'

'Do you have any idea when these systems might cease?' I asked him.

'Low pressure is currently building once more in Bay of Bengal.'

'So?'

'So it is likely to move in westerly direction from Bay of Bengal over Orissa.'

'What does that mean for monsoonal rains over the north-east in the next week, say?'

'Little chance of monsoonal rains in north-east in next week.'

'And after that?'

'This we cannot be saying.'

So that was it. Everyone I had spoken to had voiced serious doubts about my chances of seeing monsoonal rains. Certainly in the next week, and after that the likelihood of rains appeared to be anyone's guess. So much for the India Meteorological Department's long-range monsoon forecast. As far as I could see, it appeared to be anything but a normal rainfall year in Mawsynram and the areas I had on my itinerary.

I hung around in Dhaka for a few days, killing time. I could see why they reckoned its air pollution was the world's worst. Dhaka's traffic made Calcutta's look tame and positively well organized. Policemen sheltering from the sun beneath black umbrellas tried their best to keep it flowing but they were fighting a losing battle. Their plight was summed up by the first set of traffic lights I saw on arrival. Its red and green lights were on simultaneously, as if to say, 'stop, go ahead, do what you like, we know you will anyway.'

Runa said the city's population had skyrocketed in the last few decades, from a million people in 1971 to around 12 million today. The number of motor vehicles had probably grown at a similar rate but no one really knew the figures. The city's authorities had issued licences to 89,000 auto-rickshaws, but the number of unlicensed vehicles was estimated to be at least seven times greater. The government had promised to ban the three-wheelers since their two-stroke engines were a major source of contamination, but the promise had never materialized. Some said this was because unlicensed auto-rickshaws were such a significant source of income for corrupt officials that they would never get rid of them from the streets.

'The pollution is not so bad when the rains start,' Runa told me, 'it washes the air clean, you know.'

I just looked at her.

After three days of waiting, I decided to hit the road again. If it wasn't going to rain, it wasn't going to rain. It was very unsatisfactory, but there wasn't a lot I could do about it. I would just have to see the world's wettest place when it was dry.

Runa had found a driver, a man named Babu, who would take us north to the border. The roads weren't very good, he said, so it would be a couple of days' drive.

We didn't get very far on the first day. Babu was a bit of a law unto himself and had already exhibited an annoying tendency to feign deafness whenever I asked a question that he either didn't feel like answering or didn't know the answer to. He stopped on the northern outskirts of town to investigate a gaggle of people that had gathered near the road where it sloped down to some flooded fields.

'Why are we stopping, Babu?'

He just leapt out of the car.

I thought about laying down the law. I had hired his vehicle, so I should decide when we stopped. However, Babu had already disappeared into the small crowd, which rather stole my thunder. But what the hell? It wasn't as if I was in any particular hurry.

The crowd turned out to have gathered to see a group of river gypsies who were setting out by boat to an island some way off. The gypsies were of interest because they carried an assortment of snakes. They were off to the island to do a bit of public snake charming, Babu announced breathlessly when he returned.

'Would you like to go with them?' he asked. 'I can arrange it.'

We all crowded into a long wooden boat with an outboard motor for the crossing. The island was notorious in the Dhaka underworld, Babu said, as the main repository for the capital's stolen and contraband goods.

None of the island's inhabitants looked particularly delinquent to my mind, but they were all very keen to see the snakes. A large circle of people, with children squatting at the front, formed around the river gypsies almost immediately on our arrival. A grandstand view was afforded for additional kids and a number of young women by the roof of a half-finished brick building overlooking the circle.

The three river gypsies hunched down in the midst of the crowd and proceeded to unload an assortment of coloured wooden boxes from the wraps they were carrying. I counted ten boxes in total. One of the men tuned up on a flute made from an ancient gourd decorated with flecks of red paint.

Bangladesh's river gypsies, the Badhi, make their living plying from river to river selling herbal remedies and jewellery, but they are also renowned for their capabilities with snakes. They turn up in villages like this one to perform their snake-charming routine, and also offer a snake-catching service to anyone unlucky enough to find one has taken up residence in their house. As Runa related these details to me, I was reminded of a warning given to me by one of the guests at the Calcutta dinner party.

'Beware of snakes in the monsoon season,' he had said, as he proceeded to tell me how as a boy he had always been confined to bed when the rains started. 'During flood conditions, you see, snakes flee the rising waters and they frequently enter people's houses. I had to remain in bed until the water had receded and was not permitted to leave until a thorough snake hunt had been conducted throughout the house.'

The snake charmers had opened some of their boxes to release a remarkable array of serpents. There was a long yellow one, a sluggish brown one that looked more like a giant earthworm than a snake, and two cobras. The man with the gourd flute began to play an alluring tune, but none of the snakes seemed very interested in being mesmerized. The long yellow one slunk off at surprising speed towards the edge of the circle, precipitating a gasp from the line of children at the edge as they moved hastily backwards before the flute player grabbed the snake by its tail and flung it back into the middle of the circle. Having failed in its bid for freedom, the yellow snake decided to retire back into its box instead, but the flute player grabbed it by the tail

again and held it in the air. He dropped it and resumed his music, but
the yellow snake just lay there immobile and fixed the flautist with its
beady green eye.

One of the flautist's colleagues, who wore a purple headscarf tied
round his forehead, was having more success with one of the cobras.
The snake had reared its head and was flaring its hood ready to strike
as the crouching man dangled his fists a foot or so from its head.
Every time the cobra struck, the man's fists were not there.
Meanwhile, the third river gypsy had produced half a dozen small
snakes from his box, which were winding themselves round his hands
like bright green bangles. To the horrified delight of the crowd, he
proceeded to feed one of the little green monsters into his mouth.

While all this was going on, a man from the crowd beckoned the
gypsy in the purple headscarf to the side of the circle. Runa and I
could see an animated conversation ensuing, after which the gypsy
said something to his friend with the small green snakes, who had to
pull three of them from his mouth before he could answer. He squatted down to replace them in one of the wooden boxes as the purple
headscarf set about coaxing his cobras back into their boxes. In the
meantime, the flautist played on.

Babu appeared at my shoulder. 'This man has snake in his house,'
he said excitedly. It was a job for snake-busters.

Part of the crowd peeled off to follow the two river gypsies as the
man led them to his unhappy abode. Runa, Babu and I joined them.
The man's house was right on the edge of the island, his backyard
sloping down to the flooded fields. The two river gypsies checked the
first of the man's rooms, an outhouse with a corrugated iron roof.
Their survey didn't seem very thorough to me. While the man with
the purple headscarf took a brief look under a makeshift table, his
snake-swallowing colleague took a large pinch of earth from the
entrance and rubbed it quickly into a sausage between his hands. He
smelt the earth and offered it to his friend to do the same. They
moved on.

'If earth is smelling of fish, they know snake is there,' Babu whispered in my ear.

They gave the slope down to the water a brief once-over, ignoring a woodpile that to me looked like a prime site for a snake nest, and moved to the main house. The snake swallower did a bit more earth smelling at the entrance, then they disappeared inside. The crowd moved up to the door and spilled into the first of what turned out to be two rooms. The river gypsies had given the first room, evidently the kitchen, short shrift. They were in the main room, which had a large bed on one side and a neat row of cooking pots lined up above a sideboard. If the snake was anywhere, it was here, it seemed.

The owner of the house, evidently rather pleased with the attention he was getting, particularly since there was a foreigner involved, beckoned me in to his bedroom and pointed to the bed. Assuming that the bed would be the safest place from which to observe the proceedings, I jumped on. The two river gypsies had become distinctly more cautious in the way they surveyed this room.

Suddenly, there was a commotion beneath the sideboard and the gypsy with the purple headscarf darted down with his hand outstretched. He emerged holding a full-sized cobra, as long as his arm, by the tail. The snake hissed as it arched its head round to try and face the gypsy who expertly twisted his arm to keep the cobra from striking at him. The crowd at the bedroom entrance let out a short collective gasp as he grabbed the snake by the neck and began to force it into one of his coloured wooden boxes.

But the show was not over yet. The snake-swallowing gypsy had his head beneath the bed where I was cowering and emerged in a flash holding a second cobra, just as long as the first.

'Husband and wife,' Babu called from the bedroom entrance. 'Cobras are very faithful partners. Always they travel together.'

Dusk was falling as we boarded the boat for the return journey to the mainland. I asked the gypsy with the purple headscarf what would happen to the two cobras he and his colleague had caught. He said they would be trained until they could join their snake-charming display.

'Are you ever bitten during the course of your work?' I asked.

'Yes, many times.' He showed me his forearms, which were a mass of scars. 'We cut open the bite, suck out the venom and rub the wound with herbs. Then it is sealed with a cigarette or hot knife.'

'If you did nothing, how long would it take to die after a bite from one of those cobras?' I wanted to know.

'About 20 minutes,' he replied.

We left Dhaka for good the following day. The sky was grey and over-cast which was at least a step in the right direction. Two hours north, we passed through Narsingdi, a town noted for its textile industry. Row upon row of screen-printed saris were hanging out to dry on washing lines and I could hear the clack-clack-clack of the looms as we passed each factory. Swarms of bicycle rickshaws zipped back and forth piled high with rolls of fabric.

'It is known as the "Manchester of Bengal",' said Babu, but it was a Manchester of the nineteenth century.

Cows grazed by the roadsides and electricity pylons marched across the paddy fields. The road was tarmac but the potholes had been filled with fragments of red brick. While we were waiting to catch a car ferry across the Meghna river, a small girl carrying a metal vessel full of water propped expertly on her hip like a baby offered me a one taka coin and I gave her a pen in exchange. She responded with a huge smile of pearly white teeth and disappeared to show it to her friend. Ten minutes later she was back, wanting to sell me the pen for five taka. I told her to keep it, but a man who was watching offered her six and the girl looked even happier. The man also looked pretty pleased with the deal.

Every so often we had to stop for railway crossings, though I never saw any trains. The railway lines were laid on high embankments and I asked Runa if they were ever flooded. 'Very rarely,' she said, 'although it happened in the 1998 floods, and in 1988 before that.'

Babu said there had been 2 feet of water in his bedroom in 1998. 'I had to put my bed on bricks for one month and ten days. Yesterday reminded me of that time, because a snake came to stay in my bedroom,' he went on. 'He, or it might have been a she, slept on the bookcase. Every time I looked at him, or her, it just flicked its tongue. It was a cobra, normally a rather dangerous snake, as you know. But during this time we spent together I did not bother her, or him, and he, or she, did not bother me. When the floods went down, he, or she, disappeared.'

We spent the night at Srimongal, in a bungalow with rose bushes growing in the flowerbeds and a faded photograph of the Queen hanging in the dining room. The compound was surrounded by the regimented bushes of a tea garden. They marched up and down a topography that was definitely undulating but couldn't quite be described as hilly. The humidity had been building all afternoon and that evening I was rewarded with rumbles of thunder, great flashes of lightning, and then the sweet music of rain smacking the brick drive-ways round the bungalows. The downpour was all the more welcome for being unexpected. Things were definitely looking up.

By the time we neared Sylhet, our last stop before the border, the low hills were unmistakable. We arrived at lunchtime, and I wanted to forge on, eager to enter Meghalaya now that I'd at last seen some serious rainfall. But Babu insisted that we stop because the border was best crossed in the morning. I assumed he knew what he was talking about so we checked into the Parjatan Motel, run by the government tourist authority.

It was perched on its own small hill on the edge of town, set in pleasant gardens dotted with viewing shelters that looked out over the more serious Khasi Hills across the border in India. At the motel's entrance there was a sign that asked 'Why choose Parjatan?' followed by a series of answers:

It has open area and fresh air.

It is handled by professional staffs.

It is visited by people of taste.

It didn't quite live up to its billing. The dining room was empty but for a small cockroach that the waiter swept nonchalantly from our tablecloth when he arrived with the menus. He was a small, round and sweaty man who looked like a butterball. I ordered a chicken cutlet (two pieces), which came with chips.

'Drinking?' the butterball asked.

'Do you have lassi?'

The question seemed to startle him. 'No one has ordered lassi here, sir, for 25 years,' he said dismissively.

I took that as a no and ordered a bottle of mineral water instead.

The meal took just less than 25 years to arrive and when it did it was terrible. The cutlets were wafer thin, sad and burnt. They were accompanied by a plate containing eight chips. I cut into one of the cutlets and, failing to find any chicken, asked the butterball if he had made a mistake with my order.

'No,' he said definitively, 'this is chicken cutlet two pieces, served with chipped potatoes.'

'Are you sure this isn't vegetarian cutlet?' I asked. 'There doesn't appear to be any chicken here.'

The butterball looked uneasy. Despite the air-conditioning, small beads of sweat began to run down his neck towards his grubby white collar. But he remained defiant. 'Definitely chicken cutlet.'

On further investigation, I found a small strip of meat. It was about a millimetre wide and a centimetre long. Babu asked if he could examine it. He pushed aside his plate of chicken curry, which looked like a far better choice despite the fact that most of the chicken pieces were actually bones, and peered through his round glasses at the specimen I passed as if we had just discovered an exotic new species of insect. Then he exploded.

'Do you know how to run a restaurant?' he shouted at the butterball, who now looked shocked as well as decidedly uncomfortable. 'Where is the manager?' Babu demanded. Clearly relieved at the opportunity to pass the buck, the butterball scuttled away towards the kitchen. He returned presently with a younger man in tow and Babu proceeded to scream at them both in Bengali.

I put my head down and ate some of my eight chips.

After a good half hour of wild gesticulating and ferocious finger-wagging by Babu, reflected in strained expressions and anguished responses from the restaurant manager, the atmosphere calmed and the butterball and manager faded away. Babu had been pacified but was still angry.

It transpired that the meagre food rations were a result of corruption all the way up the government food chain. 'Everyone takes their cut, the regional manager, senior government executives, the suppliers, everyone except these guys, who are not senior enough yet,' Babu explained. 'I'm surprised they have any food left at all.'

A chicken actually cost 200 taka but the invoices showed that 350 taka was paid, the 150-taka difference disappearing into pockets up the chain. The hotel had to make a profit, which meant that when they received the over-expensive chicken it had to stretch a long way. Hence my virtually chicken-free cutlets and Babu's bony curry. It was the same with the chips; 24 taka was paid for a kilogram of potatoes that actually cost ten taka. The result was my plate of eight chips.

'It is terrible,' Babu exclaimed, 'scandalous, in fact. You come to my country and what do you think when faced with this shit?'

F O U R

The border crossing was hard up against the foot of the Khasi Hills that rose sharply out of the plains to disappear into a shroud of low thick clouds. A constant procession of brightly coloured Tata lorries lumbered out of the mist to cross into Bangladesh laden with gleaming black coal. As I waited for my passport details to be laboriously entered by hand into a vast ledger on the Bangladesh side, Babu pointed to an article he was reading in the *Daynik Janoahanto*, or Daily People's Voice.

'It is about lack of monsoon rains,' he said. 'First line translates as "It seems that October has arrived even before July has finished."' I had singularly failed to catch the monsoon in Bangladesh and it was time to move on. 'I hope you have better luck in India,' Babu told me.

As at the frontier coming into Bangladesh, the transition was abrupt. But this time it was not like returning to India. Going by the faces of the people it seemed more as if I had taken a shortcut into South-East Asia. We immediately became engulfed by dense jungle that glistened in the mist as the road wound its way up a series of hairpin bends into the 'Abode of the Clouds'. Mosses and lichens clung to every rock surface and delicate green ferns sprouted from every crevice. I could hear the incessant torrent of waterfalls somewhere in the distance.

As we motored on, the fog closed in. Visibility fell from 20 metres to 10, and then to less than 5. I couldn't see further than the concrete blocks that lined the road we were driving on. Beyond the blocks was just a milky void. It was an eerie nothingness that could have been hiding anything: more thick jungle, a precipitous valley, even an undiscovered ocean. It was impossible to tell. On crossing the border, I'd been briefly relieved to regain a vertical component after weeks in a two-dimensional country, but the all-enveloping fog now made Meghalaya worse. It was claustrophobic and unnerving. Driving along the thin strip of shiny tarmac that was just visible in front of the bonnet was an existence in just one dimension.

My unease wasn't helped by the driver's reluctance to employ any of the few mechanical aids available on his ancient Ambassador. The wipers were silent on the fogged windscreen and he hadn't turned on the headlights. The rear-view mirror was also useless, being covered in a thick layer of condensation. It reminded me of the interior decorator's comment at the dinner party in Calcutta about the clouds coming in through the windows. The driver was hanging out of his window, straining to see in front of him, when I asked why he didn't use the windscreen wipers.

'It's easier to see without them,' he grimaced. I couldn't grasp the logic of that remark, but I let it go. 'What about the headlights then?' I said.

'No, they just make it more difficult to see.'

The only saving grace was that he never exceeded 40 kilometres an hour and I wondered whether this was a concession to the quite obvious danger of his driving like a blind man, or because the vehicle simply couldn't go any faster. I decided on the latter, since the word danger didn't appear to feature in his vocabulary.

He swerved abruptly to avoid a figure hunched beneath an umbrella that appeared out of nowhere.

'I don't think I've ever seen fog as thick as this,' I said nervously.

'This is not thick,' the driver replied, 'when it's thick people have been known to bump into each other while out walking.'

Briefly the fog cleared as a light drizzle began to fall. The jungle had disappeared to become flat, rough grassland. It looked just like Dartmoor in the misty rain. It was cold, too, a welcome relief after the torrid heat of the Bangladeshi plains, and there were even a few bedraggled sheep grazing beside a rocky outcrop. But there were also conifers growing, and thatched houses with walls made of flattened tin cans that loomed out of the haze. Tin cans that hadn't been flattened, and were full of bright red begonias, lined their verandas.

We passed through a village. There were more people beneath umbrellas and others wearing coracle-shaped palm leaf contraptions over their heads as protection against the elements. They looked like raffia tortoise shells. They were called *knups*, my driver told me.

We drove on, past a brief glimpse of a limestone quarry, into Shillong, which had a signpost welcoming me to the Scotland of the East, the name coined during the time of the British Raj when the hill station was a popular retreat from the heat of the plains. Here we picked up my new translator, a Khasi woman named Dulci who worked as a disc jockey-cum-newsreader for the Meghalaya branch of All India Radio.

During the 20 minutes we spent in Shillong the weather changed from mist to gentle rain, then to thick fog, and back to mist again. 'They say that the weather here is like the women of Shillong,' Dulci told me with a sardonic smile, 'always changing its mind.'

Almost as soon as we left the town, the road to Mawsynram became swathed in thick fog and the landscape dissolved yet again into the miasma. 'You see the irony of it all?' mused Dulci as we crept through the twilight zone at 10 kilometres an hour, the driver once more hanging out of his window. 'When it is not raining, it is foggy. When there is no fog, it is raining.'

The afternoon dragged on and what little light was able to penetrate the fog began to fade. It was difficult to gauge how far we had travelled, but even though I had been on the road for more than five hours, I didn't think the distance could be that great since we hadn't got into fourth gear since leaving Shillong. A few minutes later, as I sensed we had begun a slight descent in our journey, Dulci asked the driver to pull over to the side of the road. She jumped out of the car and almost immediately disappeared into the fog. 'I want to show you something, Nick,' her disembodied voice called, 'your first view of Mawsynram.'

Distinctly unconvinced, I followed her into the phantom space. She was standing a few yards away, out of sight of the car, pointing.

I looked. 'Oh yes, beautiful. What a fantastic view...' I could see nothing whatsoever except the usual milky vacuum. 'I can't see anything Dulci, it's just a cloud.'

'But that's the whole point,' she said. 'It's the wettest town on Earth.'

For the briefest of moments the fog broke up and I saw a handful of houses on the far side of a valley. They were backed by a church steeple, all clinging to a grassy hillside as the clouds scudded by. Then the village melted away again into the haze. It was the only view I ever got of the wettest place on Earth.

I have to admit that I hadn't been mentally prepared for the poor visibility. When I first started researching for my journey to Mawsynram, my mind was just so boggled by the enormity of its annual rainfall that I failed to consider what this might mean for my chances of actually seeing the place. As a geographer, I found the lack of visible perspective disconcerting. Of course, there are lots of other ways of getting a hold on a sense of place, including all the other senses for a start. Sounds and smells go a long way towards building up a mental picture of where you are, quite apart from conversations with people who live there. But a good clear view of a location puts it all into perspective, and that's what I missed. It wasn't as if I couldn't see anything at all, it was just that the view was severely restricted. As

Dulci had said, when it wasn't raining, it was foggy, and when the fog eventually cleared, almost the moment we drove into the village of Mawsynram, it began to rain. As a result, I could never perceive anything further than the equivalent of the end of my short garden at home. I found it very disturbing.

But what rain. Half an hour or so before Dulci had stopped the car to show me the 'view' of the world's wettest inhabited place, a peculiar noise had started to emanate from the opaque clouds that encased us on our drive. It sounded like hundreds of castanets being played, all slightly out of sync with each other. After some consideration, I decided they might be frogs. 'Right,' said Dulci, 'They are known as *jakoid* in Khasi. You might be lucky, Nick, because they say the *jakoids* woo the rain.'

They'd certainly done that all right, because it came down in torrents. The heavens didn't open because you couldn't really see them, but they just sent forth an immense outpouring of water that was truly cosmic in its proportions. It was as if the bottom had fallen out of an ocean in the sky. It rained and it rained and it rained and it rained. It just kept on raining, non-stop for five days, an unremitting, incessant, ear-hurting deluge.

So, despite the parched frustration of my journey from Calcutta, I did, after all, get to see what I'd come for: Mawsynram, the wettest village on the planet, during a full-on monsoonal downpour. I set up the rain-gauge of my portable meteorological station in the grounds of the Public Works Department compound on the edge of the village and returned to meet the family Dulci had arranged for me to stay with.

My initial impression of Meghalaya as rather different in many ways from the rest of India was right. Politically I was still in the world's largest democracy, all right, but culturally I was closer to South-East Asia. 'The Khasis are thought to have migrated here long ago from somewhere like Cambodia or Thailand,' Dulci told me. 'Certainly many Khasi words are similar to Thai. The food too. We eat a lot of pork, and this is one of the few places in India where you can buy beef.'

But Khasi culture also came with twists of its own. The Khasis are a matrilineal society, in which inheritance passes to the youngest daughter and all the children take the mother's name. This explained why the lady of the house where I stayed, Manolin, was definitely in charge. Roy, her husband, earned the money, but it was Manolin who decided how it was spent.

And mixed in with the traditional Khasi set-up were some unmistakable ingredients left over from the time when the British ruled India. In the nineteenth century, Meghalaya became a target for Christian missionaries, many from Wales, who preached the gospel, established churches and introduced roman script. Somewhere along the line, the Khasi people became acquainted with Scottish tartan, and men and women all over Mawsynram still wander round with tartan shawls across their shoulders against the cold.

Another legacy of British rule is a fascination with English words that stretches beyond the borders of bizarre. During the course of my stay, I met a boy named Manstrong and a girl called Barents Sea. She had a best friend by the name of Latrine. I was sad to miss three sisters with the unlikely handles of Hydrogen, Oxygen and Nitrogen, and a trio of brothers named Brake, Steering and Car Horn.

Manolin's husband, Roy, was a pork butcher. He sold one pig at a time at the village market that took place twice a week in the main street, or 'station' as it was called because this was where the buses stopped. The rest of the week saw Roy travelling to other villages in search of pigs for slaughter because Mawsynram's pigs were kept for breeding only. Roy's business was affected by the monsoon in several ways, he told me. There was less demand for a start. When the rain came down in the vast quantities that it did while I was there, people who worked outdoors tended to stay at home. In consequence, they didn't receive any wages. Day labourers in the fields or at the limestone quarries saved money during the winter to tide them over the

A river gypsy entertains the crowd by swallowing one of his snakes.

Residents of Mawsynram watching the rain in the world's wettest place.

Elephants preparing to take us on a sit-down anti-poaching patrol in Kaziranga.
Hidden in this picture are several elephant leeches preparing to suck blood from
the author's right leg as soon as he sets foot in some water.

River traffic in Dhaka, not as congested as on the city's roads.

A half-time cigarette with Runa at the hadudu match.
(Ali Kazimi © Keo Films)

TOP
*Planting rice seedlings in preparation for the
monsoon's arrival in Bangladesh, a country
in just two dimensions.*

ABOVE
*Kaziranga park rangers awaiting the migration
of wild elephants from the Brahmaputra
floodplains to the Mikir Hills.*

RIGHT
*The author braving Mawsynram's elements
in his knup and tartan shawl.*

monsoon days when they couldn't work, but nonetheless they still tended to eat less meat. The other thing was that the meat went off faster in the high humidity of the monsoon. If Roy didn't sell all his pork at the market during the winter, he could usually keep it for the following market day, but if this happened in the rainy season, Roy had to don his *knup* and hawk pork chops door-to-door. 'I never have to do that in winter,' he told me.

Roy never complained about the rain, but then he was a quiet and undemonstrative man, who generally preferred to leave the talking to his lively wife. Others I spoke to in Mawsynram were slightly more voluble about the annual deluge. When I asked Jackson Marbaniang, the village headman, if the villagers felt a sense of pride in holding the record for the rainiest place in the world, he answered, 'Yes, in one way they are proud.' He paused to gaze out of the window at the cascade of water pouring from his roof. 'But in another way,' he went on slowly, 'the rain means trouble.' I waited for him to elaborate, but he seemed mesmerized by the momentous flow outside his window.

'Trouble in what sense?' I asked.

'Because when people step out of their house, to go to work or to the market, they get wet,' he replied.

It wasn't exactly what I'd been expecting, but I suppose it was a fair point. And it was one I heard time and again as people grumbled about the number of times they had to change their clothes each day after getting saturated. But perhaps the most common complaint reflected Jackson Marbaniang's demeanour as he told me about the 'trouble' of people getting wet. It was simply that the monsoon was boring. While the incessant rains were gushing from the heavens, much of the village seemed to be transfixed by a sense of seasonal lethargy. The most glaring example of this came one afternoon when I fell into conversation with a man wreathed in a plastic mac sheltering beneath the bus shelter down at the station. The electricity had been off at Roy's house all day because the power lines into the village had been brought down by the rains. I asked the man where he was off to.

'I'm not waiting for a bus,' he told me, 'I'm just watching the rain.'

'I see,' I replied, which I suppose I did in one sense.

'But you know how I comfort myself in the monsoon?' he asked rhetorically, 'I have some inner warmth.' He rummaged in the depths of his plastic mac and pulled back a flap to give me a glimpse of something that was obviously not for public display. I craned my neck to see. He was grasping a small clear plastic bag that bulged with a transparent liquid.

'What's that?' I asked.

'Rice liqueur,' he whispered conspiratorially, closing the flap in his mac and gazing back into the downpour.

Before I left him to his rain watching, I asked the man with the inner warmth what he did for a living. 'I'm a sort of electrician,' he said. 'I repair power lines.'

I sensed the lethargy in Mawsynram, but I also felt some rather less palatable effects of the rain. Manolin and Roy's three-roomed house was a solid enough structure with wooden floors and panelling on the walls. The windows had no glass in them but they had shutters that could be closed when the wind got up to blow the rain horizontally. The wood for their fire was stored below the floor to keep it dry and every morning one of their six sons, a bright little lad named Venison, disappeared below the teak floorboards to grab the fuel for the day. The house had no running water (on the inside, that is) but an ingenious method had been set up to collect the rainwater that streamed off the corrugated iron roof. It consisted of a series of bamboo poles, split down the middle, which had been arranged to act like small gutters to channel the water through a window into the kitchen, where it was collected in a series of plastic buckets. The house was warm and snug, thanks both to the kitchen fire and a charcoal brazier that was always alight and surrounded by family members drying themselves off after a dash outside through the rain. I also used the brazier to dry out the pages of my notebook and the condensation that formed every day inside my watch.

Apart from the fact that Khasi people tend to be rather short, and hence I was continually bumping my head on the beams, there was one other drawback to the house as far as I was concerned. The rain on the corrugated iron roof was very loud. It woke me up four times during my first night with a noise that sounded like huge waves crashing against a rocky shore. As the wind began to howl, they sounded more like tidal waves smashing against the roof. I surveyed the dark room from my position on the floor, expecting to see the two sons on the bed, Venison and Jefferson, equally wide awake thanks to the incredible racket. But they were sleeping like babies. I decided they must be deaf.

They must also have had very strong bladders, because the other, rather less expected outcome of the sound of all this falling water was to make me want to go to the loo. Having no internal plumbing, the house was without toilet facilities. When I first arrived, I was told that the family relieved themselves in the forest nearby. But in the middle of the night, during a torrential rainstorm of Biblical proportions, there was no way I was going to dash the few hundred metres necessary. It wasn't just the prospect of getting saturated, though that was bad enough since the charcoal brazier had burned itself out, but more the fear that the raindrops sounded so large I might be stoned to death. So every night I just lay there, crossing my legs, waiting in the vain hope for a let-up in the rain, until I drifted off to sleep again.

The volume of water falling from the sky was truly astonishing. Every morning, I made my way out to the Public Works Department compound on the edge of the village to check my rain-gauge for the previous 24-hour period. The first morning's reading was 468 mm, the next 515 mm. Mawsynram was averaging more than a foot and a half of rain a day. This was even more extraordinary when I compared it to the rainfall I was used to back home. Oxford only gets 642 mm in an average *year*.

I was fortunate, in more than one sense, that this particular climatic extreme was so spectacular. The awe-inspiring measurements

I was taking helped me to suppress the horror I felt at finally coming face-to-face with my first leeches. The short grass where I had set up my rain-gauge was infested with them and I soon became adept at reading my monitor while rubbing salt on the blood-sucking invaders (cigarettes were, of course, not an option in the torrential rain). To make matters worse, the little black stringy fiends seemed to sense my disgust and one morning I was confronted by a leech standing on the rim of the rain-gauge waving at me.

In Western Europe we enjoy four seasons, but the Indian calendar consists of three: the cold season from October to December, the hot season from January to May, and the rains of the summer monsoon from June to September. The Indian Monsoon is one of the world's great weather systems, affecting an area that extends from Tibet to the southern Indian Ocean and from eastern Africa to Malaysia. The rains are brought by warm, moist air flowing from the Indian Ocean over the Indian subcontinent, driven by differences in heating between land and sea. This differential heating is caused by contrasting energy responses of land and sea to incoming radiation from the sun. Water has a higher specific heat capacity than soil, so it is better able to disperse this heat away from its surface. Hence water does not warm up as much as land.

Air in contact with the relatively warm land absorbs the heat and rises, causing an area of low pressure (a depression) at the surface. In contrast, air in contact with the colder ocean surface absorbs less solar energy and remains cooler. Less heat is conveyed upward through the atmosphere, which compared with that over the land sinks closer to the surface. This causes a region of high pressure (an anticyclone) to develop over the Indian Ocean. It is this contrast in pressure between land and sea that drives the monsoonal circulation. All sorts of other factors are also involved, such as the heating of the Tibetan Plateau to the north of India, which is fundamental to the onset and strength of the monsoon, but essentially the rain arrives because warm, moist air is pushed from high pressure over the sea to low pressure over the land.

All of India receives most of its rainfall during the monsoon, but annual rainfall is particularly high in places where these moisture-laden monsoonal winds are forced to rise over mountains, thus cooling the air and promoting condensation of moisture to produce more rain. Hence India's zones of highest annual rainfall occur over the Western Ghats, the foothills of the eastern Himalayas and, above all, here in the Khasi Hills of Meghalaya. The zone of maximum rainfall occurs not on the mountain summits but in a relatively narrow strip on the windward side. The average annual rainfall at Mawsynram (altitude 1,401 metres) is 11,872 mm, or nearly 39 feet, making it the wettest town on Earth. Up the road in Shillong, which is just 110 metres higher in altitude than Mawsynram, they only receive an average of 2,415 mm a year.

The reasons for such spectacularly high rainfall totals at Mawsynram are thus three-fold. First, the warm moist winds of the northward-moving air from the Bay of Bengal during the monsoon, which cover an extensive area but are forced to converge into a narrower zone over the Khasi Hills, thus concentrating their moisture. Secondly, the alignment of the Khasi Hills (east to west) means they lie directly in the path of the air flow from the Bay of Bengal, producing a significant uplift (plus cooling, further condensation and thus more rain). Thirdly, uplift over the Khasi Hills is virtually continuous in the monsoon period because the lifted air is constantly being pulled up by vigorous winds in the upper atmosphere; hence the rainfall is more or less continuous, as I'd seen.

However, these same conditions also apply to the town of Cherrapunji, which was the proud holder of the record for wettest place in the world when I was at school. I remember grappling with the task of trying to draw comparative rainfall histograms that saw Cherrapunji's column disappear off the top of the graph paper. But in 1994 the record for highest annual average rainfall passed to Mawsynram. I'd read several accounts that suggested Cherrapunji was rather upset about this. Rumours were started suggesting that Mawsynram's meteorological station was sub-standard. Aspersions were cast on the quality of the equipment, and the fact that the Mawsynram observer was only a part-timer. It wasn't like that at Cherrapunji, which had a proper, full-time meteorological office.

When I asked people in Mawsynram about Cherrapunji's claims, most were diplomatic, saying that it was wet in Mawsynram but wet in Cherrapunji, too. Only occasionally was anyone more definitive. A young man named Campbell told me, 'the rain comes here first, then to Cherra further up the valley, so we get more and there's not so much left for them. It's a matter of record, Mawsynram is the wettest.'

'Valley?' I said to Dulci later, 'what valley?'

'We're up a valley here Nick, didn't you know?'

How could I have known when most of the time I couldn't see further than the end of my arm?

I wanted to look into the controversy myself, so I tried to make an appointment to meet Mawsynram's resident meteorologist whose rain-gauge was situated close to where I'd set up mine in the Public Works Department compound. He was on holiday, but he had left the daily task of taking the measurements in the capable hands of the PWD cook. The man did his best in the appalling conditions, crouching beneath his umbrella to fill his measuring cylinder time after time as the rain bucketed down all around us. Although it stood in 6 inches of water, there was nothing wrong with the equipment that I could see. Almost as importantly, there didn't appear to be any leeches. The site could just have done with a bit better drainage, that was all, but then it was in the wettest place in the world.

Although Mawsynram currently holds the record for the highest annual average rainfall total, Cherrapunji does still hold several other world rainy records. These include the highest rainfall total ever recorded in a single year (26,461 mm, or 86 feet 9 inches) between August 1860 and July 1861, and two other world records that were set on the particularly wet day of 16 June 1995: the highest ever rainfall total in a 24-hour period (1,563 mm, or 5 feet) more than twice the amount of rain falling on lowland Britain in an average year, and the highest rainfall ever recorded in a single hour (420 mm, or 17 inches).

So I decided to go to Cherrapunji. The evening before I left Mawsynram I attended a Khasi religious dance in the village hall where four young girls dressed in yellow and gold silk crept round the concrete floor in a shuffle-like motion, their feet inching forward with toes curling like caterpillars. They were laden with heavy jewellery, silver crowns on their heads and chunky coral necklaces, and encircled by men with chicken motifs on their shirts and silver quivers full of arrows on their backs. Musicians in turbans sat on the small stage and managed to triumph over the noise of the rain on the tin roof with their flutes and drums. After the dancing, there was a huge feast back at Roy's house. He had slaughtered a pig for the occasion and villagers came and went in waves for sitting upon sitting of pork and rice. Everyone was in good spirits and for one evening, at least, the lethargy of the monsoon season was dispelled.

Cherrapunji was just 16 kilometres away to the east, but it took us four hours to get there. This wasn't because we drove at 4 kilometres an hour. Our Ambassador got up to at least 20 at one point, so I assumed it was because the road wound its way round to the other side of the valley that I'd never seen. I couldn't confirm this like I normally would, with a map, because the Indian government are notoriously reluctant about making good maps available of its border areas. The reason always quoted is national security, but I found it difficult to imagine Bangladesh ever bothering to invade Meghalaya. They wouldn't be able to see it for a start.

But India has always been touchy about the north-east, a remote, sensitive border zone connected to the rest of the country only by a narrow corridor that threads its way between Bangladesh, Nepal, China and Bhutan. The north-east has also seen more than its fair share of riots, violence and terrorism aimed at the government in Delhi. The independence movement in Nagaland has long been one of India's running sores, and Meghalaya, too, has a group of Khasi freedom fighters known as the Hyniewtrep National Liberation Council (HNLC).

The name, Hyniewtrep, means seven huts or families, and derives from the legend of Khasi creation. The Creator sent 16 Khasi families down to inhabit the tummy button of the world, or Meghalaya as it is today, and established a golden tree so that they could commute back and forth to Heaven. (I guess this was so that they could go back and dry out every so often.) This was back in the days when people and animals spoke one and the same language, but the Khasis did something to upset the Creator who, in a fit of pique, felled the golden tree, so severing the link with Heaven forever. At the time that the tree was felled (some say it was a golden thread or a staircase, but it doesn't really matter), there were nine families drying off in Heaven and seven, the Hyniewtrep, left on Earth.

Indirectly, the HNLC probably also played a part in our slow progress between Mawsynram and Cherrapunji. A few miles after stopping at a petrol station, where the fuel had to be hand-pumped by the assistant in his *knup* because the electricity was off, the Ambassador began to splutter. Our driver stopped to check the engine, muttering something about adulterated petrol as he climbed back into his seat. Dulci said the HNLC had been accused of soliciting financial contributions under duress from businesses and that was why petrol was often watered down with kerosene. The HNLC denied the allegations, saying it was just crooks using their name, but attempted HNLC extortion had also been cited as the reason for the recent closure of Shillong's premier Chinese restaurant. The management refused to pay up, and decided to leave town before their premises met with an accident.

The fog cleared marginally as we ploughed on, revealing people wrapped in tartan shawls bent beneath their *knups* in paddy fields that seemed distinctly out of place surrounded by hills that looked as if they belonged with the shawls in Scotland. The mid-latitude feel was

enhanced by apple and pear trees laden with fruit and cabbages growing in neat rows on a hillside. Just outside one village, a series of
towering flat boulders stood upright on the moor, huge megaliths
that could be seen all over the Khasi region if it wasn't for the fog and
rain, Dulci told me.

Other than the adulterated petrol incident, we stopped only
once, when the scenery had disappeared again into a haze of misty
grey and we came upon a group of men wreathed in plastic sheets
who were busy clearing the road of debris from a landslip. They were
shovelling mud into a wooden handcart and levering large boulders
off the track with long metal poles in the rain. They were a Public
Works Department road maintenance team and for them the
monsoon was the busiest time of the year, their supervisor told me.
When they weren't unblocking roads from the slips triggered by rain-
soaked hillsides, they were busy clearing drains in the lower areas to
prevent flooding.

FIVE

There was a different feel to Cherrapunji after Mawsynram. Cherra was much bigger for a start. Mawsynram had had an easy-going, village atmosphere, brought about both by its size and the position of all its houses perched up on the hillside. There was just one road through the village, where the bus station was located, and from there the rest of the settlement was only accessible by foot. It was possible to drive everywhere in Cherrapunji, which was spread out across a flat limestone plateau, a bustling town that could boast a parade of proper shops, in contrast to Mawsynram's short line of permanent stalls draped in tarpaulins and plastic.

Cherrapunji was the first British outpost in this part of India, becoming the official headquarters of the British Raj in the Khasi Hills after the arrival of David Scott, the political agent of the East India Company, in 1820. I could only discern its layout the day after my arrival because night had fallen by the time we drove in and the fog was the thickest I'd seen since entering the 'Abode of the Clouds'. Dulci and I spent the night with a family who lived in a traditional Khasi house built almost entirely of bamboo, with a grass roof that provided perfect soundproofing against the rain. Its only drawback was its lack of a chimney, which meant that it generated its own internal smog, built up by a combination of the clouds drifting in through the doors (it had no windows) and the constant smoke from the open fire. Dulci said the lack of ventilation was deliberate, since the smoke kept away the mosquitoes.

The next morning, I awoke to an unusual sight: the sky. It had stopped raining during the night to leave a heavy cover of menacing grey stratus clouds, but it was not total, so that here and there I could see fragments of blue peeping through. The base of the clouds was also well off the ground, enabling me to get the perspective that I had so sorely missed in Mawsynram. But the view only went as far as the rim of the plateau, where my hosts' bamboo house was situated. I stood at its edge and could just make out a hazy hillside far off in the distance. Between the hillside and me was a gulf, which I assumed to be a gorge or valley of some sort. I couldn't be sure because although lying below me, it was full of clouds. They were dense, white fluffy cumulus that just sat there defying the usual arrangement of sky and earth.

The rain had started again by the time I arrived at the Government of India Meteorological Department at Cherrapunji, where Mr M.P. Luitel was just leaving his office to take the rainfall measurement for the previous 24 hours. His ordinary rain-gauge was of the same design as that at Mawsynram, but his station was also equipped with a self-recording rain-gauge, as well as an anemometer to measure wind speed and a Stevenson screen full of thermometers.

Mr Luitel maintained a dignified distance from any rivalry there might have been between Cherra and Mawsynram. He just said they were both very wet. He also refused to be drawn into any controversy over the Mawsynram readings. However, he did agree that the Mawsynram station probably warranted a full-time observer like himself.

'The problem, of course, is financial,' he told me when we got back into his office. It was the sort of office you'd expect of a working meteorological observer, with climatology books and papers in neat piles on his wooden desk, a bookcase stocked with more piles of paper and meteorological manuals, and photographs of cloud formations pinned to the wall above the fireplace. Hanging from the mantelpiece, held there by four large batteries, was a coloured poster of a Hindu god playing a flute astride six snakes. Occupying the wall opposite the fireplace was a large wardrobe with one door open to reveal more stacks of records. A doorway off to the left of his desk led to Mr Luitel's living quarters, another to the right led outside to the compound of meteorological instruments.

Mr Luitel told me he had been at the regional meteorological centre in Guwahati, in neighbouring Assam, before being posted for a year to Cherrapunji. It was a job he had volunteered for. 'This is because I am knowing that it is going to be a most interesting experience,' he said, his eyes lighting up. 'This place is most famous for its rainfall. People all over the world know of Cherrapunji. They may not know of Guwahati, or even Delhi, but Cherrapunji they know.'

Unfortunately, after having been in Cherra for just three months, he already wanted to go home. The strain of living in a place with so much rain was getting to him. 'These people here are accustomed to these conditions, you know. They just continue with their business when it rains. But for me I am simply stuck in this building. I cannot go out because of the rain.' His eyes had now taken on a doleful appearance.

Culturally, he also felt rather isolated, he said. The people weren't unfriendly, just rather reserved, and besides, he couldn't speak Khasi. He also missed his family who were still in Guwahati. He usually telephoned them every day, but all the phone lines out of town had been down for the last four days due to the torrential downpour. The other thing he mentioned that was getting him down made me smile in agreement. He said that the incessant rainfall made him continually think about going to the toilet.

I felt for Mr Luitel, drawn to the Khasi Hills by the allure of a meteorological phenomenon that had turned out to be his nemesis.

But at least there were only nine months to go before he could return home. His sorry tale reminded me of something I'd read about Cherrapunji during British times. When selected as a hill station sanatorium for European pensioners in the East India Company's service, the town had been equally vindictive. The story went that many were driven insane by the unremitting rainfall.

Mr Luitel's experience echoed many of my own feelings about my time in the world's wettest range of hills. I'd found the Khasis reserved at first, though very warm after a little perseverance. Their hilly abode was for me a curious combination of paddies and pine trees, *knups* and tartan shawls. In some ways it was the Scotland of the East all right, but it was a Scotland with leeches.

Like Mr Luitel, I too had been attracted by an extreme that had to be seen to be believed, but my initial delight at the cataclysmic outpouring of water had soon waned. The ceaseless torrent had become a high-pressure version of the Chinese water torture. For the Khasis I met, life went on despite the weather, but more for some than for others. Roy just kept on selling his pork without so much as a word of protest. However, I couldn't forget the intent look on the face of Mawsynram's village headman as he gazed out at the rain and told me that the monsoon meant trouble, or the electrician who stood in the bus shelter watching the deluge when he should have been out repairing the power lines. For them, surviving the monsoon season appeared to rely on a sort of mental hibernation.

But on my final afternoon in Cherra, I came across what could be described as an antidote to the seasonal lethargy. It was a game that is best described as a cross between archery and darts, known simply as 'arrow'. In essence that's all it was, just an interesting Khasi sport that involved opposing two-man teams throwing arrows like javelins at small bamboo targets. But there was also a whole lot more to the game than that.

I learnt the basics of its other dimension from a young secondary school literature teacher named Ïasaid. He was a short man with a large vocabulary, picked up, he told me, from studying the *Oxford English Dictionary*. He was the sort of character who should have had a nervous tic, with an air about him of being permanently perplexed. It was as if he carried all the metaphysical problems of Meghalaya on his shoulders and he was worried that he might have to pick up some more before solving those he already had.

Ïasaid told me that arrow was really about para-psychology. Certainly the game itself was just a game, but it was what came before that was really important. The players just threw the arrows, but they only did so after a thinker from either side had come to an agreement about how this particular game should be played.

'First the two parties come to an agreement,' he said. 'A typical start to such an agreement is for the first thinker to provide his own arrows, and then the other thinker also.' I nodded; I was following him so far.

'The agreement may continue for as long as is necessary. Just like in a court of law, it is down to the verbal jousting that goes on between the two thinkers. In the agreement there must be no flaw at all. It must be perfect. If you lose in the agreement you will lose the game.'

He was beginning to lose me. 'If your thinker loses the argument in the agreement his team will lose the actual throwing of the arrows?' I asked.

'Yes,' he said definitively, 'you will not win.'

I paused. 'Why is that?' I asked. 'Because the throwers get some sort of handicap written into the agreement?'

'A handicap of sorts, but only of the mental kind.'

'I see,' I said, which I didn't at all.

'In the agreement you can do tongue fu,' Ïasaid continued.

'Tongue fu?'

'Yes, a sort of verbal kung fu.'

Now I was completely lost. 'So how does tongue fu work exactly?' I asked tentatively.

'It is just logic, like a game of chess. You try to kill your opponent's idea, to gain advantage in the agreement. It is crucial never to say "yes" while making the agreement. If you say "yes", you will lose. You have to keep the agreement going.'

It seemed like a Khasi variety of sports psychology, but this was a highly formalized pre-match verbal jousting that appeared to dictate the outcome of the match itself. I was familiar with football managers at home trying to out-psych opponents before a game, but what perplexed me was Ïasaid's complete certainty that the outcome of the agreement would irrevocably dictate the outcome of the match itself. If that was the case, I wondered, then why bother throwing the arrows at all?

'Because your team will still have a chance, resting on the terms of the agreement,' Ïasaid told me.

I was floundering. 'I'm sorry, I don't understand,' I said.

'Here is an example,' Ïasaid replied, 'Once in the competition, one of the men throwing the arrows, his *dhoti*, or loincloth, dropped off and everything shows. The thinker from the opposite side found fault with him by saying that this is outside the agreement. You see, no part of the agreement said that a thrower could remove his *dhoti*. So that man who lost his *dhoti*, he consistently lost.'

At last, I thought I was getting it. 'He was disqualified, you mean?' I said.

'No, not disqualified, he just consistently lost in the throwing of the arrows.'

So it really was all in the mind. I reckoned I had just about grasped it, but I still didn't understand how it could happen.

I soon found out. Ïasaid took me to a foggy piece of ground on the edge of Cherrapunji where a match was scheduled. A small crowd had gathered, sheltering against the light drizzle beneath umbrellas and *knups*. He managed to get me on to one of the two-man teams, throwing the arrows for a small hamlet just outside Cherra against the home side. Two elderly men were introduced to me as the rival thinkers. The Cherrapunji thinker had a shock of white hair and carried a black umbrella. My team's thinker, who held a red umbrella, had deep wrinkles in his face and looked more kindly. They set about making the agreement and after 20 minutes they broke off.

'The agreement is set,' Ïasaid told me, 'you will throw the arrows with the red mark.' He looked over towards the two thinkers, who were gathering up their arrows. 'This man with the white hair is more cunning,' Ïasaid added, referring to the opposition's thinker, 'because he makes your thinker obey.' The negotiations for the agreement had been in Khasi, so I had no idea what they'd said. 'You will lose,' Ïasaid announced.

The two teams gathered around to place their bets. The Khasis love gambling and everyone put in some money. I was becoming slightly irritated by Ïasaid's conviction that my team would lose before we had even started, so I threw 20 rupees into the pot for my team to win.

Each team provided their own target, a cylinder made of tightly packed grass wrapped in bamboo mounted on a stick, and a referee staked out the targets opposite each other, about 20 metres apart. The four throwers would all line up and dispatch their arrows towards one target and then move to the other end to throw at the second one.

Each thrower was issued with ten arrows by his thinker. My team went down on our haunches into a huddle. My thinker handed me ten long wooden arrows, each with a piece of red tape round its shaft. With his hand still on the bunch of arrows he looked deep into my eyes. 'Your job is to throw these arrows,' he said gravely. 'Clear your mind and concentrate. Think of nothing else but the arrows.'

The four of us lined up and took aim. By this time, the fog was so thick I could scarcely see the tiny target at the other end of the range. It was more like throwing a javelin than a dart, but while the three Khasis were able to hurl their arrows in such a way that they flew straight through the air, mine wobbled all over the place. The first few fell far short of the target, but with an increase in effort I found my line. After ten arrows each, however, our opponents had hit the target twice. My team was two down.

Having thrown all our arrows, we recovered them from the grass at the other end and turned to aim at the second target. The Cherrapunji team made two more direct hits in quick succession. I was trying to focus my mind on throwing, but the knowledge that we had already lost in the agreement kept nagging at the back of my mind. The only chance we had left, it seemed, was for one of the opposition to lose his *dhoti*. My teammate hit the target ... 4–1. We each had four arrows left.

One of the opposition's arrows flew through the air, grazed the target, and fell away. There was a sharp intake of breath from the crowd. I threw mine and missed again. My teammate threw and struck the target a second time. The crowd clapped ... 4–2. Three arrows left.

We all missed. Since I had little chance of ever actually hitting the target, it was all down to my teammate scoring with his last two, and the opposition missing with theirs. We all missed again. With his final arrow, my teammate struck home, but we had lost 4–3. We all shook hands. Iasaid had been right. It seemed that we'd been predestined to lose. He came over and congratulated me on my throwing, even though I had not hit the target once. He was holding some banknotes. Unbeknown to me, he had put ten rupees on the opposition to win.

I still wasn't sure I'd completely grasped the full intricacies of the thinkers' mental gymnastics, but I was sure that the para-psychology of the arrows had been concocted, at least in part, to keep the Khasis sane during the monsoon.

I left Meghalaya and drove further north, into the neighbouring state of Assam. I'd seen the rains, but there was still one aspect of the monsoon that I was keen to experience. Having missed any significant flooding in Bangladesh, I was heading for the Brahmaputra River, which spills out on to its floodplain at this time of year.

Descending from the Khasi Hills felt like returning to India after my sojourn in the 'Abode of the Clouds'. I was back in the land of rickshaws, notably absent from Mawsynram and Cherrapunji, and revisiting the muggy heat of the plains. I was aiming for Kaziranga, a national park set on the banks of the Brahmaputra, a land of alluvial swamps and elephant grass. It is also one of the last homes of the Indian one-horned rhinoceros, the species that Marco Polo thought was a unicorn.

Like rhinos the world over, Kaziranga's are on the endangered list, so the main task of the park's rangers is to patrol the swamps on the lookout for poachers. I joined a group of three rangers for a week in their encampment deep inside the park. Their base had reed and clay walls, its wooden floor raised on brick pillars 2 metres above the ground against the floodwaters. In one direction was a swollen river, in the others swamp, dense woodland and elephant grass that towered 2 or 3 metres above the ground. Asian open billed storks roosted at the tops of the tallest trees.

The rangers stayed out at the base for about a month at a time. When going out on duty, they took basic supplies of rice and oil with them but they largely led a self-sufficient life in the wilds. They kept a few chickens at the base and grew marrows on a bamboo frame. A lemon tree also grew nearby. Otherwise they foraged for the stalks of the rattan palm, which, when stripped of its thorns, could be eaten raw or made into a curry, and the tips of ferns, which they fried.

Kaziranga is home to a large number of wild animals, including elephants, Indian bison, swamp deer, gibbons, buffaloes and tigers, but it is the one-horned rhinoceros that attracts the poachers. Its single black horn can be sold illegally for unimaginable wealth for use in traditional Chinese medicine. Poachers often worked at night, I was told, digging pits for a rhino to fall into and returning later to hack off its horn with an axe. The poachers preferred this method to using their guns because a rifle shot was likely to bring unwelcome attention from the park rangers. The rangers themselves carried their rifles wherever they went. When I asked one of them what the procedure was should he come across a poacher, he answered, 'If we can arrest them, we do. If not, we shoot them.' Two of my three companions had been involved in shoot-outs with poachers in the previous 12 months. Both complained that the poachers usually had better guns than theirs.

Patrols took place mainly on foot. There was something primeval about the landscape we walked and waded through. I got the feeling that this was no place for men, an alien environment, more waist-deep swamp than solid ground, where the grass outgrew the people. Marching through the grass felt incredibly claustrophobic. We could only walk on narrow paths walled with swards that loomed up all around, leaving nothing else to see but the trail in front of us and a ribbon of blue sky above. It was almost as bad as the fog in Meghalaya. I was back in a one-dimensional world again.

I assumed these paths had been trampled by previous patrols. A few had, one of the rangers told me, but most had been created either by a rhino, an elephant or a buffalo.

'Aren't they rather dangerous then?' I asked Jagannath, a good-natured man with a wide moustache and a ready smile.

'Yes,' Jagannath replied simply.

I asked him what I should do if we encountered a rhino, and Jagannath said that usually it was easy to scare them away. 'But if rhino charges, the best thing to do is to run.'

I thought he was having me on until later when we came to a stretch of deep chocolate-brown water and, before plunging in, Jagannath and his colleague, Borah, both removed their canvas boots. I asked them why, and Borah said it was easier to run and climb a tree in bare feet should a rhino charge.

We encountered no fewer than four of the beasts on my first afternoon out. Three we spied from a distance standing waist deep in the water at the other side of a wide river. They looked like prehistoric tanks having a bath. The fourth was rather closer. It appeared before us as we rounded an almost imperceptible bend in the run through the grass we were following, standing with its back to us about 30 metres away. It just looked very solid and immovable and I could clearly see the thick armour-plating on its hind legs. But Jagannath and Borah unshouldered their rifles and advanced slowly shouting 'Ha!' as if they were laughing at it, and the rhino slowly turned and pushed its way through the grass.

I'd read that rhinos can't actually see very well, and have been known to charge at trees, which viewed in one way is risible. But in another, it provides little solace because a person might well look very similar to a tree to a partially sighted giant mammal. However, the apparent ease with which the rangers dispatched the specimen in the grass, just by laughing at it, eased my mind somewhat. Until, that is, I discovered that they bite.

That evening the rangers showed me the scars they had picked up from close encounters with these antediluvian creatures. Negou had been bitten on the upper arm. Still missing one bone, which had been crushed beyond salvation, he had spent no less than three years in hospital after the attack. Borah turned his head to show me where he had been bitten above his right ear.

The rangers were risking their lives to save a species that was actually more of a danger to them than the poachers they were protecting it from.

The thought of being charged and then bitten by two tonnes of angry leviathan was bad enough, but a greater everyday menace to me were the leeches. Like the grass and the rhinos, the leeches in Kaziranga were gigantic. In fact, Jagannath called them elephant leeches and funnily enough, the first one I saw was stuck fast to the leg of an elephant that I was about to board to go out on a sit-down patrol. The leech just hung there sucking blood, looking slimy and repulsive.

Thicker than my thumb and nearly twice as long, it looked like a giant vampire slug.

'They also go on water buffalo,' Jagannath said as the elephant's minder, or *mahout*, swept the leech away into the grass with his stick.

'Do they ever attack people?' I asked cautiously.

'Very rarely,' said Jagannath.

'So it does happen?' I wanted to get the facts straight.

'Yes, but very rarely,' came the reply.

That afternoon, the first time I set foot in some water, which didn't even come up to my knees, I got three of the big fat bastards on my right leg. They made the stringy leeches in Meghalaya look positively friendly.

But despite the leeches and rhinos and the claustrophobic grasses, Kaziranga was also a magical wilderness. The stretches of muddy water were alive with jumping fish and a thousand dragonflies that darted hither and thither in a glitter of luminous orange and electric blue. The skies provided daily exhibitions of towering cumulonimbus clouds etched against a hazy background of Himalayan foothills, and when dusk fell I lay beneath my mosquito net marvelling at the fire-flies dancing to the night music of the jungle.

One day we were called to assist in policing the migration of a family of wild elephants who were moving from the floodplains as the waters rose, crossing a road and passing some villages on their seasonal passage to the Mikir Hills. I had glimpsed the life of the rangers in their waterlogged park and admired them for a bravery that they were too modest to acknowledge.

Although it was not until the morning of my final day that I saw rain again, its arrival was announced by a colossal explosion. For a brief moment, I thought that it was a bomb going off, but it was only Heaven declaring war on Earth. The heavy artillery of thunder boomed as the rain began to fall, followed by the cracks of gunshot, one after another, a volley of ten shots rendering the sky. Flashes of lightning ignited the heavy clouds, illuminating the downpour with brief, bright explosions. I could feel the reverberations in the air as extended peals of thunder ripped through the sky and disappeared into the distance like the sounds of aircraft passing overhead. More heavy guns flashed and crashed as the rain came down, steady and torrential like the monsoon should be.

As the thunder passed, it sounded more like heavy furniture being moved up above, or giant bowling balls rolling away down a celestial alley. But little by little, in a sort of audible slow motion, the heavenly noises faded and left just the sound of the rain.

Index

Plain of Patience, Atacama Desert
112, 114, 115, 119
poaching 246–7, 248
precipitation
Arica x, 93, 94, 95–6
Atacama Desert 106–12, 113,
123–8
Mawsynram x, 190, 213, 233, 239
Pribaikalsky National Park, Siberia
16, 20, 22
Puna de Atacama, Chile 69, 70, 93

Quillagua, Chile 124, 125, 126–9

rainfall
Atacama Desert 111–12, 123–4,
126–7
Mawsynram x, 190, 213, 233, 239
Ralph M. Parsons Company 185, 186
Red Sea 181, 182
reindeer herders 57–8, 59–64
rhinos 246–8
rickshaw wallahs 196
river gypsies (Badhi) 215–19
Rodrigo (fisherman) 105, 111–12
Roy (Khasi host) 228–9, 230, 235,
241
Royal Geographical Society 135
Runa (translator) 192–4, 197, 200,
201, 202, 203, 204, 205, 206,
209, 214, 215, 216, 217, 219
Russia *see* Siberia; Soviet Union
Russo–Japanese war 19–20

Saba River 175
sables 22
Sahara Desert, North Africa 114,
181–2
Salar de Atacama, Chile 122
salt lakes 74, 75, 76, 90, 182–4,
185–6
salt trade 170, 171, 182–4
San Josè River 93, 94
San Miguel de Azapa museum, Arica
97, 98–101, 102–3
San Pedro de Atacama, Chile 69,
70–3
Santoro, Calogero 98–101, 102, 103
Sasha (interpreter) 33, 34
Saudi Arabia 151
Scott, David 238
Shillong, India 225, 233, 236
Shura (reindeer herder) 58, 59–60
Siberia x, 1–65
alcohol consumption 17–19, 22,
23, 24, 53
Angarsk 8–14
clothing 25–6, 48–50, 60–1
exiles 29–31
Irkutsk 3, 4–8, 15–17, 27, 58
Lake Baikal 5, 8, 16, 17, 18–21
Nezhdaninskoye 31–7
reindeer herders 57–8, 59–64
sense of community 58–9
size 39
summer 64–5
temperatures 42–3, 55–6

Tomtor 55–6
  wildlife 22–3
  Yakutsk 25–8, 31, 32, 33
Sierra Gorda, Chile 124, 125, 126
snakes 215–19, 220
Soviet Union 6, 30, 53–4, 57, 139
Srimongal, Bangladesh 220
Stalin, Joseph 15, 29–30, 31, 40
steam harvesting 156, 160
Sylhet, Bangladesh 220–2

taiga forest 17, 25, 42
Taparacá, University of 97, 98
  see also San Miguel de Azapa
    museum
Thesiger, Wilfred 135, 136, 145,
  149, 166
Tigray People's Liberation Front
  (TPLF) 169–70
Tigray (Region Number One),
  Ethiopia 169–70
Times of India, The (newspaper) 189,
  211–12
toasts 17–19, 39
Tomtor, Siberia 55–6

urine recycling 118

Venison (Khasi child) 230, 231

walrus clubs 8–14
War of the Pacific 113

water supplies
  Chile 113, 118
  Ethiopia 156, 160
  Oymyakon 53–4
  see also precipitation; rainfall
West Bengal, India 211–12
'white gold' 120
  see also nitrate deposits
wildlife
  Bangladeshi 202, 204–6, 215–19,
    220
  Chilean 105–6
  Indian 246–9
  Siberian 22–3
Williams, David 62
winds, desert 176, 179–80, 181, 182
wolves 23
World Meteorological Organization
  129

Yakutia, Russia 28–30, 32, 58, 59,
  64–5
  see also Yakutsk
Yakutsk, Siberia 25–8, 31, 32, 33
Yohannès, Zewditou 142, 143

Zahel (guide) 73, 74–5, 76, 78, 79,
  80, 88
Zeus (Chilean soldier) 114, 115,
  116–17, 118–19